Elizabeth Ellicott Lea
(1793–1858)

A QUAKER WOMAN'S COOKBOOK

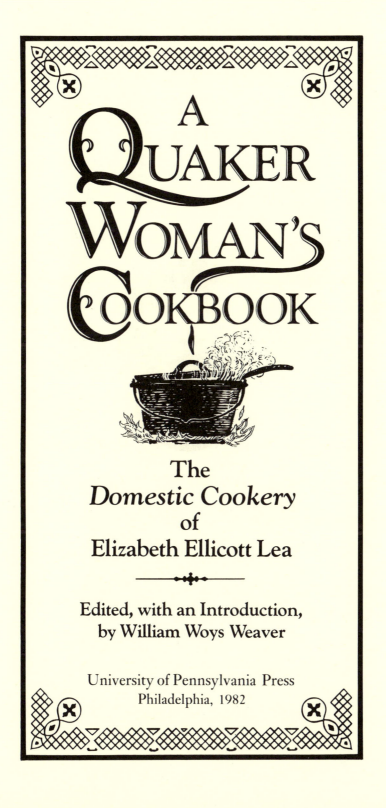

The
Domestic Cookery
of
Elizabeth Ellicott Lea

Edited, with an Introduction,
by William Woys Weaver

University of Pennsylvania Press
Philadelphia, 1982

Published by the
University of Pennsylvania Press

The Introduction and Glossary are
copyright © 1982 by William Woys Weaver
All rights reserved

Library of Congress Card No. 82–60260
ISBN 0–8122–7848–8

*Domestic Cookery: Useful Receipts, and Hints to
Young Housekeepers,* by Elizabeth E. Lea was
first published in 1845 by the author. The
subsequent eighteen editions were published by
Cushings and Bailey in Baltimore, Maryland.

Printed in the United States of America

For
my grandmother, Grace Hickman Weaver,
an expert Quaker cook and a most
understanding Friend

CONTENTS

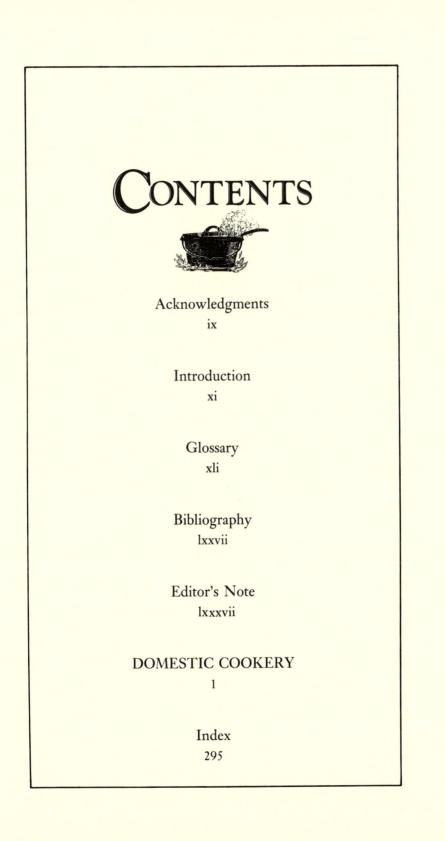

ACKNOWLEDGMENTS

This edition of *Domestic Cookery* would not have been possible without the help of several individuals whose kindness, generosity, and support were essential in reconstructing the life and times of Elizabeth Ellicott Lea and in guiding my project to press. I shall always be grateful to John McGuigan of the University of Pennsylvania Press for his astuteness as an editor and his unflagging interest in subjects relating to material culture—a refreshing combination. Likewise, Karen Hess must be thanked for her helpful comments and suggestions on technical matters relating to food origins.

Special mention should be made of Elizabeth Lea Oliver of Haverford, Pennsylvania, who was a great help in shoring up matters of Lea genealogy. Her unfailing interest in the project was at all times a much appreciated moral boost. Jane Sween, librarian of the Montgomery County Historical Society, Rockville, Maryland, must be thanked for her assistance in locating material on Walnut Hill. Mr. and Mrs. Barry Goodman of Walnut Hill were most generous in their willingness to show me Elizabeth Lea's house as it exists today. Samuel Cooper of Colora Friends Meeting, Colora, Maryland, and Elizabeth Haviland of Brookeville, Maryland, were extremely helpful in putting me in touch with individuals in Sandy Spring who were familiar with Elizabeth E. Lea and her cookbook.

Through Samuel Cooper and Elizabeth Haviland, I found Martha Nesbitt, an energetic local historian who became a valued correspondant, an enthusiastic research assistant, and my most reliable informant. Martha is a rare and marvelous person, and it was she who led me to Deborah Iddings Wilson whose generous offering of Elizabeth E. Lea's photograph provided me with a frontispiece for this book. It was accepted with the same affectionate regard that these

Friends share for the rich and bountiful heritage that has made the people of Sandy Spring so very special.

Roughwood
Thanksgiving 1981   *WILLIAM WOYS WEAVER*

INTRODUCTION

Elizabeth Ellicott Lea had every reason to lay aside the cause of housewifery and often remarked that she would rather be doing something else. For she was well educated, born to a good family, and a liberal Quaker—especially liberal when it came to slavery and social reform. She was also financially independent, so she answered to no one but herself. And yet, her sentiments doubtless agreed with the philosophy expressed in a period book review: "It is not wearing breeches or howling at negro meetings, that improves the female mind, but the calm culture of her faculties."[1] Thus, Elizabeth Lea's calling was at the hearth.

Widowed at an early age, left with the responsibility of managing a farm and raising a family near Sandy Spring, Maryland, and failing in health, Elizabeth Lea developed a special concern for newlyweds who entered into marriage knowing absolutely nothing about it—a bitter pill she herself once tasted. She made this her life's passion, and as a result, wrote *Domestic Cookery*, ostensibly as a handbook for inexperienced brides.

She published the first edition at her own expense in 1845. By 1879, it had run through nineteen editions. Her book was an honest approach to cookery as well as a unique statement about early American culture, and in particular about the Quakerism of its author. Most of all, in terms of its own times, the book worked. It had all of those solid merits of reliability that came to be associated, for better or for worse, with the label "Quaker," that is, in a commercial sense, a thing of quality. Yet it was different from the other period cookbooks of Quaker authorship, most notably Elizabeth Nicholson's *Economical Cook and House-Book* (Philadelphia, 1855), and

---

1. Review of Maria and Emily Grey's *Thoughts on Self-Culture* (Boston, 1851) in *The United States Magazine* XXVIII:156 (June, 1851): 572.

Hannah Widdifield's *New Cook Book* (Philadelphia, 1856).

An Orthodox Philadelphia Friend, Elizabeth Nicholson made lavish use of references to cooking implements and groceries made or sold by local Quaker merchants whose addresses were shrewdly included in the cookbook. This, together with Quaker dating and terminology, set her cookbook apart as something not only Philadelphian, but also peculiarly "for Friends." Elizabeth Lea made no attempt to advertise the fact that she was Quaker or that her cookbook was prepared from a Quaker point of view. Her work rested on its own merits and on those merits alone. Nowhere is this substantiated better than in the fact that *Domestic Cookery* was widely plagiarized, even by Elizabeth Nicholson.[2]

Hannah Widdifield's book, which appeared posthumously, was actually the work of her daughters Sarah and Mary.[3] It reflected the urban tastes of a family engaged as professional cooks and confectioners in Philadelphia. Technically, the book was superior to most of its competitors—Quaker or otherwise—and because it struck a balance between regional dishes and fashionable cuisine, it was hugely successful on the national level. In fact, there was nothing "Quaker" about it.

Elizabeth Lea's cookbook fell somewhere between Nicholson and Widdifield, for the Quaker personality of her work, while there, does not appear directly on the surface. In fact, Elizabeth Lea's Quakerism is often tenuous. This is because there is a real philosophical contradiction in the view promoted by several later writers that Quakerism also produced a distinct branch of cookery. Quakerism is simply a way of thinking, a perception of truth. It does not reveal itself in a definite cuisine because Quaker cookery has more to do with nuance than with flavor; it is more in the spirit of the serving than in the spice. Much to her credit, Elizabeth Lea was fully aware of this. The real strength of her work rested on its regionalisms.

---

2. See, for example, "To Broil Shad," in Elizabeth Nicholson, *The Economical Cook and House-Book* (Philadelphia, 1855), p. 19.

3. I am indebted to Nancy Klavans of Merion, Pennsylvania, for genealogical material on Hannah Widdifield.

What is remarkable about Elizabeth Lea's cookbook is that a Quaker widow in Maryland has compiled a collection of recipes that forms one of the most varied samplings of the rural American folk cookery of her era. This rural emphasis was both intentional and an inadvertent reflection of Elizabeth Lea's own milieu. From the motto on her title page—"The Source of Liberal Deeds is Wise Economy"—it is evident that the author had perceived the subject of cookery from a philosophical stance different from most of her more famous contemporaries, such as Eliza Leslie, Sarah Josepha Hale, or Lydia Maria Child. These personages compiled cookbooks to take advantage of a lucrative market. They were not confectioners or chefs or even simple housewives. Cookbook writing was truly secondary to the serious literary endeavors on which these women staked their reputations, as even Eliza Leslie begrudgingly admitted in her autobiography.[4]

Elizabeth E. Lea was not even a writer. Her cookbook was a labor of love compiled largely at her bedside with the help of Rebecca Russell (1786–1888), a Quaker nurse of Pennsylvania birth who came to Sandy Spring in 1829 to care for Elizabeth's ailing husband.[5] Thomas Lea died young anyway, and instead of four months, Rebecca Russell stayed fifty-nine years. In a real sense, *Domestic Cookery* was the product of the indestructible friendship that developed between these two unique personalities. For Rebecca Russell became Elizabeth's companion, confidante, and co-sufferer in the ups and downs of the family fortunes at Sandy Spring. And with the hawkeye of a spinster schoolmarm, she edited the manuscript of Elizabeth Lea's cookbook.

Both women were deeply religious, a fact that has some bearing on the Quaker aspects of this cookbook. Stranded by circumstance on their lonely farmstead near Sandy Spring, far from railroads, far from concourse with large towns, far from the humanity to whom liberal deeds were best directed, the

---

4. See "Letter to Mrs. Alice B. Neal," in *The Female Prose Writers of America,* John S. Hart, ed. (Philadelphia, 1855), pp. 27–32.

5. For a biographical sketch, see "Rebecca Russell," *Friends' Intelligencer and Journal* (Jan. 19, 1889), pp. 43–44.

women turned inward and evidently took up the ancient charge:

> Do the duty that lies nearest thee,
> Wisely improve the present: it is thine.[6]

Domestic Cookery, then, became a subtle form of ministry, for this theme, above all else, underlies Elizabeth Lea's life. As a guidebook on wise economy, it was the foundation upon which liberality could be possible. So her book was both a kitchen sermon and a tool. If, by today's standards, her recipes seem overly plain, then remember that rural eating habits before the Civil War were generally simple. Practicality, economy, and simplicity at the table were not new themes in American culinary literature during this period. But here we are dealing with a Quaker, and in Quaker terms, there is nothing so complex as simplicity.

Elizabeth Ellicott Lea and Her Quaker World

Much of the content of Elizabeth Lea's *Domestic Cookery* is a reflection of the web of influences which made up the Quaker world in which she lived. It was a close-knit world of friends and relatives, and very rarely did Elizabeth Lea leave it. Even in Sandy Spring, a settlement composed largely of Quakers, Elizabeth Lea kept mostly to herself.

She was born at Ellicott City, Maryland, on December 6, 1793, a daughter of George Ellicott and Elizabeth Brooke, parents who came from two of Maryland's wealthiest and most distinguished Quaker families. Since the early eighteenth century, the Brookes owned huge tracts of land in Montgomery County; the Ellicotts, on the other hand, had come down from Bucks County, Pennsylvania, and built Ellicott City in 1772 as a mill town on the Patapsco River, about ten miles west of

---

6. Jane P. Rushmore, *The Quaker Way* (Philadelphia, n.d.), p. 3.

Baltimore. George Ellicott's house, erected in 1789, where Elizabeth was born, is still standing and is now part of a historic district within Ellicott City.[7]

By virtue of this fortunate birth, Elizabeth grew up at the hub of a community whose commercial and family connections spread out across the United States and brought her into contact with the leading political and financial figures of her time. Because she was a member of a Quaker family deeply committed to civic affairs, her childhood was constantly enlivened by visits of influential Quakers from across the country and from abroad.

Her father, in particular, was interested in the welfare of racial minorities. He was the patron and friend of Benjamin Banneker (1732–1804), a black mathematician who grew up near Ellicott City and in later years published a famous almanac.[8] George Ellicott was also committed to work on behalf of the American Indians. His visit among the Wyandots and Delawares in 1799 was well known nationally and was even included as general reading matter for Quakers in the *Friends' Miscellany*.[9] More importantly, George Ellicott wrote a recommendation to Congress which resulted in a law prohibiting the sale of alcoholic beverages to the Indians on the rationale that alcohol was being misused by whites to drug the Indians out of land, not to mention its devastating psychological affects on their culture. This stance on temperance was fully in accord with the strictures of the Quaker discipline of Baltimore Yearly Meeting, which warned that alcohol, by introducing a "defection from simplicity of the heart," created "imaginary wants" and should be avoided.[10] Significantly, alcohol does not figure as a social beverage in any of Elizabeth Lea's recipes.

---

7. For a description of Ellicott City, see Celia M. Holland, *Ellicott City. Maryland's 18th Century Mill Town* (Ellicott City, Md., 1968).

8. See Silvio A. Bedini, *The Life of Benjamin Banneker* (New York, 1972).

9. See "Narrative of a Journey to Sandusky," *Friends' Miscellany* VII:7 (Oct., 1835): 290–336.

10. Baltimore Yearly Meeting, *Discipline of the Yearly Meeting of Friends, Held in Baltimore* (Baltimore, 1806), p. 71.

Elizabeth Lea's sisters and brothers also became prominent. For example, her sister Martha Ellicott Tyson (1795–
1873) carried on the family's social concerns by writing one of
the earliest and most accurate accounts of Benjamin Banneker's life and career. She worked for the abolition of slavery,
took an active role in Indian affairs, and after the Civil War
wrote a history of Ellicott Mills. As a recorded minister in
Little Falls Friends Meeting and one of the founders of
Swarthmore College, Martha was memorialized after her death
by Baltimore Yearly Meeting.[11]

Needless to say, Elizabeth Lea was considerably overshad-
owed by her more famous and wealthier kin, and because she
wrote a cookbook—not worthy enough to be considered so-
cially redeeming by nineteenth-century standards—her contri-
bution has remained largely forgotten until now. In fact, outside of Sandy Spring, Maryland, it is difficult today to locate
individuals who are familiar with her book. And yet, through
her *Domestic Cookery*, Elizabeth Lea's influence went far beyond her immediate world.

On November 18, 1812, Elizabeth married Thomas Lea
according to Quaker custom in Elkridge Friends Meeting-
house on "Quaker Hill" at Ellicott City—a good enough reason to include "Elkridge Huckleberry Pudding" in her cookbook many years later. Her husband was the son of Thomas
Lea and Sarah Tatnall of Wilmington, Delaware. Like the
Ellicotts, the Leas were a prominent Quaker milling family.
They owned and operated flour mills in Brandywine Village
north of Wilmington.[12] It was there that Thomas Lea and his
new wife settled to live. It was there that seven children were
born.

Life in Delaware brought Elizabeth Lea into direct contact with the large, almost homogeneous Quaker communities
that stretched north from Wilmington into Chester County,

11. Baltimore Yearly Meeting, *Memorials Concerning Several Ministers and Others, Deceased* (Baltimore, 1875), p. 168.

12. A full account of the Leas, including genealogical data on Eliza-
beth E. Lea, appears in James H. Lea and George H. Lea, *Ancestry and Posterity of John Lea* (New York, 1906).

Pennsylvania. It was from this area that a great many of her recipes seem to originate. This is not surprising considering that in 1805 Elizabeth had attended Westtown School and after her marriage had many Lea family connections up and down the Brandywine Valley. In addition, there were numerous Ellicott associations with New Garden Township in Chester County, which also happened to be Rebecca Russell's birthplace.

Through marriage and purchase, Thomas Ellicott, one of Elizabeth's cousins, acquired a large tract of land in the New Garden "Wastelands" near Avondale.[13] Part of this tract was used as a farm and private resort by the family and Quaker friends; other parts were developed for milling purposes. The Avondale watering hole became one place where Ellicotts North and South could congregate to exchange news and family recipes, to rest, and sometimes even to die in the privacy of family surroundings, as in the case of young John Ellicott of Philadelphia, who went there for reasons of health but never recovered.[14]

Perhaps even more influential than her Avondale relatives was Elizabeth's own Aunt Sarah Harvey, the wife of Jonathan Ellicott. Born in Bucks County, Pennsylvania, Aunt Sarah brought a vast storehouse of culinary information to Maryland where she became well known for her profuse entertaining, her home economy, and her culinary feats. Doubtless, between the cream cheese and lemon butter, the pepper mangoes and rusks, there is a great deal of Aunt Sarah in Elizabeth's cookbook. In fact, Elizabeth Lea's recipe for "Potato Pudding" (p. 89) is known in Bucks County as "Quarterly Meeting Pie." It is a potato pudding baked in a pie shell.

Elizabeth's quiet life in the polite circles of Delaware and Pennsylvania Friends was not one of hardship. Quaker shipping in Wilmington and Philadelphia kept tables within the Quaker network well stocked with things unobtainable in many parts of the country, such as fresh pineapples from the

    13. See Ann Hagerty, *Once Upon a Time in New Garden Township* (Kennett Square, Pa., 1977), pp. 75–76.
    14. *Friends' Intelligencer* X:45 (Jan. 28, 1854): 707, 711.

Caribbean, Seville oranges, and winter grapes from the Canary Islands, even when Philadelphia grocers went without. And only a few miles from Elizabeth's home were the Chalybeate Springs which in those days was a fashionable spa, a second Saratoga, where the wealthy gathered to socialize and drink mineral tinctured water, among other things. Even the most temperance-minded Quakers did not object to mineral water or late night "teas." Such was life in and around Brandywine Mills.

All of this was cut short in 1822 when Elizabeth's first cousin, Hannah Chandlee Pierce, moved to Sandy Spring, Maryland, to settle on a large farm inherited from her mother, Deborah Brooke. Hannah's husband encouraged the Leas to follow and settle at Walnut Hill, a farm which Elizabeth's mother had given her—both tracts being family subdivisions of Charley Forest, one of the vast Brooke plantations in Montgomery County.[15]

Thus, in the spring of 1823, using the same ox-drawn wagon that brought the Pierces to Maryland, Elizabeth Lea, her husband, and seven children set out for Sandy Spring laden with furniture and accompanied by no less than four horses, six cows, a bull, twelve sheep, and some chickens.[16] In a letter to Joshua Pierce, Thomas Lea remarked that "when my stock arrives it will make the Maryland Farmers open their eyes."[17] Evidently he was right, for each animal was a showpiece. The Leas, it seems, had come prepared for rugged living. And rugged living it was.

William Forster, an English Quaker, noted in 1820 during a trip through the region that "the country seems running back again into wilderness. Thousands of acres are overgrown with brambles and young forest-trees. Things wearing such a for-

---

15. The Brooke holdings are extensively covered in Thomas Boyd, *History of Montgomery County, Maryland* (Clarksburg, Md., 1879).

16. Roger Brooke Farquhar, *Old Homes and History of Montgomery County, Maryland* (Washington, D.C., 1962), p. 318.

17. Private communication with Martha Nesbitt, dated Sandy Spring, December 8, 1980. Martha Nesbitt possesses an extensive collection of material on Elizabeth E. Lea and early Sandy Spring, including Joshua Pierce's *Day Book*.

lorn appearance is indescribably affecting to one's spirits."[18] This decaying and abandoned farmland had been worn out by overcropping tobacco. Most of the local population had moved West to Kentucky and Missouri.[19] Only in the redlands around Brookeville and Sandy Spring, where tobacco had never been grown as extensively, were Quaker farmers able to bring the soil back to fertility. Thus, through hard work, the Leas saw inviting possibilities.

Life at Walnut Hill

Walnut Hill was little more than half a mile from Brooke's Black Meadow, the farm where Hannah Pierce had set up household. This proximity was important to both Hannah and Elizabeth Lea because they were kinfolk and friends. And having grown up in less makeshift surroundings, they comforted one another over the hardships of Sandy Spring. They exchanged woes, they exchanged gossip, and they exchanged recipes. In fact, according to family traditions, Hannah Pierce later tested many of the recipes in *Domestic Cookery* on her own hearth.[20] It was through her descendant Deborah Iddings Wilson that the only known photograph of Elizabeth Lea has come to light. It is the same photograph reproduced as a frontispiece for this edition of the cookbook.

Joshua Pierce's *Day Book,* covering the years 1822–1849, records in minute detail how extensively these two families were interconnected, how they borrowed money back and forth (there was no bank in Sandy Spring until 1868), and how they cooperated in money-making schemes.[21] But in addition, the Pierces and Leas erected a school halfway between the two farms. Here their children were educated, and here, not sur-

---

18. Benjamin Seebohm, ed., *Memoirs of William Forster* (London, 1865), I, p. 296.
19. Thomas Scharf, *History of Western Maryland* (Philadelphia, 1882), II, p. 653.
20. Private communication with Deborah Iddings Wilson, dated Columbia, Maryland, Sept. 15, 1980.
21. The original *Day Book* is in the possession of Martha Nesbitt of Sandy Spring.

prisingly, blossomed friendships that later developed into the intermarriage of their offspring.

Walnut Hill itself, overlooking the Hawlings River, consisted of over 200 acres, part of which Thomas Lea shrewdly developed into apple orchards. Thus apples, and cider in particular, became the economic mainstay of the farm. This might explain why Elizabeth Lea included fourteen recipes for apples in her cookbook, not to mention a long and excellent recipe for making cider, and two recipes for making apple butter.

The brick farmhouse, built about 1820, was not very large for a family that continued to grow. Yet it was not until about 1844—fifteen years after Thomas Lea's death—that the dwelling was extended, probably with some of the money Elizabeth realized in selling off 110 acres of the farm the year before. It was this new surge in cash that also probably enabled her to pay for printing the first edition of her cookbook in 1845.

The house at Walnut Hill is still standing and is well maintained. Elizabeth Lea's kitchen, where all of the recipes were tried and tested, is still extant, although it now serves as a dining room. An iron and brass-decorated wall oven manufactured by H. Reid of Baltimore is also still in place. It is said that Elizabeth Lea installed this oven to test her baking recipes.[22] Perhaps it is simply enough to note that in her chapter on bread, Elizabeth Lea includes extensive directions for heating and baking in such an oven. Her exacting advice serves as one of the few truly reliable American sources for baking in this traditional manner.

Above the old kitchen is a small bedroom where Elizabeth Lea wrote much of her cookbook. According to descendants, and a colorful account of her in the *Baltimore Sun* in 1905, the bedridden authoress was obliged to shout down recipes and corrections to Rebecca Russell or the family cook, whose duty it was to execute them properly.[23] For, bedridden or not, Elizabeth Lea was a large woman, strong-willed, not easily put off by inconveniences or weak sensibilities. Over each detail she

---

22. Maryland State Historic Sites Survey, *ACHS Summary Form* (1979), *"Walnut Hill," 23/89,* pp. 1 and 5.
23. *Baltimore Sun,* Dec. 24, 1905.

maintained a firm hand. Since her cookbook underwent revisions in 1846 and again in 1851, one can imagine that the shouting continued sporadically for a number of years. Yes, Elizabeth Lea also published two remedies for sore throat.

The broader implications of her cookbook were not lost on her children. The gnawing anguish over ignorance in matrimony was sidestepped by five of her nine children; they simply never married. But the three siblings who did (the fourth died young), all married before Elizabeth Lea published her cookbook, and no doubt in doing so, extended their mother's reasons and range for recipe gathering. Mary Lea in particular seems to have exercised considerable influence. She was Elizabeth's only daughter who married.

Mary became the wife of Henry Stabler in 1842. Rebecca Russell moved in with the couple to serve as a nurse and housekeeper after they settled at Roslyn, a farm within walking distance of Walnut Hill. Henry Stabler was the son of Edward Stabler of Alexandria, Virginia, a druggist and influential Quaker minister—leader, in fact, of the Temperance movement within Baltimore Yearly Meeting.[24] The original apothecary shop which Edward Stabler established in 1792 on South Fairfax Street in Alexandria is now preserved as a historic site because it was here that he sold medicine to George Washington, his most famous customer.[25] Doubtless, some of the Virginia recipes and the ingenious herbal remedies in the medical portion of Elizabeth Lea's cookbook trace to this Stabler family connection.

The Stabler connection also figures in another facet of the cookbook and its story, for Mary Lea Stabler's brother-in-law, Edward H. Stabler, continued the family drug business and operated a large store first on Market Street, then later at 120 Pratt Street Wharf in Baltimore.[26] There he sold not only

---

24. See William Stabler, *A Memoir of the Life of Edward Stabler* (Philadelphia, 1846).

25. Gay Montague Moore, *Seaport in Virginia* (Richmond, Va., 1949), pp. 195–96.

26. Richard J. Matchett, *Matchett's Baltimore Director for 1853–1854* (Baltimore, 1853), p. 47 advertisements.

drugs, but Quaker books as well, and for many years served as agent for the *Friends' Miscellany.* By the 1850s, his firm had grown large enough to afford full-page advertisements in the annual city directories. The back covers of these directories are often covered with notices for Stabler's "Diarrhoea Cordial" and "Anodyne Cherry Expectorant," two of many widely favored patent medicines made by the firm. This medical connection would be ephemeral as far as *Domestic Cookery* is concerned—Elizabeth Lea did *not* publish the family formulas!— were it not for the fact that the first edition of the cookbook was coddled into print by a Baltimore physician.

The 1845 edition of *Domestic Cookery* was sold through Dr. Henry Colburn, a dental surgeon and partner in the firm of Knight & Colburn, which operated a medical bookstore at 128 Baltimore Street in Baltimore.[27] Dr. Colburn was a distinguished city physician. His connection with Elizabeth Lea is now obscure, but certainly his very name served as a recommendation for her book.

It may be that Dr. Colburn had a professional connection with Edward H. Stabler & Company, either as a customer or as an agent. For that matter, he may have been Elizabeth Lea's dentist. This much is certain: for business reasons unrelated to the cookbook, the partnership of Knight & Colburn was dissolved and Dr. Colburn got out of the book trade altogether. However, the popularity of Elizabeth Lea's book evidently prompted Joseph Cushing, Jr., another Baltimore publisher, to pick up the rights to it. As the principal in Cushing & Brother (later Cushings & Bailey), a major city firm, he was able to convince Elizabeth Lea to enlarge her work from 180 pages to 247 for the second edition in 1846.[28] The third edition, which appeared in 1851, was enlarged to 310 pages with the addition of such non-culinary material as the remarks on the treatment of servants, the directions for carving meat, and the advice on flower gardening. It was this "new" work that was copy-

---

27. Richard J. Matchett, *Matchett's Baltimore Director for 1840* (Baltimore, 1840), pp. 100 and 218.

28. Eleanor Lowenstein, *Bibliography of American Cookery Books 1742–1860* (Worcester, Mass., and New York, 1972), p. 62.

righted in 1851 and which remained unchanged until it went out of print in 1879.

Unfortunately for Elizabeth E. Lea, the watchful care of her family and faithful servants and the best medical connections in Maryland were not enough to insure her against declining health. The success of her cookbook came at a time when money could do no good. She was simply too sick to enjoy it. Eventually, her condition sank to such a point that on December 21, 1858, her son, Edward Lea, and his wife, Deborah Pierce, set up a cemetery for the use of the Lea family— now Woodside Cemetery near Sandy Spring. Nine days later, on the morning of December 30th, Elizabeth Lea died. Shortly afterwards, she was buried at Woodside. Thus, even in death, Elizabeth Lea was set apart from the Quaker community around her.

Because she had been bedridden for so many years, Elizabeth had not been a regular attender at meeting, but her death was duly recorded in the *Record of Births, Deaths, and Membership* of Sandy Spring Friends Meeting.[29] The exact nature of her illness, however, remains a mystery, even though a long obituary appeared in the *Friends' Intelligencer* for January 15, 1859. It provided a brief sketch of her life and recounted the vicissitudes and sorrows of her protracted illness, the days and nights of suffering, and her reliance on reading from the Bible shortly before her passing. It made no mention of her popular cookbook.

Christianity in the Kitchen

The *Friends' Weekly Intelligencer* carried great weight within the Hicksite Quaker community to which Elizabeth Lea belonged, a community that was scattered throughout the United States. The omission of her cookbook both in reviews and in her obituary was probably a conscious one in spite of

---

29. The original record book, for the years 1730–1895, is now in the collection of the Friends Historical Library at Swarthmore College, Swarthmore, Pennsylvania.

a general loyalty on the part of the editors to Friends and their literary works. While it is true that in general only works of a more spiritual or controversial nature received notice, the *Intelligencer* did carry advertisements for ice cream saloons and updates on the agricultural market with food prices, hints on housekeeping, and sometimes even a few recipes. In light of this, the utter omission of *Domestic Cookery* does strike a peculiar note. But there is, perhaps, an explanation.

In 1847, the *Intelligencer* noted without apology that it was not in the practice of publishing culinary recipes.[30] True, only now and then did this editorial policy waver. Yet this does not in itself explain the apparent disinterest in Elizabeth Lea's cookbook.

During the 1840s, Friends were only beginning to discover the science of diet as an extension of their larger religious concerns. Homeopathy, vegetarianism, Grahamite cookery, and other rationalistic systems were gaining the attention of the more radical Hicksite wing of the Society. Favorable articles on these various positions appeared from time to time in the *Intelligencer*. The usual editorial theme was that Friends were awake to excesses in drinking but neglectful in their diets of what was natural and good.

This theme was emphasized over and over in material reprinted in the *Intelligencer* from Lydia Maria Child's *American Frugal Housewife*.[31] The material that found its way into the *Intelligencer* was chosen because one of the editors, Edward Parrish, felt that Friends could unite with its tenor. Actually, it was the best kind of publicity Mrs. Child could have gotten, pure and simple.

Judging from book reviews and other reprinted matter in the *Intelligencer*, Friends united with nearly everything Lydia Maria Child wrote. She had become a champion of social causes close to the hearts of Quaker radicals—anti-slavery and women's rights, for example—and was a serious author in her

---

30. *Friends' Weekly Intelligencer* IV:1 (April 3, 1847): 5.
31. For example "Travelling and Public Amusements," *Friends' Weekly Intelligencer* II:20 (Aug. 16, 1845): 155–56.

own right who devoted much attention to morality on the home front. Several years later, her life of the Quaker Isaac T. Hopper became basic reading among Friends.[32] Although not a Quaker herself, Mrs. Child became the darling of Quaker society and an approved "Quaker" author. The merits of her cookbook had little to do with it.

Unfortunately, Elizabeth Lea could not cash in on a public personality like Lydia Maria Child's or on an "approved" reformist reputation. Elizabeth Lea was totally unknown and lacked the feverish intellectual enthusiasm of other accepted writers, such as Mary Mann, whose very name became a shibboleth among Quaker food faddists.

In January of 1858, the *Intelligencer* reprinted a long extract from Mary Mann's *Physiological Cookery Book.*[33] Mary Mann was the wife of Horace Mann, a well-known Unitarian educator, so theologically she was on ground close to Hicksite Quakerism. In her book, she attacked American diet with the zeal of an Abolitionist. The extract in the *Intelligencer* focused on her main theme: holiness and health, what she called the "gospel of the body." "There is no more prolific, indeed, there is no *such* prolific cause of bad morals as abuses of diet." "It is a good omen that practical physiologists, even now, begin to feel ashamed of ill health."[34] She was, perhaps, only one step away from Christian Science, but her missionary techniques for dietary conversion certainly find their modern counterparts in commercial food advertising and in American advertising in general.

Quakers applauded her cookbook because it seemed to be a novel approach to diet that squared most aspects of consumption with biblical morality and common sense—no easy task. Mrs. Mann abstained from the use of saleratus (old-fashioned baking soda), from butter, from lard, and from all fatty sub-

---

32. Lydia Maria Child, *Isaac T. Hopper: A True Life* (Boston, 1853).
33. "Economy in the Kitchen," *Friends' Weekly Intelligencer* XIV:43 (Jan. 9, 1858): 685–87. Mrs. Mann's cookbook was published in 1857 by Ticknor & Fields of Boston.
34. "Economy in the Kitchen," *Friends' Weekly Intelligencer* XIV:43 (Jan. 9, 1858): 685.

stances. Unwittingly, she championed a low-cholesterol diet by abjuring such trendy Victorian favorites as bride cake, plum pudding, and turtle soup, all found, incidentally, in Elizabeth Lea's cookbook. It was this high-principled, uncompromising reformist spirit found in works like Mrs. Mann's that so dulled the appeal of Elizabeth E. Lea's homey recipes in the eyes of Quaker editors. Yet reviews in the *Intelligencer* were one thing; kitchen practice was quite another.

In perusing the manuscript cookbook of Ann Aston Warder (1781–1871), a prominent Ohio Quaker who grew up in Germantown, Pennsylvania, we see at work a set of values entirely different from Mrs. Mann's. Like Elizabeth Lea, Ann Warder came from the Quaker aristocracy.[35]

Neatly written in 1844 for her daughter-in-law, the book records a whole generation of recipes collected from relatives, from classes at Mrs. Goodfellow's cooking school in Philadelphia, and from years of personal experience.[36] In short, the recipes are the sum total of what Ann Warder actually cooked and served at home and what she felt were worthwhile to pass on to the next generation. As a selection, her recipes are strikingly similar to those in Elizabeth Lea's cookbook. In a few cases, such as Deshler's Salve, they are basically the same. So in this respect, Elizabeth Lea's *Domestic Cookery* has the personal quality of a mother's recipe scrapbook rather than a polished treatise after the manner of Mrs. Mann. While this may have detracted from the social merits of Elizabeth Lea's book in the eyes of Quaker intellectuals, it did add an aspect to her work which is not found in many other American cookbooks of the period: that is, a noticeable "folk" perception in the selection and composition of her recipes. For her cookery, if anything, was matter-of-fact in its simplicity, not over-intellectualized or studied. Her cookery was traditional. Her folk recipes were in some cases outright poverty food. So from

35. See Mary McGregor Miller, *The Warder Family* (Springfield, Ohio, 1957).
36. The original cookbook is in the possession of the editor.

the standpoint of methodical, scientific cookery as it was then perceived, Elizabeth Lea offered nothing new or healthful, no broad moralizing, no overriding social intentions, nothing more noble than her concern for inexperienced brides, a concern that was far from unique in cookbook literature.

This explains to a large extent why the Quaker press simply ignored *Domestic Cookery*. It also brings us full circle to a question mentioned earlier: Is there a Quaker cookery? Is there a unique cuisine waiting for us between the covers of books like N. J. Clayton's *Quaker Cook Book* (San Francisco, 1883)? Or is this just a confusion of terms, an outgrowth of the commercial exploitation of the word "Quaker" as a synonym for pure?

The Swedish minister Israel Acrelius, living in Delaware in the early eighteenth century, once referred to puddings and dumplings as "Quakers' food."[37] In Central Pennsylvania, dried-beef gravy is still commonly called "Quaker gravy." There are many similar examples, none of which carry the implicit meaning of pure or natural or even plain. Rather, the distinction is cast along cultural boundaries, that is, as seen from an ethnological standpoint. Puddings and dumplings, dried-beef gravy, these are also traditional foods for many Anglo-Americans. And yet, there seems to be some significance in the fact that most of the Quakers who came to the Middle Atlantic region came primarily from Western England and Wales. For they preserved a number of food preferences traceable to that part of the British Isles. In this respect, rural Quaker cookery, particularly during the seventeenth and eighteenth centuries, may have differed somewhat from that of non-Quaker neighbors. There is evidence to suggest this in Elizabeth Lea's cookbook. But of course, this is an aspect of cookery which is not a product of Quakerism, but of the people themselves. It has to do with their cultural identity, their culinary roots.

---

37. J. Thomas Scharf, *History of Delaware 1609–1888* (Philadelphia, 1888), I, p. 158.

"Domestic Cookery" as a Folk-Cultural Document

In looking at historical folk cookery in this country, that is, the everyday cookery of the common man, we are naturally faced with serious dilemmas if we trust cookbooks alone. This applies to the study of food all over the world, since cookbooks record only a small fraction of what is known at a particular time. This is quite unavoidable because cookbooks usually reflect the tastes of a very limited segment of society, as viewed through the conscious or unconscious editing of the book's author or compiler. The first requirement, of course, is that this segment of society must be literate. Thus, the cookery of the literate class becomes something different from that of the unlettered class, and this is where cookery diverges from workaday sustenance to something akin to an art. The question is: Can a cookbook like *Domestic Cookery* serve as a folk-cultural document? This is a disturbing question for many scholars in the field of American folklife studies, since American folk scholarship tends to emphasize oral aspects of the culture.

Part of the difficulty lies in the fact that food is material culture, like a basket or a votive painting. The only difference is that it is temporary. The cookbook gives food permanence only in that it preserves the formulas, the way a songbook preserves sound. To this extent, the cookbook can only serve as a guide. But additionally, it can also lend itself to detailed analysis and interpretation as a historical object. This is where *Domestic Cookery* is extremely useful to research today.

In Europe, the term *Volkskunde* (folklife research) covers all aspects of everyday life, a broad approach which makes room for printed sources, even ephemera, because European scholarship is well aware that everyday people are never totally ignorant of the printed world around them. In terms of cookery, Edith Hörandner of the University of Vienna has used the *Volkskunde* approach in her important study of cookbooks: "The Recipe Book as a Cultural and Socio-Historical Document."[38]

---

38. See *Food in Perspective,* Alexander Fenton and Trefor M. Owen, eds. (Edinburgh, 1981), pp. 119–44.

In dealing with the historic folk cookery of Lower Austria, Dr. Hörandner has been faced with the same problems that confront American researchers: How is it possible to reconstruct the cookery of a given era when there is no one left to interview? The answer, of course, demands that the problem be approached from several viewpoints, among them the viewpoint of period cookbooks.

Dr. Hörandner has noted that certain types of cookbooks served as "memory aids" to the oral cooking traditions that accompanied them. In other words, cooks would write down only those things they felt they were most likely to forget. Manuscript cookbooks are often compiled this way. Ann Warder's cookbook of 1844, already mentioned, was compiled to pass on *everything* that she as a cook considered useful to remember—easy and difficult recipes alike. Elizabeth Lea's *Domestic Cookery* resembles the Warder manuscript in this respect, but Elizabeth Lea emphasizes the simple recipes, the everyday things which people took for granted. She does not call her recipes folk recipes. She does not state that such-and-such a cook dictated a particular recipe to her, or for that matter, that a given dish might be considered old-fashioned or even poverty food. These things she leaves unsaid. She simply records. So the broader implications of her work must be clarified by exhaustive research in scores of other period sources. The important point is that Elizabeth Lea emphasized the everyday cookery of the Middle Atlantic states, and this is why I have called her book a folk-cultural document.

In the glossary which follows this introduction, a number of dishes and terms have been traced to some type of folk source or set against a broader folk-cultural context. In this case, the glossary is not intended to be exhaustive, but simply to be a key to help the reader understand the book and use it for further research. Yet theoretically, the glossary could be expanded to include every term and dish concept in the text. This, of course, would take years of painstaking research, but this is why *Domestic Cookery* should be of continuing interest to folklife scholars as well as food and cultural historians. It can be used as a kind of acid test for researchers who may want to set it against the vast array of materials they have assembled from other sources.

"Domestic Cookery" as a Product of Middle Atlantic Culture

Some culinary historians will take great pains to labor over the fact that a recipe in one cookbook may include six eggs, while in another only four. This has to do with the art of cookery and does not have direct bearing on the folk-cultural aspects, unless of course, there is a cultural reason for fewer eggs. Broadly speaking, the folklife scholar must treat dishes on a more general level, as a dish or food concept. This includes not only ingredients and methods of preparation, but also such things as serving patterns, time of day, the occasion, and so forth. It encompasses every known aspect of a given dish.

Organically, *Domestic Cookery* is an arrangement of dish concepts, some more abbreviated than others. Most of this material is drawn from two geographic sub-regions within the Middle Atlantic states: the Tidewater South, centering on the Chesapeake Bay; and Southeastern Pennsylvania, including the Delaware Basin. These are two areas of early settlement where transplanted Old World cultures underwent significant alteration as the result of local adaptation and innovation. Because of the migration of early settlers, these new, American-born influences spread even deeper into the South and the Midwest.[39] Even though it was published during the middle of the last century, *Domestic Cookery* is in many ways a summary of Middle Atlantic cooking traditions as they developed in the one hundred years preceding the appearance of the book, for a great many of the recipes have parallel roots in the oral cooking traditions of this region.

The material Elizabeth Lea chose to include in her cookbook shows evidence of food acculturation from a number of directions. This cultural diversification is one of the character-

---

39. These themes are well covered in Henry Glassie's *Pattern in the Material Folk Culture of the Eastern United States* (Philadelphia, 1968).

istics of Middle Atlantic culture. Naturally, some of the oldest
influences can be traced to the American Indians, who not
only passed along indigenous ingredients, and in some cases
cooking techniques, but dish concepts as well: the combination
of green corn and meat in a stew, for example.[40] The most
obvious foods of native origin in *Domestic Cookery* are poke;
green corn soup; several squash dishes; terrapin (without the
wine and seasonings); all of the pumpkin recipes with the
exception of pumpkin preserve; and a number of cornmeal
dishes, including some of the breads and puddings. Also of
Indian origin are several of the home remedies using native
plants, such as the sassafras and lily root poultices, and the tea
made with spicewood berries, the latter called "an ancient
Indian remedy" in Samuel Stearns' *American Herbal.*[41] In
Elizabeth Lea's time, such remedies could be found in the oral
folk traditions of both the blacks and whites, as well as in
popular household medical books.

However, some of the remedies may be entirely home-
made, as in the case of Elizabeth Lea's "Elecampane and Horehound Syrup," which appears to be her own adaptation of
Hance's "Compound Syrup of Horehound," a patent medicine produced and sold by the Quaker druggist Seth B. Hance
of Baltimore.[42] His advertisements, often in the form of dog-
gerel poems, were popular in the *Baltimore Sun* during the
1840s. Also in this category are Deshler's (Nipple) Salve, Hux-
ham's Bark Tincture, and Warner's Cordial, all adaptations of
old patent medicines. On a number of occasions, Elizabeth Lea
refers to country nurses; doubtless she had Rebecca Russell in
mind, for her personal knowledge of herbal remedies and
Thomsonian medicine certainly provided the book with some
of the raw material which makes the medical section so full and

---

40. Several Indian foods acculturated by the whites in the Middle
Atlantic area are discussed in John Witthoft and Bonita Freeman-Witthoft,
"Lenape Indian Fall Harvest," *Frontiers* (Fall, 1975).
41. Samuel Stearns, *American Herbal* (Walpole, N.H., 1801), p. 143.
42. In 1851, Hance's shop was located at 108 Baltimore Street. See
Richard J. Matchett, *Matchett's Baltimore Director for 1851* (Baltimore, 1851),
p. 116.

unique, and so appealing to scholars of American folk and popular medicine.[43]

With blacks living all around her in Maryland, their foods and foodways did not go unnoticed by Elizabeth Lea. Yet it is difficult, using her cookbook alone, to separate dishes of the black community from those of the poor whites. For in Maryland, the diet of both groups was in many ways quite similar. Okra, however, might serve as a typical example, since it is known to have an established African origin. Yet exactly how popular it was among Maryland's whites during this period remains to be seen. Like gumbo soup, which also appears in *Domestic Cookery*, it may have found its way to Sandy Spring by roundabout means, for it is known that Deborah Pierce, Elizabeth Lea's friend and neighbor, had a Creole servant. Furthermore, during the 1830s and 1840s, there was a surge of interest throughout the Middle Atlantic area in a number of Creole foods made fashionable through nationally sold cookbooks and travel accounts. The appearance of okra and gumbo in many ways parallels the appearance of tomato dishes, which before that time were almost completely unknown in the North. Okra, gumbo, and tomatoes, however, form an acculturation complex, for they appear to have traveled, if not together, then certainly not very far apart.

The popularization of certain Creole foods might be attributed to the revolution which was occurring at the time in Mississippi River trade. With the growth of railroads, both Baltimore and Philadelphia became important depots for trade moving west and down the Ohio. It was by this means that many Pennsylvania-German foods moved out of Southeastern Pennsylvania. But even earlier, in the eighteenth century, German settlers followed the valleys of the Blue Ridge and Allegheny Mountains and carried their foods and foodways south into areas far removed from the original Pennsylvania "Dutch" country.

---

43. For a better perspective of Elizabeth Lea's medical contributions, it would be helpful to refer to a recent essay by Bruno Gebhard, "The Interrelationship of Scientific and Folk Medicine in the United States since 1850," in *American Folk Medicine*, Wayland Hand, ed. (Berkeley/Los Angeles/London, 1976), pp. 87–98.

Maryland, in particular, became heavily populated with Germans in its northwestern counties. Of all of the non-English groups, the Pennsylvania-German influence is one of the heaviest in Elizabeth Lea's cookbook. Apple butter (conceptually different from English apple marmalade), as well as pumpkin preserve made the same way, bacon dumplings, "bologna" sausage, sauerkraut, mush flannel cakes, dried green corn, gingerbread nuts, liver sausage, rye mush, scrapple, and certain types of souse, all are traditionally associated with Pennsylvania-German cookery.[44] They are all found in *Domestic Cookery*, and many of these foods became so popular outside Pennsylvania-German communites that their origins have been attributed to other groups. Scrapple is probably the best known example of this.

The Anglo-American foods found in *Domestic Cookery* represent a number of diverse influences from the folk level to the more sophisticated cooking manuals of the early nineteenth century. Foods associated with the Quakers fall into both categories.

It is perhaps a peculiarity of early American Quakerism —its generally cautious and conservative approach to change —that led to a preservation of English eating habits among its members long after they had disappeared among Anglo-Americans elsewhere. For one thing, Quakers preferred to drink tea while most Americans preferred coffee. Their preference for afternoon teas and lavish evening tea parties kept in demand an enormous number of tea cakes, loaf cakes, currant breads, cookies, tea biscuits, and such accoutrements as lemon butter, cream cheese, and ice cream. Such foods can hardly be called "folk," since the pomp and ceremony of formal tea is but an eighteenth-century convention. But while recipes for most tea party delectables can be found in fashionable eighteenth- and nineteenth-century cookbooks, a few of these foods do claim genealogies with folk roots.

Foremost on Quaker tables would be cream cheese, which is hardly more than curds pressed until almost fully dehy-

---

44. See, for example, Ann Hark and Preston A. Barba, *Pennsylvania German Cookery* (Allentown, Pa., 1950).

drated, as Elizabeth Lea's recipe demonstrates. No artificial thickeners are necessary. This is a simple folk food made in parts of western England even today.

The historic yeoman cookery of rural England was in all events extremely plain.[45] When it was introduced to Maryland in the seventeenth century, the cultural shock rested with the English, not with the Indians, for the indigenous foods provided a far greater variety than what the English had known on a day-to-day basis at home. In technology, however, native American cookery had many similarities to its European counterparts. Indian baking was generally done in the ashes on the "hearth" or cooking place. On the folk level, this is where most of the baking was done in the British Isles, as it still is in underdeveloped parts of Britain and Ireland.[46] Thus, a number of hearth foods were assimilated by the English settlers at a very early date. This happened, for example, with the American Indian flat cakes made of cornmeal. The substitution of cornmeal for traditional oatmeal or barley was simple, since Indian flat cakes and British Isles flat cakes were almost identical.

In Maryland and Virginia, this transfer resulted in the development of a corn cookery based on British Isles food models using other grains. Corn, especially in the form of hominy, was generally a poverty food in Pennsylvania, but became a staple in tidewater Maryland. Hoe cakes and journey cakes, both found in *Domestic Cookery*, are British Isles hearth cakes utilizing cornmeal instead of oatmeal or barley.

From this it would appear that acculturation always occurs first where cultural barriers are the weakest, or conversely, where there are greatest similarities. This may explain why the Pennsylvania Germans, who baked almost exclusively in bake-ovens or on the tops of plate stoves, did not assume many Indian breads into their diet. Furthermore, cornmeal did not

45. See Jay A. Anderson, "Yeoman Foodways in Stuart England" (Ph.D. dissertation, University of Pennsylvania, Philadelphia, 1972).

46. Alexander Fenton, "Hafer- und Gerstenmehl als Hauptgegenstand der schottischen Nahrungsforschung," *Ethnologia Scandinavica* (Lund, 1971), pp. 149–57.

lend itself to the traditional dough foods which they preferred.[47]

As for other culinary traditions from the British Isles,
Domestic Cookery takes into account such cultural preference
foods as gruel and porridge, pones, muffins, and pies, and
includes several recipes for mutton. In addition to this, there
are also a number of foods which suggest connections with
other English-speaking regions farther south. Molasses beer, a
light, popular plantation beverage in the seventeenth and early
eighteenth centuries, was served as a substitute for traditional
English ale, since West Indian molasses was cheap and readily
available. Elizabeth Lea's unusually large number of rice
recipes were no doubt possible because of Maryland's trade
connections with the Deep South.

From eighteenth-century British Empire sources, mostly
through cookbooks, we find a number of East Indian dishes
reinterpreted in the form of yellow pickles, pepper mangoes,
and catsups. The yellow pickles in *Domestic Cookery* are called
"Virginia Yellow Pickles" because Elizabeth Lea's recipe is an
improvement of one published in Mary Randolph's *Virginia
Housewife.*

This brings us to the subject of printed sources, for certainly Elizabeth Lea was not ignorant of the vast array of
cookbooks and household receipt books that were available in
her day. In any event, tracing her recipes to specific works is
not simple, since she was meticulous enough to test and in most
cases improve nearly all of the recipes in her cookbook—an
admirable streak of honesty at a time when most cookbook
writers plagiarized without comment or apology.

On a regional level, Mary Randolph's *Virginia Housewife*
(Washington, D.C., 1824) was doubtless the strongest compet-
itor of *Domestic Cookery.* It also ran through many more editions. Nationally, the market was already cluttered by 1845–
1846 with works by Eliza Leslie of Philadelphia, Catharine

---

47. This aspect of Pennsylvania German diet is discussed in William
Woys Weaver, *"Die Geschickte Hausfrau:* The First Ethnic Cookbook in the
United States," *Food in Perspective* (Edinburgh, 1981), pp. 353–56.

Beecher, Eliza Acton (as improved by Sarah J. Hale), and many others. Yet the *Virginia Housewife* and *Domestic Cookery* share a number of similarities not found in the nationally marketed works. This may reflect both the peculiarities of regional taste as well as the fact that both Elizabeth Lea and Mary Randolph were familiar with Maria Rundell's *New System of Domestic Cookery* and drew on this work for some of their material.[48] Mary Randolph in particular leaned heavily on Rundell.

Richard Briggs' *New Art of Cookery* (London, 1788), reprinted at Philadelphia in 1794, was always popular among Philadelphia Quakers. And through Mrs. Goodfellow's cooking school, his influence went far beyond the owners of his book. He includes, incidentally, most of the basic ice cream recipes which later made Philadelphia famous. Elizabeth Lea includes four recipes for authentic Philadelphia ice cream—no milk allowed. But her recipe for ice custard with vanilla is probably the most antique in the frozen dessert category, even though vanilla flavoring did not become popular with Philadelphia gourmets until after 1800. Before then, lemon was by far the most popular flavor, pineapple the most recherché.

Another direct source for some of Elizabeth Lea's material was Turner & Fisher's *House-Keeper's Almanac*, which every year included a variety of recipes plagiarized from earlier cookbooks, agricultural journals, and even from other almanacs. Elizabeth Lea's recipe for tomato figs is taken, in part *verbatim*, from the *House-Keeper's Almanac* for 1846.[49]

All of these overlapping sources make the analysis of the

48. The first American edition of *A New System of Domestic Cookery* appeared at Boston in 1807 and was sold widely. It was reprinted at Philadelphia and Richmond the same year. The first Baltimore edition, called *American Domestic Cookery*, appeared in 1819. In spite of the shorter title, it followed the 1807 edition almost word for word.

49. *Turner's Improved House-Keeper's Almanac* was published annually in the 1840s and 1850s at Philadelphia by Turner & Fisher, who also issued it simultaneously in other cities. There were special editions for New England, the Middle States, the South and West. The Southern edition was sold at Baltimore by J. B. Keller, 3 South Gay Street. See his advertisement in the *Baltimore Sun*, January 2, 1845.

recipes in *Domestic Cookery* a fascinating study in itself. More important, however, is their sum total; for, oral or archaic, printed or popular, together they form a statement about their own times in terms of social custom, food habits, and taste preferences—all useful for understanding the origins of our own situation today.

The fact is, during its heyday, *Domestic Cookery* was extremely well received. Recipes from the collection show up in a variety of unexpected places, for example, in the cookbook kept by Thomas Jefferson's granddaughters.[50] However, industrialization and massive shifts in diet after the Civil War gradually rendered Elizabeth Lea's cookbook out of date. For in general Mid-Atlantic traditional cookery experienced a decline as cheap sugar, factory-made foods, and certain kitchen appliances became more widely available.[51]

Locally, the Civil War destroyed the thin economic base of Maryland's planter class. A new cookbook by Mrs. Benjamin Chew Howard (1801–91), called *Fifty Years in a Maryland Kitchen* (Baltimore, 1873), emerged in time for the Centennial and its turn toward colonial nostalgia and myth. If Mrs. Howard's cookbook acquired the sanctification of a history seen through somewhat colored spectacles, hers was also a book which became an institution and a social model for the next one hundred years. Elizabeth Lea, on the other hand, made no attempt to romanticize the cookery of old Maryland. Her own secluded lifestyle had none of the glamor of Mrs. Howard's, much less the lore. But where Mrs. Howard laid out silver settings for fox–hunting Episcopalians, Elizabeth Lea sat all of Maryland together: the blacks, the Indians, the Germans, the Irish, and the poor whites from Chincoteague to Swallow Falls.

50. Marie Kimball, *Thomas Jefferson's Cook Book* (Charlottesville, Va., 1976). See, for example, "Huckleberry Pudding," p. 99.
51. See, for example, Edward F. Keuchel, "Master of the Art of Canning: Baltimore 1860–1900," *Maryland History Magazine* LXVII (Winter, 1972): 351–62.

GLOSSARY

This glossary is intended to sharpen with further detail some of the concepts touched upon in the introduction to this book. It is also meant to serve as an explanation for unfamiliar or archaic food items in the text of Elizabeth Lea's *Domestic Cookery*. Special emphasis has been given to regional dishes or foods of folk origin with the hope that this will render the original text more useful to the researcher and more interesting to the general reader. For those who would like to experiment with some of the recipes in *Domestic Cookery*, some advice on weights and measures may be found under *Measurements* in the glossary.

A

APPLE BUTTER

This is an acculturated folk food introduced to Anglo-Americans in the Middle Atlantic region by the Pennsylvania Germans. The Pennsylvania Germans call it *Latwaerrick*, from German *Latwerge*, which is derived in turn from Latin *electuarium*. In flavor and consistency, it is not the same as English apple marmalade, although the two are related. One of the main differences is in the proportion of sugar to fruit pulp, apple butter having much less sugar than marmalade. Apple butter was also traditionally spiced with fennel seed, ground cloves, and nutmeg.

During the Middle Ages, a German *Latwerge* could be any of several thick, partially dehydrated preparations of slowly cooked fruit. Because it was generally cooked with sugar, at the time treated as an internal medicine, *Latwerge* was once only available through apothecaries. By the sixteenth century, however, the concept of *Latwerge* as food had become part of German folk cookery. It is still made in several areas of Austria, Switzerland, and Germany.

In the Pfalz, from which most Pennsylvania Germans originate, *Latwerge* is usually made from plums or pears. Apple *Latwerge* appears to be an adaptation to American conditions, since plums and pears were generally scarce in the Middle Atlantic region during the early part of the eighteenth century.

Among the Quakers, apple butter was acculturated from the Germans at a very early date, but it was generally called cider cheese in local dialect—a cheese being any sort of food thickened or partially dehydrated by slow cooking or pressing, as in the case of cream cheese (see p. 182), head cheese, and lemon cheese (also called lemon butter).

According to the Orthodox Quaker Mary Larkin Thomas, born in New Garden Township, Chester County, Pennsylvania, in 1886: "If there were no apple sauce and apple butter on the table, my father would ask for it. He expected it at every meal. It is a necessity." She continued: "On the third floor at the farm we had a meat room, and mother kept a stone jar there . . . which was full of apple butter. I remember going up and scooping it out just like any butter; it was that thick, and maybe more than a year old."

For a technical comparison with Elizabeth Lea's recipe, full directions for making Pennsylvania German apple butter may be found in the *Libanon Demokrat* for October 17, 1851.

REF.: Anna Bergner, *Pfälzer Kochbuch* (Mannheim, 1858), p. 549; "Das Latwerge Kochen," *Libanon Demokrat* (Lebanon, Pa.), October 17, 1851; *Interview,* Mary Larkin Thomas, Oct. 5, 1977; Laura B. Straron, "Applebutter Making as Practiced by Our Ancestors," *Papers Read Before the Bucks County Historical Society* IV (1917): 331–33; Hans Wiswe, *Kulturgeschichte der Kochkunst* (Munich, 1970), p. 211.

APPLE DUMPLINGS

The recipe in Elizabeth Lea's *Domestic Cookery* is conceptually the same dish mentioned by Peter Kalm in 1754. It is difficult to imagine that Kalm's Swedish readers were so unfamiliar with such a universally known dish as apple dumplings that he felt obliged to publish the recipe. But his observation supports evidence found in many other period sources that boiled apple dumplings were a standard (daily/seasonal) feature of Middle Atlantic folk cookery. Originally a medieval dessert food, apple dumplings were usually prepared during the eighteenth and nineteenth centuries as a light supper in themselves, a one-dish meal served hot with sugar, cream, and butter. For this reason, they were particularly well suited as meals for children.

The method of preparation described by Elizabeth Lea (p. 97), by which whole apples were encased in dough (pie crust) and boiled, is also commonly found in English period cookbooks; Hannah Glasse, in her *Art of Cookery* (1796), provides two similar recipes. But since this type of dumpling was also made by the Pennsylvania Germans and may be found in German culinary literature, it is evident that the dish was introduced simultaneously by both English and German-speaking groups. Its cultural role was thus fortified from two directions.

REF.: Bridget Ann Henisch, *Fast and Feast: Food in Medieval Society* (University Park, Pa., 1978); Sam Bowers Hilliard, *Hog Meat and Hoecake* (Carbondale, Ill., 1972), p. 55; Peter Kalm, *Travels in North America* (New York, 1966), I, p. 173; Johanna Maria van Winter, *Van Soeter Cokene* (Haarlem, 1976); Hannah Glasse, *The Art of Cookery Made Plain and Easy* (London, 1796), pp. 256 and 257.

APPLE FRITTERS

Fritters, like sweet dumplings, were originally medieval dessert foods that gradually became accessible to the lower classes, often in association with a particular religious or secular feast. In the Quaker counties of Southeastern Pennsylvania and Northern Delaware, and in the Quaker settlements in Northern and Western Maryland, orange fritters were particularly popular around Christmas, even among established church groups. The Quakers themselves generally served the fritters at New Year's, since they did not observe Christmas. In the case of rural Friends, who may have seen oranges only once a year at any rate, the ubiquitous apple fritter took its place.

REF.: *Chester and Delaware Federalist*, Dec. 13, 1809.

ARROWROOT

Before the perfection and widespread use of commercial cornstarch, arrowroot *(Maranta arundinacea)* was a popular thickening agent for foods. As an ingredient in hydropathic and homeopathic cookery, which gained considerable vogue among Quakers during the nineteenth century, arrowroot was also treated as a highly nourishing food in its own right, and was served either in gruel or pudding form to infants and invalids.

During the eighteenth and nineteenth centuries, most domestically consumed arrowroot was imported from the West Indies, but by 1845, arrowroot plantations had been established in Camden County, Georgia. An article in the *Friends' Weekly Intelligencer* that year praised this initiative as a great improvement over previous and sometimes unpredictable foreign trade arrangements. From a consumer standpoint, it meant cheaper arrowroot. However, the success of the Georgia experiment was short lived, for in the following decade Abolitionist boycotts of articles of trade produced by slave labor sent the Camden County plantations into financial ruin.

REF.: R. T. Trall, *The New Hydropathic Cook-Book* (New York, 1854), p. 190; *Friends' Weekly Intelligencer* II:8 (June 24, 1845): 61.

B

BACON DUMPLINGS

Although bacon dumplings are certainly known in British cookery, in terms of Maryland cookery they are traditionally associated with the Maryland Germans. As a folk dish, they trace their beginnings to the period between 1500 and 1600 when major shifts in food consumption occurred that changed several basic aspects of German diet. One of these shifts was a gradual decline in meat consumption on a per capita basis, and in its place, greater emphasis on *Mehlspeisen* (foods in which flour or dough is a major ingredient). *Mehlspeisen* became characteristic of South German cookery in particular.

According to the German food specialist Günter Wiegelmann, meat dumplings with liver or bacon were strictly a feature of upper-class cookery until about 1600, after which time they became increasingly associated with peasant (rural) cookery. In the context of folk cookery, the meat dumpling became a substitute for meat. But even for the peasants, such dumplings were not served every day. Like meat, they were reserved, rather, for Sunday dinners or festive occasions. This pattern was continued in Pennsylvania and Maryland by the German settlers, to whom Elizabeth Lea was doubtless indebted for her recipe.

REF.: Günter Wiegelmann, *Alltags- und Festspeisen* (Marburg, 1967), pp. 37–39; H. J. Teuteberg and Günter Wiegelmann, *Der Wandel der Nahrungsgewohnheiten unter der Einfluss der Industrialisierung* (Göttingen, 1972), especially "Die Rolle der Fleischkost in der Volksernährung," pp. 97–105.

BACON FRAISE

In the introduction, I proposed that Elizabeth Lea's cookbook is a synthesis of Middle Atlantic folk cookery as it developed over the century or so preceding the appearance of *Domestic Cookery*. Nowhere is this more evident than in Elizabeth Lea's recipe for bacon fraise (p. 22), a dish which is associated more with the seventeenth century than with the eighteenth in American colonial cookery.

The name of this dish is evidently borrowed from medieval French *fraiser*, although the dish itself has many counterparts in Mediterranean cookery, the Italian *frittata* among them. In substance, the fraise, like the *frittata*, is a glorified pancake, and was evidently introduced into English court cookery during the late Middle Ages. It subsequently filtered down into the folk level and by the seventeenth century took on a number of regional variations. Since bacon was a standard meat substitute in English yeoman cookery, the bacon fraise may be considered a standard folk dish.

The popularity of the fraise in rural diet is evident from the fact that it may be prepared very easily on a hearth. Thus, recipes continued to appear in such agricultural works as Richard Bradley's *Country Housewife* (1736). However, as a dish for fashionable cookbooks of the eighteenth century, the fraise was generally omitted. This makes its appearance in *Domestic Cookery* all the more interesting. Furthermore, in her directions for the recipe, Elizabeth Lea has preserved an old-dialect expression which was once commonly used among Pennsylvania Quakers, particularly those of Delaware and Chester County: "be careful in turning, that the bacon does not come to the pan." Come, in this sense, is used to mean stick or adhere and is probably related to the expression of making butter "come" (thicken), since the butter, when coming, begins to adhere to the churn. Perhaps this is one of Rebecca Russell's contributions to Lea's cookbook, since the expression was doubtless commonly used in her native New Garden, Chester County.

REF.: Richard Bradley, "Bacon Froize," *The Country Housewife and Lady's Director* (London, 1736), II, p. 51.

BALTIMORE OYSTER PIE

There is no question that the Chesapeake Bay offered Marylanders a ready source for excellent oysters. According to Matchett's *Baltimore Director*, William A. Redding & Company, 26 Hill Street, offered the most extensive selection of "fresh Cove" oysters in Elizabeth Lea's day. They came hermetically sealed in jars, freshly spiced, pickled, or put up in their own juices.

Characteristic of the entire Middle Atlantic region, not just Baltimore, is the use of oysters combined with a nineteenth-century Anglo-American preference for what the English term "savory" pies—pies filled with some sort of fish, poultry, or meat. On the folk level, savory pies took the place of the one-meal stew; at affluent tables, they formed part of a larger selection of pies usually served in combination with a variety of other dishes.

The pie, as a species of dish, came to the New World from the British Isles. Its development as a folk food there parallels the shift in meat consumption that occurred in Germany (*see* Bacon Dumplings), a shift away from meat toward greater reliance on dishes utilizing flour or dough. In Germany, the dough was placed in the stew, in the form of dumplings; in Britain, the stew was placed in the dough, in the form of savory pies. In both cases, dumplings and pies were features of upper-class cookery during the Middle Ages.

REF.: James Wharton, *Bounty of the Chesapeake* (Newport News, Va., 1957); Richard J. Matchett, *Matchett's Baltimore Director for 1853–1854* (Baltimore, 1853), p. 45 of advertisements; William Henderson, "Fish Pies," *The Housekeeper's Instructor* (London, 1805), pp. 193–95.

BEANS, WHITE (FOR SOUP)

Beans and bacon is an ancient combination in British cookery. References to soups made with these ingredients can be found in English culinary literature dating from the Middle Ages. Yet Elizabeth Lea's recipe (p. 34), an excellent example of folk cookery, appears to be of Pennsylvania-German or Maryland-German origin, for "soup beans" as they are still called in Pennsylvania were also known to the Germans.

Lea refers to a "little thickening" without explanation, but this was generally understood to be browned flour, the most universally preferred thickener in Pennsylvania-German cookery. Lea herself provides a recipe for browned flour (see p. 22) elsewhere in the cookbook. Browned flour, in combination with dumplings, as Elizabeth Lea suggests, is still a typically Pennsylvania-German approach to bean soup, fully a meal in itself, and a cheap way to feed a large family, as she even states in her recipe. However, for those interested in cooking techniques, the Pennsylvania Germans generally ran the cooked beans through a sieve or collander before adding the dumplings. The thickness of this purée could be controlled by adding meat stock, hot milk, or water. Elizabeth Lea leaves the beans whole.

REF.: George Girardey, "Bohnen Suppe," *Höchst Nützliches Handbuch über Kochkunst* (Cincinnati, 1842), p. 12; Georg von Martens, *Die Gartenbohnen* (Ravensburg, 1869).

BEEF, DRIED

Like oatmeal, salt meat—particularly dry-salted beef or pork —was once a basic item of food in the rural households of Western England and Wales. This traditional preference for salt meat was brought to the New World and preserved among the rural Quakers of the Middle Atlantic region.

In general, dried beef was made in the fall and eaten the following summer, since fresh beef was not usually available during hot weather. As a food item, it was made at home or bought from numerous commercial producers. Several Quaker-owned firms in Baltimore and Philadelphia processed dried beef for the shipping industry as well as for domestic consumption. Quaker dried beef could be purchased in country stores almost everywhere in Maryland and Pennsylvania, and it was partly through this association that dried beef became so firmly labeled as a Quaker food in the Middle Atlantic region. It is not surprising then that Elizabeth Lea should include a long and excellent recipe for making it, along with a number of serving suggestions (p. 172).

REF.: S. Minwell Tibbott, "Traditional Foods in Wales at the Beginning of the 20th Century," *Kansatieteellinen Arkisto 26* (Helsinki, 1975), pp. 268–69.

BIRD'S NEST PUDDING

There is no Chinese connection here. This is merely one of those odd novelty dishes that gained widespread popularity in the nineteenth century, for it was, in every sense, a cook's *tour de force.* Many years later, in her *Philadelphia Cookbook,* Sarah Tyson Rorer admitted that every recipe for bird's nest pudding was "just as troublesome as it reads, but beautiful when done." In Elizabeth Lea's household, where there were several daughters learning to cook, this touch of Victoriana was doubtless an all-day exercise in expertise and patience, but a perfect way to impress young gentlemen callers.

REF.: Sarah Tyson Rorer, *Philadelphia Cookbook* (Philadelphia, 1886), p. 399.

BLACK CAKE

This is a commercial cake of British origin which remained popular in the United States until the end of the nineteenth century. In England, it is called bride, wedding, or christening cake. A well-known recipe published by William Henderson in the *Housekeeper's Instructor* was the same as that used by the firm of Tupp and Perry in Oxford Street, London. Henderson's recipe was reprinted many times in American cookbooks.

In New England, this cake is usually called wedding cake or black cake and evidently served the same purpose there as it did in England: a cake for high occasions. In the Middle Atlantic region, black cake was more commonly called Dutch cake and was sold either in large "wheels" or in small loaves, particularly at Christmas. In the South, however, it acquired the name fruit cake, and is still produced commercially under that label.

Whatever the name, recipes for this type of cake do not often appear in manuscript Quaker cookbooks. It was either much easier to buy the commercial versions, or it simply did not fit into Quaker custom. Friends did not encourage lavish wedding entertainments (marriage was a religious service and little more), christening was out of the question theologically, and they certainly did not observe Christmas.

REF.: William Henderson, *The Housekeeper's Instructor* (London, 1805), p. 213; "Days and Times," *Discipline of the Yearly Meeting of Friends, Held in Baltimore* (Baltimore, 1806), pp. 30–31.

BOLOGNA SAUSAGE

Bologna sausage is a rich English pudding made from beef suet, pork, bacon, beef, and veal highly seasoned and boiled or poached in a gut until thick. It is an adaptation of the *mortadella* sausage of Bologna, hence the name. In most respects, the English version is only vaguely similar to its Italian ancestor.

William Henderson's *Housekeeper's Instructor* provides a standard English recipe. It is this same recipe that later appeared under bologna sausage in Mary Randolph's *Virginia Housewife*. Anglo-Americans, however, extended the name to include other types of spicy beef sausage, in particular, the sweet, smoked beef sausage made by the Pennsylvania Germans. In Pennsylvania-German dialect, this sausage is called *Summerwarscht* or summer sausage. *Summerwarscht* in no way resembles the original *mortadella* of Bologna. It is still made the traditional way in parts of the Rhineland-Pfalz, where the Pennsylvania-German recipes may have originated. Summer sausage is *never* boiled, and it is *never* served hot, since this would ruin both the flavor and texture of the sausage.

Although she calls it bologna sausage (p. 170), Elizabeth Lea has actually provided us with a recipe for *Summerwarscht*. This is evidence in itself of just how extensively *Summerwarscht* (by whatever name) was acculturated by non-German groups in the Middle Atlantic area. For certainly everywhere that Pennsylvania Quakers settled, whether in Maryland, Virginia, or Ohio, they took summer sausage with them and treated it as their own.

REF.: William Henderson, *The Housekeeper's Instructor* (London, 1805), p. 298; Mary Randolph, *The Virginia Housewife* (Philadelphia, 1851), p. 55; Thomas F. DeVoe, *The Market Assistant* (New York, 1867), p. 102; Erich Lissner, *Wurstologia oder Es Geht um die Wurst* (Frankfurt, 1939).

BRANDY PAPERS

This was usually cooking parchment (but sometimes writing paper) thoroughly soaked in brandy and tied down over crocks or jars or preserves. The brandied paper acted as an antiseptic and deterrent against vermin. It did not keep out air. See, for example, Elizabeth Lea's recipe for quince jelly (p. 137). This method has now been replaced by paraffin or vacuum sealing.

BREAD

See Dutch-Oven Loaf.

BRITANNIA WARE

This is a species of pewter that contains no lead. It is usually a compound of tin, antimony, and copper. As a metal for household utensils, britannia ware was popular during the first half of the nineteenth century, particularly for tea and coffee pots. From a health standpoint, it was often extremely dangerous due to the high content of copper found in some brands. Both tea and coffee contain strong acids that can react with the metal to produce poisonous precipitates. Holmes & Sons of Baltimore were the largest retailers of britannia ware in Maryland while *Domestic Cookery* was at the height of its popularity. Elizabeth Lea's directions for the care of Britannia ware, however, are based on those published by Lydia Maria Child in her *American Frugal Housewife.*

REF.: Lydia Maria Child, *American Frugal Housewife* (Boston, 1833), p. 10.

BROWN FLOUR

There are three basic methods for preparing brown flour: (1) roasting unground wheat in a bakeoven (as the Pennsylvania Germans do with corn), and then, afterwards, grinding it to a fine brown powder; (2) scorching flour in a heavy iron skillet or kettle, as Elizabeth Lea suggests; or (3) frying flour in butter or lard and using it immediately—the most common method among the Pennsylvania Germans. Fried flour appears as *braun geröstetes Mehl* in the old and once very popular Pennsylvania German cookbook *Die Geschickte Hausfrau* ("The Handy Housewife"). Elizabeth Lea's method, however, is a substitute for roasting the wheat whole in a bakeoven. The advantage of her method is that quantities of flour could be browned ahead of time and stored until needed. In the German areas of Pennsylvania, there are still cooks who scorch flour by this means. When done properly, the scorching flour often fills the kitchen with smoke, as I have observed on more than one occasion in the course of fieldwork.

Browned flour and the preference for it in cookery is a feature of South German cuisine that was brought to America by the Pennsylvania and Maryland Germans. They, in turn, introduced it to their English-speaking neighbors. It was once as much a feature of the cookery in the German counties of Maryland as cornmeal cookery was a feature of the Tidewater area. Brown flour was as basic as salt, for it was used as a thickener in soups and sauces, as a filler in meat pies, and as an additive to bread—particularly rye bread—when cooks wanted to stretch a few extra loaves from their dough.

REF.: Friederike Löffler, "Eine Gebrennte Suppe" [Browned Flour Soup], *Ökonomisches Handbuch für Frauenzimmer* (Stuttgart, 1795), p. 9; Gustav S. Peters, *Die Geschickte Hausfrau* (Harrisburg, Pa., 1848), p. 5; William Woys Weaver, "Die Geschickte Hausfrau: The First Ethnic Cookbook in the United States," *Food in Perspective* (Edinburgh, 1981), pp. 343–63.

BUCKWHEAT CAKES

Buckwheat has had a long association with Quaker cookery in Maryland, Delaware, and Pennsylvania. In Sandy Spring, where Elizabeth Lea lived, the farmland remained relatively fertile, and wheat and buckwheat, rather than corn, served as local staples. According to James Lemon, however, buckwheat was generally consumed by the less affluent, even during the eighteenth century when it was most popular.

A regional preference for buckwheat, generally in the form of buckwheat cakes, was probably a continuation of a widespread buckwheat culture introduced by the Holland Dutch in the seventeenth century. According to surveys by J. Dyneley Prince and others, *bukwait* was one of the most common food terms in New World Dutch dialect. Buckwheat was likewise noted by the Swedish traveler Peter Kalm who wrote that it was by far one of the most popular winter breakfast foods in Philadelphia—in this case, in the form of buckwheat cakes.

Philadelphia appears to fall toward the southern end of the old seventeenth-century buckwheat "belt" which encompassed the tidewater farmlands of the Delaware Valley as far south as New Castle. In the other direction, it extended northward through New Jersey and into the Hudson Valley.

In the Delaware Basin, buckwheat was a major ingredient in scrapple (see p. 171), a Lower Rhineland dish which, like buckwheat itself, seems to have gained acceptance among all social levels within the region. Isaac Norris, a Philadelphia Quaker who was certainly not among the colony's impoverished, recorded in his farm account for 1723 that he had sowed buckwheat in a field where "it was last year abundant." Norris' estate was only a few miles from Germantown where the production of scrapple had been a home industry since the 1680s.

In time, the acceptance of buckwheat as a breakfast cereal, especially in the form of cakes, muffins, scrapples, and the like, became so much a feature of general American cookery that it might be cited as one of our points of divergence from traditional

British diet. For in terms of British-American cookery, buckwheat always remained an American peculiarity. This was evident even in Elizabeth Lea's lifetime.

In 1846, shortly after she published the first edition of *Domestic Cookery,* there was a well-publicized effort to introduce buckwheat to the British public in order to stave off the effects of the potato famine. According to a long article in the May, 1846 *Friends' Weekly Intelligencer,* a large propaganda campaign was launched in Britain to promote buckwheat in spite of the fact that until that time it was mostly viewed there as fodder—a social stigma not easily overcome in any society. An editor of a British newspaper who tasted buckwheat cakes later remarked in print that they were "so totally different in flavour from anything English, that no words can describe their peculiar excellence." An article in the *American Farmer* later that same year was a little more Yankee in its assessment of buckwheat: "the very name of which makes the mouth water."

REF.: James T. Lemon, *The Best Poor Man's Country* (Baltimore, 1972), p. 157; Peter Kalm, *Travels in North America* (New York, 1966), I, p. 184; William T. Parsons, "Orders What's to Be Done at the Plantation: The Isaac Norris Farm Accounts, 1713–1734," *Pennsylvania Folklife* XXVII:1 (Fall, 1977): 10–18; *Friends' Weekly Intelligencer* II:6 (May 9, 1846): 46; *American Farmer* (Baltimore) II:1 (July, 1846): 2; J. Dyneley Prince, "The Jersey Dutch Dialect," *Dialect Notes,* III, Part 6 (1910): 470.

C, D

CHERRY CORDIAL

This is Elizabeth Lea's version of cherry bounce, a popular social drink in colonial times, which in the nineteenth century became an acceptable tonic for monthly "female complaints." Elizabeth Lea's choice of the word "cordial," the addition of ethyl alcohol (rather than rum or rye), and the very large quantity of sugar all suggest this medical application. The social drink, made with rum in Maryland and rye in Pennsylvania, was infinitely easier to make and infinitely easier to drink than Elizabeth Lea's concoction (p. 147).

We are reminded here of the author's firm stance on temperance, which is carried through in her other cordial recipes. Thus, her lemon brandy (p. 147) is a flavoring for cakes and puddings; her blackberry cordial (p. 148), a medicine for children in the summer; and her elderberry wine (p. 150), a remedy for "summer disease," or common diarrhea.

CHICKENS STEWED WITH NEW CORN

Elizabeth Lea's recipe (p. 29) offers two variations of the same thing: a chicken-corn pot pie, and a chicken-corn soup with dumplings. Both of these dishes are white adaptations of similar native American stews.

The Delaware Indians, whose historic homeland included parts of Maryland, had a highly developed stew cookery. Their earthenware cooking pots (the average size held about three gallons) were particularly well suited for stew making; and according to archeology, the traditional "hornets' nest" shape of these pots was developed perhaps a thousand years ago, but with many subsequent refinements in neck and rim design and decoration. Many eighteenth-century journals, such as those of David Brainerd and John Bartram, make special mention of Delaware stews combining green corn with some type of meat. Instead of chicken, however, the Indians generally used a mixture of fish and eel, dog, opossum, or the meat of some other small game. The natural sweetness of new corn provided a rich contrast to the meat. And like the Pennsylvania Germans, the Indians also added a variety of dumplings, some made with cornmeal and nut paste, others with corn and beans tied up in small bundles, using the husks in place of dough.

It is significant that in the Quaker counties in the immediate vicinity of Philadelphia, where a more homogeneous "English" cookery prevailed, chicken-corn soup was not widely consumed and therefore cannot be associated with the Anglo-Quaker element. John Witthoft and Bonita Freeman-Witthoft have pointed out in their survey of Delaware (Lenape) Indian harvest foods, that many dishes like chicken-corn soup came into Anglo-American diet through a middle group, in this case, through the Pennsylvania Germans. Yet aside from the European substitution of chicken, the dish remains remarkably similar to its pre-Columbian ancestor.

REF.: John Heckewelder, "Food and Cookery," in *An Account of the Indian Nations, Who Once Inhabited Pennsylvania and the Neighboring States* (Philadelphia, 1818), p. 187; David Brainerd, *An Account of the Life of the Late Reverend Mr. David Brainerd* (Boston, 1749); John Bartram, *Observations on the Inhabitants* (London, 1751), particularly p. 60; John Witthoft and Bonita Freeman-Witthoft, "Lenape Indian Fall Harvest," *Frontiers* (Fall, 1975), pp. 9–13; Herbert Kraft, "Indian Prehistory of New Jersey," in *A Delaware Indian Symposium* (Harrisburg, Pa., 1974), pp. 1–55.

CIDER CAKE

This is a popular early American box cake that evolved out of soft gingerbread, with cider and sugar taking the place of molasses. The basic recipe (p. 120), although altered somewhat, appeared earlier in Eliza Leslie's *Seventy-Five Receipts* (Boston, 1828). Ultimately, the recipe may have originated at Elizabeth Goodfellow's cooking school (circa 1809–1844) in Philadelphia, where Eliza Leslie collected recipes and learned to cook.

REF.: Eliza Leslie, *Seventy-Five Receipts* (Boston, 1828), p. 63.

COLD SLAW

The name of this dish (p. 51) is the result of an attempt to anglicize *kolslaa*, the New World Dutch term for cabbage salad. It is a misnomer because the *kol* (cabbage) is not cold. For one thing, the hot dressing warms it up. Furthermore, this recipe is probably not of Dutch origin, although it belongs to a large family of salads which are related to the Dutch species.

Salads with hot dressings are a Northern European adaptation of the oil-and-vinegar salad which moved northward out of the Mediterranean area during the Middle Ages. The concept seems to have been dispersed first through the monasteries, then it passed to the tables of the upper classes, and finally, after much local adaptation, it found its way into folk diet. In place of olive oil, melted fat, hot butter, eggs, even sour cream were appropriated as binders for the vinegar. Of course, this gave rise to a wide variety of dressings and produced a genre of salad that was quite different from its Italian model.

In terms of Maryland and Elizabeth Lea's world in particular, salads with hot dressings were probably introduced by the Germans who settled there in the eighteenth century. In general, such "hot" salads were eaten as meals in themselves during the period of the "six-weeks' want"—February to March—when stocks of stored vegetables were low and gardens were not yet planted.

REF.: Günter Wiegelmann, "Das Gebiet der Neuerungen des 16. und 17. Jahrhunderts," *Alltags- und Festspeisen* (Marburg, 1967), pp. 230–32; J. Dyneley Prince, "The Jersey Dutch Dialect," *Dialect Notes* III, Part 6 (1910): 470.

CORN BANNOCK, CORN CAKE, CORN MEAL BREAD

In 1781, while traveling through Maryland, Baron von Closen noted that "the only grain produced here is maize (Turkish wheat), from which bread and some thin cakes, like those of Brittany, are made, which are not very tempting to me." The baron was an unwitting ethnologist, for in his off-hand observation, there surface three significant points relating to the study of Mid-Atlantic foods and foodways.

The first and most obvious observation is that Tidewater Maryland, like Virginia, developed a corn-based diet. This was a diet centered on white corn. In western Maryland, where Elizabeth Lea lived, most people preferred roasted yellow corn. The reasons for this difference are not clear at present, but since white corn was the cheapest grain available in Tidewater Maryland, perhaps the very nature of the plantation system, which used it as a food crop for the slave population, encouraged both blacks and poor whites to substitute it for grains that had been used in traditional Old World dishes. The extensive use of white corn gave rise to the appearance of the corn breads, corn bannocks, corn muffins, corn cakes, and other corn dishes now associated with Tidewater cookery. But on the rather bald and sandy soils of the Tidewater area, this was subsistence cookery at best. For when the corn crop failed, everyone suffered, as the *American Farmer* noted in 1846 when Maryland's lower counties were in the grip of famine.

Von Closen's second observation, that the thin cakes he saw were like those of Brittany, is rather on target, since the flat cake, as it appeared in Western Europe, is thought by ethnologists to be of Celtic origin. As Kevin O'Danachair has pointed out, it is a traditional food in Ireland, Wales, Scotland, and those parts of continental Europe—like Brittany—where Celtic foodways still persist on the folk level.

The third important point made by von Closen is that corn-meal cookery did not appeal to him. He was not speaking as an aristocrat, but rather as a German. He was referring to a cultural preference. Naturally, because of its texture, cornmeal does not work in German cookery, which is based on wheat flour. Except for mush, the Pennsylvania Germans did not care for plain cornmeal any more than did von Closen. They roasted the corn in their bakeovens, then ground it to a fine, brown, nutty powder, which was commonly used as an adulterant in rye flour. Elizabeth Lea was certainly familiar with this type of cornmeal because, commercially, the Lea mills in Delaware held almost a complete monopoly over kiln-dried cornmeal for the period 1800–1850. The Leas were able to satisfy domestic markets as well as markets in the West Indies, but their product was not guaranteed against competition or shifting patterns of taste. For when Pennsylvania Germans moved into areas where the soil was poor and wheat could not be grown, they turned to the use of white corn. As a result, they were forced to give up their traditional baked foods, and roasted cornmeal lost its cultural appeal.

Maryland, however, played an important role during the nineteenth century in disseminating cornmeal cookery northward. Most of the slaves who escaped to Pennsylvania and New Jersey came generally from Maryland's Eastern Shore or from neighboring areas of Virginia. Once in free territory, they often found employment as cooks. These black cooks introduced many households to traditional cornmeal dishes. Their story is one of the more fascinating but unwritten chapters in the history of Middle Atlantic cookery.

REF.: Evelyn M. Acomb, ed., *The Revolutionary Journal of Baron Ludwig von Closen* (Chapel Hill, 1958), p. 130; Aubrey C. Land, "Economic Base and Social Structure: The Northern Chesapeake in the Eighteenth Century," *Journal of Economic History* XXV:4 (1965): 639–59; Kevin O'Danachair, "Bread in Ireland," in *Food in Perspective* (Edinburgh, 1981), pp. 57–67; "Suffering at Home," *American Farmer* I (June, 1846): 368; James W. Thomson, "Indian Corn: Experiments in Manufacturing Corn Meal," *Monthly Journal of Agriculture* II:1 (July, 1846): 40–41; Vera A. Foster Rollo, *The Negro in Maryland: A Short History* (Baltimore, 1972).

CREAM CHEESE

Cream cheese was and still is a popular food in the Philadelphia region, but it is not a Philadelphia invention, as the name of Elizabeth Lea's recipe might suggest. The technique for making cream cheese was brought to Pennsylvania on a large scale during the late 1600s by the English and Welsh settlers. However, the Dutch, who had settled much earlier in the Lower Delaware Valley, were also culturally familiar with cream cheese, so there may be grounds for suggesting an earlier date of introduction. Regardless of who introduced it, the best "Philadelphia" cream cheese in the eighteenth and early nineteenth centuries was imported directly from Holland. Advertisements for these cheeses are not rare. Thomas Mackie, a Philadelphia merchant, for example, advertised Dutch cream cheeses in *Poulson's American Daily Advertiser* in 1805. Poulson's *Advertiser* went out to most of the East Coast ports, so in commercial terms "Philadelphia" cream cheese may have been more a label of convenience than a reference to point of manufacture.

The modern species of cream cheese is in no way similar to the old-fashioned varieties—Dutch or domestic, and in no way superior to it. In its most ancient and purest form, cream cheese was not a true "made" cheese, at least in the sense that no heat was involved, no rennet was used, and no curds were separated. Mary Smith, in her *Complete House-Keeper,* provides the basic folk recipe, whereby fresh cream is simply allowed to drain between clean linens for two weeks or until thick. True cream cheese is thus nothing more than partially dehydrated sour cream.

It was in this same archaic vernacular sense that the term cheese was applied to other thick dehydrated foods, such as walnut cheese, lemon butter (see p. 136)—also called lemon cheese, apple butter (see p. 143)—also called cider cheese, and damson cheese, a preparation of plums, similar to apple butter, which was commonly found in provincial English cookbooks, among them, *The Frugal Housewife.*

Elizabeth Lea's recipe (p. 182), which uses milk instead of cream, necessarily calls for the separation of the curds, but it is a traditional recipe, one which replaced the older method in the nineteenth century.

REF.: *Poulson's American Daily Advertiser,* Mar. 21, 1805; Mary Smith, *The Complete House-Keeper* (New Castle, England, 1786), p. 313; *The Frugal Housewife* (Devonport, England, ca. 1840), p. 24.

CRULLER

In the nineteenth century, the term "cruller" was considered a provincialism of New York origin. It meant a doughnut. Today, the word varies somewhat in meaning throughout the United States—different people have different ideas as to what constitutes a proper cruller. In the 1840s, however, it was generally a doughnut with a hole, that is, a form of fried Fastnacht cake.

The term itself stems from the Holland Dutch verb *krullen*, also variously written *krollen* and *kruyllen*. It seems to have wandered into American cookbook vocabulary through the Holland Dutch element in New York. The specific meaning of *krullen* is apparent in the meaning of a related word, *Krüllkoken* (*"krullen"* cakes) in Oldenburg dialect, which is similar to Holland Dutch. Annemarie Wurmbach has explained that certain Fastnachts, or "Shrove-Tuesday" cakes, were called *Krüllkoken* because after frying, they were *rolled* in sugar. A cruller, then, is a fat-cake rolled in sugar.

REF.: Henry Reeves, "Our Provincialisms," *Lippincott's Magazine* III (Mar., 1869): 313; Annemarie Wurmbach, "Kuchen-Fladen-Torte," *Zeitschrift für Volkskunde* LVI:1 (1960): 20–40; for Dutch food and social customs relating to Shrove Tuesday, see Jos. Schrijnen, *Nederlandsche Volkskunde* (Zutphen, n.d.), I: 154–66.

CURRANT WINE

Among temperance-minded Quakers, wine was considered the more acceptable alternative to distilled liquors. For many years before the Civil War, Quaker writers, such as David Lloyd, author of the widely read *Economy of Agriculture*, promoted viticulture and the perfection of domestic table wines. But fruit wines made at home were always particularly acceptable, and in Elizabeth Lea's case, an ingredient in her medical repertoire.

REF.: David Lloyd, *Economy of Agriculture* (Germantown, Pa., 1832), pp. 85–93.

DUTCH-OVEN LOAF

Baking bread in an iron kettle on the hearth is one of the most consistent and most ancient features of folk cookery in the British Isles. It is a method of baking which in some areas predates the appearance of the domed brick bakeoven, in Wales, for example, while in other regions, it served as an alternative for individuals who did not possess or could not afford a brick oven. For even in England during the seventeenth and early eighteenth centuries, bakeovens were usually found only in manor-house kitchens, to which rural cooks were obliged to take their bread for baking, and thus subject it to a tithe. Possession of a domed bakeoven, therefore, carried with it considerable status. A Dutch oven did not.

The Quaker settlers in South Jersey, Pennsylvania, and Maryland—even Elizabeth Lea's own ancestors—came mostly from the western counties of England, particularly Cheshire, and Wales. Rural Quaker cookery in the Mid-Atlantic region reflected this origin, and the use of a Dutch oven, which Quakers sometimes called "pot ovens," was prevalent at least until the advent of iron cookstoves.

As an accessory for baking bread, the Dutch oven was perhaps most commonly found among the Scotch-Irish of Western Pennsylvania, Ohio, West Virginia, and the hill country of Western Maryland. It is absolutely necessary for the preparation of soda bread.

It is significant to note that within the context of the broader regional culture in which Elizabeth Lea lived, there was a large class of poor whites and blacks who depended upon hearth baking as their sole source of bread. It is interesting that Lea's recipe (pp. 59–60) took this into account, because very few period cookbooks, American or British, devote much space to it. "Baking in dirt," as some Welsh cooks characterize it (the pot is covered with ashes), was generally considered primitive by the 1840s and an unappetizing way to go about the business of bread baking, regardless of the delightful "hearthy" flavor.

REF.: Trefor M. Owen, "The Ethnological Study of Food in Wales," *Folk and Farm* (Dublin, 1976), pp. 218–28; S. Minwell Tibbott, *Welsh Fare* (Cowbridge and Bridgend, Wales, 1976); Alwyn D. Rees, *Life in a Welsh Countryside* (Cardiff, 1975).

E, F, G, H

FOX GRAPE

Wild grapes abound in Maryland, and fox grapes are still among the most popular of the wild varieties for making jellies and jams (Lea, p. 136). Among the Quakers, fox grapes were also called raccoon grapes. Some Quaker farmers allowed the vines to grow over the tops of apple trees and could thus force each vine to produce as much as seventy-five bushels of grapes per year.

REF.: *Friends' Weekly Intelligencer* IV:51 (Mar. 18, 1848): 407.

GILL

From Middle Latin *gellus* and *gillo,* but more directly, from Old French *gille:* a liquid measure equal to ½ cup. In nineteenth-century America, it was used in connection with the measurement of wines and spirits, as in the case of measuring out brandy for vanilla (Lea, p. 107). *See* Measurements.

GRAHAM BREAD

In 1840, Sylvester Graham (1794–1851), an American vegetarian who advocated radical changes in eating habits, developed the flour now known as Graham flour. It was made from unsifted whole wheat flour, and like homeopathic cookery, became one of the leading fads of the period. Progressive Quakers, always interested in scientific reforms and social improvement, openly advocated many of Graham's ideas. Considering Elizabeth Lea's interest in health, it is not surprising to find a Grahamite recipe (p. 61) in her cookbook.

GREEN CORN

This is an older term for sweet corn or corn that has not yet fully matured. Boiled green corn (p. 44) was originally an American Indian dish. Toward the end of August, the Mohican Indians celebrated their annual Feast of the Green Corn, at which time many corn dishes were served. Other East Coast tribes, like the Delawares and Nanticokes, had their own corn-related festivals.

REF.: Clark Wissler, "Aboriginal Maize Culture as a Typical Culture-Complex," *American Journal of Sociology* XXII (1916): 656–60; "Food Products of the North American Indians," *Report of the U.S. Commissioner of Agriculture, 1870* (Washington, D.C., 1871).

HARVEST BEER

In its most limited sense, a harvest beer is any "small" beer (a beer low in alcoholic content) served to field hands during their breaks. It is not a specific recipe. Elizabeth Lea's recipe (p. 152), however, is an honest variation of molasses beer (p. 153), but to be safe she has supplied us with recipes for both.

Among the Quakers and non-Quakers alike, molasses beer was one of the most popular summer field drinks served during the colonial period. After the Revolution, when stiff levies were placed on imports, especially on wine, rye whisky, because of its relative cheapness, generally replaced molasses beer in Maryland and Pennsylvania. In New Jersey, it was replaced by apple jack. The Quakers resisted the temptation to serve spirits to their workhands, but by the 1840s, even molasses beer, like lemonade, was something drunk only by old ladies and children. Temperance advocates and Elizabeth E. Lea tried to put it back in the fields.

I, J, K, L

ICE CREAM

As early as 1744 ice cream was being served in Maryland, but then, only as a great rarity enjoyed by a wealthy few. Ice cream gained popularity in England and its colonies through the Italians, who introduced Arabic sorbets in the 1600s and greatly improved upon them. For a long time, ice creams and other frozen desserts were foods limited only to the highest aristocracy in Europe, and even in the late eighteenth century, they were not available at large. By the nineteenth century, however, ice cream had become something of a social institution in America, along with iced drinks and other cold summer foods.

Elizabeth Lea's recipe (p. 108) is an excellent and quite authentic recipe for Philadelphia ice cream—no *milk* allowed. Frozen creams and whips became fashionable in Philadelphia while the city served as the nation's capital in the 1790s. Foreign diplomats brought private cooks well acquainted with the latest Paris techniques for making ice creams, and many French cooks established themselves in the city to work in private homes or as caterers. They were important in making Philadelphia ice cream famous. But there was more to it than just good cooks.

At the time, Quaker farmers in Delaware and Chester Counties (west of the city) produced some of the richest butter, cream, and milk in the country—an accomplishment that went unchallenged until well after the Civil War. By simply taking a standard ice cream recipe from Richard Briggs's *New Art of Cookery,* and using only the very richest *fresh* country cream, it is still possible to reproduce the ice creams that once made Philadelphia famous. But for country Friends living in places like Sandy Spring, in the days when ice cream did not travel well, Elizabeth Lea's recipes are an equal substitute for the Philadelphia species, and every one of them true to the name.

REF.: Richard Briggs, *New Art of Cookery* (Philadelphia, 1792); W. S. Stallings, "Ice Cream and Water Ices in 17th and 18th Century England," *Petits Propos Culinaires 3—Supplement* (London, 1979), pp. 1–32; J. Stevens Cox, *Ice-Creams of Queen Victoria's Reign* (St. Peter Port, Guernsey, England, 1970).

JOURNEY CAKE

These once-popular hearth cakes of British Isles origin were standard fare for travelers, both as a fast food served at inns and as a snack for eating along the way—hence the name. They were also eaten by the poor throughout the eastern United States, serving the same purpose as the tortilla in Mexico. Father Mathew, the popular temperance advocate in Ireland, tried to introduce American cornmeal journey cakes to the local population during the potato famine, but without success.

REF.: *Friends' Weekly Intelligecer* III:6 (May 9, 1846): 46; Kevin O'Danachair, "Our Daily Bread," *Biatas* (June, 1959), pp. 204–8 and 225; Kevin O'Danachair, "Bread," *Ulster Folklife* IV (1958): 29–32.

LEMON BUTTER

There are various methods for making this dish, but in general it is a thick custard of milk, eggs, butter, sugar, and lemon. It is still made in Scotland and Wales under its older name, lemon cheese, although some commercial varieties generally leave a bad impression of the dish.

Lemon butter, of all the foods mentioned in *Domestic Cookery*, is perhaps the one dish that Quakers in the Middle Atlantic states identify as a symbol of their cookery, even though recipes for it are common enough in seventeenth- and eighteenth-century English cookbooks—usually under the name of lemon cream. As a dish, its popularity predates that of ice cream, but among Quakers it is not a dessert. It is simply eaten as a spread, pudding, or side dish. Elizabeth Lea suggests eating it on bread.

Less popular, but made in exactly the same manner, was orange butter, which in the late eighteenth and early nineteenth centuries was mostly eaten around Christmas and New Year's.

Among Quakers, the serving of lemon butter is still viewed as a high compliment, since it is extremely rich, expensive, and rather difficult to get right, for much of its success depends on its consistency. Today, lemon butter is sometimes served at Quaker picnics, but on high occasions it is best served in a crystal bowl set down in crushed ice.

REF.: Eliza Smith, "Lemon-Cream," *The Compleat Housewife* (London, 1753), p. 185; Frances Harriet McDougall, "Lemon Cream," *The Housekeeper's Book* (Philadelphia, 1838). pp. 151–52; "Lemon Cream," *Cookery as It Should Be* (Philadelphia, 1855), p. 307; Isabella Beeton, "Lemon Cream," *The Book of Household Management* (London, 1861), pp. 726–27.

LOAF SUGAR

See Sugar.

M

MANGOES

This popular nineteenth-century pickle traces its origin to India, to a true mango pickle, which is called *bafena* among the Parsees. The recipe became popular in England during the eighteenth century, mostly as a less expensive substitute for the real imported article. The pickle was popularized in this country through English cookbooks. Cookbook writers often used the term "mango" rather loosely in connection with any fruit or vegetable that could be successfully stuffed and pickled according to the recipe.

In Pennsylvania and western Maryland, mangoes were generally made with green bell peppers. In Tidewater Maryland, where the growing season was longer and soil conditions were ideal for melon culture, muskmelons provided the most popular form of local mango. Elizabeth Lea's recipe (p. 156), which calls for muskmelons, is similar to the mango recipe published in Mary Randolph's *Virginia Housewife*. Like most mango pickles, her pickle was served as a condiment with roasts. At banquets, it was sometimes served as a separate salad course.

REF.: William Woys Weaver, "Food Acculturation and the First Pennsylvania-German Cookbook," *Journal of American Culture* II:3 (Fall, 1979): 425–27.

MARYLAND BISCUIT

This is another name for the folk food called "beaten biscuits," beaten because they were kneaded with a hammer or pestle instead of adding yeast to make them rise. This type of biscuit appears very early in the Chesapeake area, and may trace its origin to the British Isles. In Maryland, however, the beaten biscuit is a popular symbol of local cookery. Mary Randolph included a recipe in her *Virginia Housewife*. She calls the biscuits "Apoquiniminc Cakes." (Appoquinnimink is in New Castle County, Delaware.)

REF.: Mary Randolph, *The Virginia Housewife* (Philadelphia, 1851), p. 139.

MARYLAND CORN CAKE
See Corn Bannock.

MEASUREMENTS
Like modern European recipes using metric measurements, early American recipes often rely more on weight than on volume. Once one is accustomed to thinking in this idiom, it is usually possible to cook directly from *Domestic Cookery* without much difficulty. "Heaped" measurements generally mean half again as much.

```
cupful = 16 tablespoons or 1 cup
gill = ½ cup or 8 tablespoons
glassful = in Lea, another term for wineglass
handful = 1 ounce
pint = 2 cups
saltspoon = ¼ teaspoon
small spoonful = 4 saltspoons or 1 teaspoon
spoonful = 3 teaspoons or 1 tablespoon
teacupful = allow 5 ounces
wineglass = 4 tablespoons or ½ gill
```

MOLASSES BEER
See Harvest Beer.

MUSH, MUSH FLANNEL CAKES, RYE MUSH
Mush is a colloquial term for cornmeal porridge, one of the few cornmeal dishes that even the Pennsylvania Germans learned to eat with gusto. In New England, mush was called hasty pudding; in New York, it was called suppan; and in England, stirabout.

Suppan is the Delaware Indian term for the dish, a term borrowed from the Indians by the New York Dutch in the seventeenth century. While suppan may have been a humble porridge by European standards, it was by no means a humble food for the Indians, for it apparently served them in many ways. They must have equated it with hospitality or a symbol of hospitality because it played a significant ceremonial role at feasts and treaties. Among the Delawares, for example, it was eaten the morning after the Annual Ceremony as a kind of send-off breakfast for visitors.

The role of suppan as a breakfast food was continued by European settlers, who substituted it for the other cereal porridges they had known in the Old World. Even though this adaptation was widespread, and even though Delaware and its related languages were once broadly distributed across Maryland, Delaware, Pennsylvania, and New Jersey, most Europeans in this region preferred to call the dish mush rather than suppan. Mush, in fact, is now considered a Pennsylvania regionalism, and it is interesting that Elizabeth Lea preferred this usage herself.

REF.: Mark R. Harrington, "A Preliminary Sketch of Lenape Culture," *American Anthropologist* XV (1913): 229; Don Yoder, "Pennsylvanians Called It Mush," *Pennsylvania Folklife* XIII:2 (Winter, 1962):27–49.

N, P

NEW YEAR'S CAKE

This name is somewhat misleading. The ingredients, as Elizabeth Lea has ordered them, make a stiff cookie which was once popular in Pennsylvania and Delaware under the name of apees cake. It is closely related to the springerle but was sold by street vendors the year around. For rural Quakers it was a special treat for children at New Year's, which may explain the name Elizabeth Lea has used for it. The cookie, however, is not related to the crumb cake which is now sold under the name of Apees in Berks County, Pennsylvania.

Elizabeth Lea's recipe is a direct adaptation of the Apees recipe published by Eliza Leslie in 1828, and which later appeared in Turner and Fisher's *Kitchen Companion*. Like hard gingerbread, apees cookies were originally stamped with designs of animals, hearts, and other ornamental figures.

REF.: Eliza Leslie, *Seventy-Five Receipts* (Boston, 1828), p. 57; Turner and Fisher, *The Kitchen Companion, and House-Keeper's Own Book* (Philadelphia, 1844); Alfred L. Shoemaker, "About Apees," *Pennsylvania Dutchman* V:13 (Mar. 1, 1954): 5.

PEACHES IN CIDER

This recipe (p. 140) is a preservation method related to the process for making apple butter. It is a folk technique that does not appear in many period cookbooks.

PICKLED CABBAGE

This is Elizabeth E. Lea's recipe (p. 162) for sauerkraut, a dish popular in the German counties of Maryland. It was not popular among the Quakers because they did not like the odor, at least that is a common explanation. For those who did not object to sauerkraut, but who did not want to go through the trouble of making it, William Bodemann on Howard Street in Baltimore made and sold fresh sauerkraut in Elizabeth Lea's day. His price, according to advertisements in the *Baltimore Sun,* was a remarkable 12½ cents per gallon. Bodemann, a German, owned a "Preserving and Pickling House" that was once a well-known food emporium in Maryland.

REF.: Eleanor Fein Reishtein, "Minutes of the West Grove Housekeepers Association As Source Material for Folklife Studies," *Pennsylvania Folklife* XXI:1 (Autumn, 1971): 21.

POT PIE

Elizabeth Lea's recipe (p. 28), which calls for lining a Dutch oven with pastry and covering the stew inside with a pastry lid, is a folk variant of the more elaborate free-standing meat pies once so popular in medieval English cookery. Elizabeth Lea's version was a common Anglo-American form that appeared at an early date in the Chesapeake area. It was also popular among the Quakers farther north.

In Pennsylvania, however, pot pie was generally a fricassee of meat or poultry with dumplings—not a true pie. In the Deep South, this was called chicken with dumplings. Among the Pennsylvania Germans, a pot pie *(Bottboi)* was the large square dumpling or noodle that was dropped into the fricassee, also the name of the dish itself. This version seems to have moved south during the eighteenth century and may be a Pennsylvania-German or general New World innovation, since a fricassee, as it is known in the British Isles, does not contain dumplings or noodles.

R

RICE SPONGE CAKE

Before the perfection of milling flour in the late 1800s, only winter wheat was thought suitable for fine baked goods, and even then, it had to be double sifted through flannel bags at the mill and sifted once or twice again just prior to using. Rice flour, however, was much finer and much lighter. Thus, in the South, where humidity was always working against a "good bake," rice flour was often preferred to that of wheat. This was especially true for sponge cakes. Although more expensive, rice sponge cake was considered the lightest and most delicate sponge cake one could make.

The recipe (p. 116) which Elizabeth Lea published is a simplified version of a much longer and more elaborate recipe in Turner and Fisher's *Housekeeper's Almanac* for 1846.

RUSK

This was a particularly popular form of small bread or roll among the Quakers and was usually served at breakfast or at afternoon tea. In flavor, traditional Quaker rusks should be only faintly sweet; in color, they should be deep yellow (from the eggs) and the tops should be dark brown. In the country, they were usually eaten fresh, although, technically, a true rusk should be dry and brittle. The dry rusks were broken up in breakfast coffee or tea.

At one time, rusks were a fairly widespread feature of urban Anglo-American cookery, at least on the East Coast. They were introduced from England, where they were popularly served as shipboard fare—dried rusks could be laid down in tins and kept for some time. The name itself, however, is of foreign origin and may be derived from the Spanish or Portuguese *rosca,* a twist or roll of bread. Such small breads often served as part of traveling fare for Spanish and Portuguese sailors.

S

SALERATUS BISCUIT

This is the British name for soda cake or soda cracker. During the nineteenth century, saleratus was generally potassium bicarbonate or sodium bicarbonate. Today, it is usually the latter and is usually sold commercially under the name of "baking" soda.

SALTSPOON

See Measurements.

SCRAPPLE

Traditional Pennsylvania scrapple is a pot pudding made by thickening a butcher's broth *(Metzelsuppe)* with scraps of meat and buckwheat flour. After the pudding "sets," it is sliced and fried like sausage. It is for this reason that Henrietta Davidis includes her recipe for frying scrapple in the sausage section of her popular German cookbook.

A brief look at any of the hundreds of German recipes for scrapple will show that the only major difference between the Pennsylvania dish and its European parent is the addition of cornmeal. In the Lower Rhineland, where Pennsylvania scrapple originated, scrapple makers use buckwheat flour exclusively, although blood is sometimes added for richer consistency and a darker color. Many Germans consider scrapple a Westphalian dish, and it is possible, even today, to find it on the menus of Westphalian inns specializing in local cookery.

In Westphalia, scrapple is generally called *Panhas* (the term has many variant spellings). It is also known by this name in Pennsylvania-German dialect, but it is evidently a loan word, since it does not appear in Pfälzer dialect, the closest German model to Pennsylvania "Dutch." The term, like the dish, was probably introduced to Pennsylvania by the Crefelders who settled Germantown in the late 1600s. Crefelders and Westphalians speak a very similar dialect and share a number of cultural characteristics with their Holland-Dutch neighbors. *Panhas* and its close relatives, such as the *Stoppa Grötta* ("pudding grits") of Osnabrück, are all parts of a complex of pot puddings that serve as an important component of Lower Rhineland folk diet.

In his "American Glossary" (1936), R. H. Thornton recognized scrapple as a Pennsylvania-German food; he also assigned a Pennsylvania-German origin to the term. (He did not discuss *Panhas*.) His useful study has been largely overlooked by culinary journalists, and this has resulted in a wide variety of explanations for scrapple, some as amusing as they are farfetched.

Part of the confusion has arisen from the fact that the word scrapple appears in English dialect, although in very different contexts. It is also a cognate with a wide variety of Lower Rhineland and Holland-Dutch dialect terms which are much closer in meaning to "scrapple" as it is used in Pennsylvania.

Wright's *English Dialect Dictionary* notes that the word scrapple appears in Yorkshire dialect as a term for scraps or odds and ends. He also mentions that the term "scrapple cake" was used to describe any thin oat cake. Unfortunately, this usage was never very common, even in Yorkshire, and speakers more often said "scrapplings" instead. Pennsylvania scrapple, as such, was unknown. Just the same, it may be worth noting that many of the early Quaker settlers in West Jersey (the lower counties) came from Yorkshire and that their settlement at Salem (1675) was a bustling community quite some time before Philadelphia grew to comparable size.

Henry Hexham's *Netherduytch Dictionarie* (1648) lists a number of related Holland-Dutch terms: *schrabbe* (a scraping), *schrabben* (to scrape or scratch), *schrapsel* and *schrapel* (a snipping, scrap or scraping). The last term is pronounced like English scrapple. Holland-Dutch dialect also combines *schrapel* to form words like *schrapelkoekje* (a little scrapple cake), used in the very same sense that scrapple is used in Philadelphia. It is also used euphemistically for a baby born very late in married life. This is similar to "flash in the pan," one of the euphemistic meanings of *Panhas*.

Panhas itself may have its root in old Holland Dutch or in one of the related Lower Rhine German dialects, for it is a combination of *pann* + *harst*, something pan roasted or pan fried. Marcus Lambert, in his Pennsylvania-German dictionary (1924), attempted to explain the origin of *Panhas*, but like the dish itself, included scraps of Ersatz etymology. He was followed by Preston Barba, who provided a more scholarly explanation of *Panhas*, or *Pannhaas* as he spelled it, when he collaborated with Ann Hark in writing *Pennsylvania German Cookery*. Barba, however, rejected scrapple as an alternative term for *Panhas* even though he called his *Panhas* recipe "Scrapple" in the cookbook. It is no wonder that food historians have been confused. All the more so because it is quite probable that scrapple is merely an American dialect approximation of a similar word of Lower Rhineland origin.

Actually, there is no material difference between *Panhas* and scrapple. In Pennsylvania, these are both terms for the same dish. A comparison between Elizabeth Lea's recipe for scrapple and *any* Pennsylvania-German recipe for *Panhas* will certainly bear this out. In addition, most antique Pennsylvania recipes called for parched cornmeal, which is true to its original purpose as an adulterant, in this case, as an adulterant in buckwheat.

While on the subject of ingredients, perhaps it would be appropriate here to share an observation on modern scrapple and its many approximations. There are a number of commercial products sold today under the name of scrapple, but several of these "scrapples" do not contain buckwheat—the basic cereal ingredient—so the consumer would do well to read the labels and reject as spurious any product that omits it. Buckwheat defines the traditional flavor of the dish, so it is questionable whether the thing is truly scrapple or *Panhas* without it.

REF.: Henrietta Davidis, *Praktisches Kochbuch für die gewöhnliche und feinere Küche* (Bielefeld/Leipzig, 1898), pp. 159–60; R. H. Thornton, "An American Glossary," *Dialect Notes*, VI, Parts 12–13 (1936): 562; Joseph Wright, *The English Dialect Dictionary* (London, 1904), V, pp. 272–73; Henry Hexham, *A Copious English and Netherduytch Dictionarie* (Rotterdam, 1648); J. A. N. Knuttel, *Woordenboek der Nederlandsche Taal* (s'-Gravenhage/ Leiden, 1936), XIV, cols. 996–97; Marcus Lambert, *A Dictionary of the Non-English Words of the Pennsylvania-German Dialect* (Lancaster, Pa., 1924), pp. 117–18; Ann Hark and Preston A. Barba, *Pennsylvania German Cookery* (Allentown, Pa., 1950), p. 43; Susan J. Ellis, "Traditional Food in the Commercial Market: The History of Pennsylvania Scrapple," *Pennsylvania Folklife* XXII:3 (Spring, 1973):10–21.

SMEARCASE

This is Elizabeth E. Lea's phonetic spelling of the Pennsylvania-German dialect word *Schmierkees*, better known as cottage cheese. By definition, *Schmierkees* is any sort of cheese that can be spread on bread—*schmieren* means "to spread." Cottage cheese was the commonest sort, but in Elizabeth Lea's day, there were also many others. Yet in spite of the Pennsylvania-German name, "smearcase" as Elizabeth Lea made it was probably not of German origin. Traditional cottage cheese throughout the Middle Atlantic region was similar to Scottish "hung milk," although our milk was first scalded before hanging. From that point, the method of preparation was practically the same.

REF.: Alexander Fenton, "Traditional Elements in the Diet of the Northern Isles of Scotland," *Kansatieteellinen Arkisto 26* (Helsinki, 1975), p. 70.

SOUSE

The name of Elizabeth Lea's recipe (p. 171) is misleading, since this is actually a recipe for making pickled pig's feet or "soused" pig's feet. It is not the sour pork aspic that is still popular among the Maryland Germans and sold simply as "souse."

SUGAR

In several cases, Elizabeth Lea mentions loaf sugar or configurations of sugar that are now unfamiliar. In her recipe for black cake (p. 121), for example, she calls for brown sugar rolled fine.

In general, white cane sugar was retailed in hard cones of various weights. These cones were called loaves. They had to be cut with shears, boiled, the liquid skimmed of insects and other particles, and reduced to crystalline form again. To make powdered sugar, one was required to roll white sugar with a heavy wooden roller that looked much like a fat pastry roller. Some sugar rollers were made of heavy glass in order to produce a finer texture.

Sugar came in several grades, the cheapest being Muscovado, a dark, sticky, unrefined sugar that tasted like molasses and was used in coffee, pies, cookies, and heavy cakes. Lighter grades of brown sugar, similar to Demerara in sweetness, were also available. It was a grade of crystallized brown sugar like Demerara that Elizabeth Lea was using in her black cake recipe. Unfortunately, the Demerara sugar that is sold today is a raw sugar treated with sulphuric acid and cannot be used as a substitute. Turbinado sugar, sold in health food stores, might make the best alternative—all for the sake of authenticity, of course.

T

THOMSONIAN MEDICINE

This is a practice of medicine based on botanical cures as advocated by Samuel Thomson. A self-taught American botanist, Thomson wrote the *New Guide to Health*, a book which appeared in 1822 and immediately found a place in American popular medicine. The *Guide* was reprinted several times and was even translated into German at Lancaster, Ohio, in 1828. Many of Thomson's cures found their way into almanacs, handbooks on farriery, and household apothecary manuals.

TIN KITCHEN

Elizabeth Lea uses this (p. 14) as another term for a reflector oven, also called a Dutch oven in some localities. The tin kitchen, or reflector oven, was placed before the fire and used for roasting, but sometimes also for baking muffins or rolls.

TOMATO FIGS

Tomato figs, or sun-dried tomatoes, using the pear or plum varieties, were once prepared in many sections of the Middle Atlantic region. Although invented as a health food, the "figs" usually served the double purpose of emergency food or a diet supplement for lower income rural families. There was little work involved in their preparation and much of the nutritional value of the tomatoes was retained.

According to Josiah T. Marshall in his *Farmer's and Emigrant's Hand-Book*, a Mrs. Steiger of Washington, D.C., attempted to patent tomato figs in the early 1840s, but without success. Her recipe was published and widely copied. It later appeared in the *House-Keeper's Almanac* for 1846, from which Elizabeth Lea adapted her recipe (p. 145).

REF.: Josiah T. Marshall, *The Farmer's and Emigrant's Hand-Book* (New York, 1845), p. 158; Turner and Fisher, *Turner's Improved House-Keeper's Almanac* (New York and Philadelphia, 1846).

TOMATOES, FRICASSEED

This is Elizabeth Lea's version (p. 48) of fried tomato gravy, an extremely popular breakfast and supper dish among the Quakers. The gravy was usually served on toast.

WASH FOR HEARTHS

Made with red ochre and buttermilk, this wash for brick hearths (p. 215) dates at least from the eighteenth century. Generally, it was common practice once a year (usually in the spring) to wash the hearths to cover the blackened areas. It was considered a matter of kitchen cleanliness. In Pennsylvania and the German areas of Maryland, this same red wash was also applied to the exteriors of brick buildings, a practice which still survives in the form of red paint.

WINEGLASS

See Measurements.

BIBLIOGRAPHY

Published Sources

Acomb, Evelyn M., ed. *The Revolutionary Journal of Baron Ludwig von Closen.* Chapel Hill: University of North Carolina Press, 1958.

The American Farmer (Baltimore: Samuel Sands), I:12 (June, 1846); II:1 (July, 1846).

Annals of Sandy Spring, III (Baltimore: King Brothers, 1909); V (Westminster, Md.: Times Printing Co., 1929).

Baltimore Sun, Jan. 1, 1845; Jan. 2, 1845; Dec. 24, 1905.

Baltimore Yearly Meeting. *Discipline of the Yearly Meeting of Friends, Held in Baltimore.* Baltimore: Printed by John Hewes, 1806.

Baltimore Yearly Meeting. *Memorials Concerning Several Ministers and Others, Deceased.* Baltimore: Innes and Company, 1875.

Bartram, John. *Observations on the Inhabitants, Climate, Soil, Rivers, Productions, Animals, and Other Matters Worth of Notice: North America* London: J. Whiston and B. White, 1751.

Bedini, Silvio A. *The Life of Benjamin Banneker.* New York: Charles Scribner's Sons, 1972.

Beeton, Isabella. *The Book of Household Management.* London: S. O. Beeton, 1861.

Bergner, Anna. *Pfälzer Kochbuch.* Mannheim: Tobias Löffler, 1858.

Boyd, Thomas H. S. *History of Montgomery County, Maryland, from Its Earliest Settlement in 1650 to 1879.* Baltimore: Regional Publishing Company, 1968. Reprint of the Clarksburg, Md., edition of 1879.

Bradley, Richard. *The Country Housewife and Lady's Director.* London: Printed for D. Browne, 1736.

Brainerd, David. *An Account of the Life of the Late Reverend Mr. David Brainerd.* Boston: Printed for D. Henchman, 1749.

Briggs, Richard. *The New Art of Cookery, According to the Present*

Practice. Philadelphia: W. Spotswood, R. Campbell, and B. Johnson, 1792.

The Chester and Delaware Federalist (West Chester, Pa.), Dec. 13, 1809.

Child, Lydia Maria. *American Frugal Housewife.* Boston: Carter and Hendee, 1833. Originally called *The Frugal Housewife,* first issued in 1829.

Child, Lydia Maria. *Isaac T. Hopper: A True Life.* Boston: John P. Jewett & Co., 1853.

Clayton, N. J. *Clayton's Quaker Cook-Book. Being a Practical Treatise on the Culinary Art Adapted to the Tastes and Wants of All Classes.* San Francisco: Women's Cooperative Printing Office, 1883.

Cookery as It Should Be: A New Manual of the Dining Room and Kitchen, for Persons in Moderate Circumstances. Philadelphia: Willis P. Hazard, 1855.

Cox, J. Stevens. *Ice-Creams of Queen Victoria's Reign.* St. Peter Port, Guernsey, England: Toucan Press, 1970.

Davidis, Henrietta. *Praktisches Kochbuch für die gewöhnliche und feinere Küche.* Bielefeld/Leipzig: Zwenka-Verlag, 1898.

DeVoe, Thomas F. *The Market Assistant.* New York: The Riverside Press, 1867.

Ellis, Susan J. "Traditional Food in the Commercial Market: The History of Pennsylvania Scrapple." *Pennsylvania Folklife* XXII:3 (Spring, 1973):10–21.

Farquhar, Roger Brooke. *Old Homes and History of Montgomery County, Maryland.* Washington, D.C.: Judd & Detweiler, 1962.

Fenton, Alexander. "Hafer- und Gerstenmehl als Hauptgegenstand der schottischen Nahrungsforschung." *Ethnologia Scandinavica* (Lund, 1971), pp. 149–57.

Fenton, Alexander. "Traditional Elements in the Diet of the Northern Isles of Scotland." *Kansatieteellinen Arkisto 26* (Helsinki, 1975), pp. 64–78.

Fenton, Alexander, and Trefor M. Owen, eds. *Food in Perspective: Proceedings of the Third International Conference on Ethnological Food Research.* Edinburgh: John Donald, 1981.

Ferguson, Alice, and H. G. Ferguson. *The Piscataway Indians of Southern Maryland.* Accokeek, Md.: A.F. Foundation, 1960.

"Food Products of the North American Indians." *Report of the U.S. Commissioner of Agriculture, 1870.* Washington, D.C.: U.S. Government Printing Office, 1871.

Friends' Miscellany, John Comly and Isaac Comly, eds. I-XII (1828–1839).

Friends' Weekly Intelligencer (Philadelphia), later *Friends' Intelligencer and Journal* II:6 (May 9, 1845); II:8 (June 24, 1845); II:20 (Aug. 16, 1845); III:6 (May 9, 1846); IV:1 (Apr. 3, 1847); IV:51 (Mar. 18, 1848); X:45 (Jan. 28, 1854); XIV:43 (Jan. 9, 1858); XV:44 (Jan. 15, 1859); XLVI:3 (Jan. 19, 1889).

The Frugal Housewife; or, Housekeeper's and Servant's Guide. Devonport, England: Printed by Elias Keys, ca. 1840.

Gebhard, Bruno. "The Interrelationship of Scientific and Folk Medicine in the United States of America since 1850," *American Folk Medicine* (Berkeley, 1976), pp. 87–98.

Girardey, George. *Höchst Nützliches Handbuch über Kochkunst.* Cincinnati: J. A. James, 1842.

Glasse, Hannah. *The Art of Cookery Made Plain and Easy.* London: T. Longman, 1796.

Glassie, Henry. *Pattern in the Material Folk Culture of the Eastern United States.* Philadelphia: University of Pennsylvania Press, 1968.

Hagerty, Ann. *Once Upon a Time in New Garden Township.* Kennett Square, Pa.: KNA Press, 1977.

Hallowell, A. Irving. "The Impact of the American Indian on American Culture." *American Anthropologist* LIX (Apr., 1957): 201–17.

Hand, Wayland, ed. *American Folk Medicine.* Berkeley/Los Angeles/London: University of California Press, 1976.

Hark, Ann, and Preston A. Barba. *Pennsylvania German Cookery.* Allentown, Pa.: Schlechter's, 1950.

Harrington, Mark R. "A Preliminary Sketch of Lenape Culture." *American Anthropologist* XV (1913): 208–35.

Hart, John S., ed. *The Female Prose Writers of America.* Philadelphia: E. H. Butler & Co., 1855.

Heckewelder, John. *An Account of the Indian Nations, Who Once Inhabited Pennsylvania and the Neighboring States.* Philadelphia: Abraham Small, 1818.

Henderson, William. *The Housekeeper's Instructor; or, Universal Family Cook.* London: J. Stratford, 1805.

Henisch, Bridget Ann. *Fast and Feast: Food in Medieval Society.* University Park, Pa.: Pennsylvania State University Press, 1978.

Hexham, Henry. *A Copious English and Netherduytsch Dictionarie/ Het Groot Woorden-Boeck.* Rotterdam: Aernout Leers, 1648.

Hilliard, Sam Bowers. *Hog Meat and Hoecake.* Carbondale, Ill.: Southern Illinois University Press, 1972.

Holland, Celia M. *Ellicott City: Maryland's 18th Century Mill Town.* Ellicott City, Md.: n.p., 1968.

Hörandner, Edith. "The Recipe Book as a Cultural and Socio-Historical Document." *Food in Perspective* (Edinburgh, 1981), pp. 119–44.

Howard, Jane Grant (Gilmor). *Fifty Years in a Maryland Kitchen.* Baltimore: Turnbull Brothers, 1873.

Jacobson, Phebe R. *Quaker Records in Maryland.* Annapolis, Md.: The Hall of Records Commission, 1966.

Janney, Samuel M. *Memoirs of Samuel M. Janney, Late of Lincoln,*

Loudon County, Va. Philadelphia: Friends' Book Association, 1881.

Kalm, Peter. *Travels in North America.* 2 vols. New York: Dover Publications, 1966.

Keucliel, Edward F. "Master of the Art of Canning: Baltimore 1860–1900." *Maryland History Magazine* LXVII (Winter, 1972): 351–62.

Kimball, Marie. *Thomas Jefferson's Cook Book.* Charlottesville, Va.: University Press of Virginia, 1976.

Knuttel, J.A.N. *Woordenboek der Nederlandsche Taal.* s'-Gravenhage: Martinus Nijhoff/Leiden: A.W. Sijthoff's Uitg. Mij N.V., 1936.

Kraft, Herbert E., ed. *A Delaware Indian Symposium.* Harrisburg, Pa.: Pennsylvania Historical and Museum Commission, 1974.

Lambert, Marcus B. *A Dictionary of the Non-English Words of the Pennsylvania-German Dialect, with an Appendix.* Lancaster, Pa.: Pennsylvania-German Society, 1924.

Land, Aubrey C. "Economic Base and Social Structure: The Northern Chesapeake in the Eighteenth Century." *Journal of Economic History* XXV:4 (1965): 639–59.

Lea, Elizabeth Ellicott. *Domestic Cookery, Useful Receipts, and Hints to Young Housekeepers.* Baltimore: H. Colburn, 1845.

Lea, Elizabeth Ellicott. *Domestic Cookery, Useful Receipts, and Hints to Young Housekeepers.* Baltimore: Cushing & Bro., 1846.

Lea, Elizabeth Ellicott. *Domestic Cookery, Useful Receipts, and Hints to Young Housekeepers.* Baltimore: Cushing & Bailey, 1851.

Lea, James H., and George H. *Ancestry and Posterity of John Lea.* New York: Lea Brothers & Co., 1906.

Lemon, James T. *The Best Poor Man's Country.* Baltimore: Johns Hopkins University Press, 1972.

Leslie, Eliza. *Seventy-Five Receipts for Pastry, Cakes, and Sweetmeats.* Boston: Munroe and Francis, 1828.

Libanon Demokrat (Lebanon, Pa.), Oct. 17, 1851.

Lissner, Erich. *Wurstologia oder Es Geht um die Wurst.* Frankfurt: Hauserpresse, Hans Schaefer, 1939.

Lloyd, David. *Economy of Agriculture: Being a Series of Compendious Essays on Different Branches of Farming.* Germantown, Pa.: P. R. Freas & Co., 1832.

Löffler, Friederike. *Ökonomisches Handbuch für Frauenzimmer.* Stuttgart: Johann Friedrich Steinkopf, 1795.

Lowenstein, Eleanor. *Bibliography of American Cookery Books 1742–1860.* New York and Worcester, Mass.: American Antiquarian Society and the Corner Bookshop, 1972.

McDougall, Frances Harriet. *The Housekeeper's Book.* Philadelphia: William Marshall & Co., 1838.

Mann, Mary Tyler. *Christianity in the Kitchen: A Physiological Cook Book.* Boston: Ticknor & Fields, 1857.

Marshall, Josiah T. *The Farmer's and Emigrant's Hand-Book.* New York: D. Appleton & Co., 1845.

Matchett, Richard J. *Matchett's Baltimore Director for 1840.* Baltimore: R. J. Matchett, 1840.

Matchett, Richard J. *Matchett's Baltimore Director for 1851.* Baltimore: R. J. Matchett, 1851.

Matchett, Richard J. *Matchett's Baltimore Director for 1853–1854.* Baltimore: R. J. Matchett, 1853.

Meyer, Mary Keysor. *Genealogical Research in Maryland: A Guide.* Baltimore: Maryland Historical Society, 1972.

Miller, Mary McGregor. *The Warder Family: A Short History.* Springfield, Ohio: Clark County Historical Society, 1957.

Moore, Gay Montague. *Seaport in Virginia: George Washington's Alexandria.* Richmond, Va.: Garrett and Massie, 1949.

Nicholson, Elizabeth. *The Economical Cook and House-Book.* Philadelphia: Willis P. Hazard, 1855.

O'Danachair, Kevin. "Bread." *Ulster Folklife* IV (1958): 29–32.

O'Danachair, Kevin. "Bread in Ireland." *Food in Perspective* (Edinburgh, 1981), pp. 57–67.

O'Danachair, Kevin. "Our Daily Bread." *Biatas* (June, 1959), pp. 204–8.

Owen, Trefor M. "The Ethnological Study of Food in Wales." *Folk and Farm.* Dublin: Royal Society of Antiquaries of Ireland, 1976.

Parsons, William T. "Orders What's to Be Done at the Plantation: The Isaac Norris Farm Accounts, 1713–1734." *Pennsylvania Folklife* XXVII:1 (Fall, 1977).

Peters, Gustav Sigismund. *Die Geschickte Hausfrau.* Harrisburg, Pa.: Lutz and Scheffer, 1848.

Poulson's American Daily Advertiser (Philadelphia), Mar. 21, 1805.

Prince, J. Dyneley. "The Jersey Dutch Dialect." *Dialect Notes,* III, Part 6 (1910): 459–84.

Randolph, Mary. *The Virginia House-Wife.* Washington, D.C.: Davis and Force, 1824.

Randolph, Mary. *The Virginia Housewife.* Philadelphia: E. H. Butler, 1851.

Rees, Alwyn D. *Life in a Welsh Countryside.* Cardiff: University of Wales Press, 1975.

Reeves, Henry. "Our Provincialisms." *Lippincott's Magazine* III (Mar., 1869): 310–21.

Reishtein, Eleanor Fein. "Minutes of the West Grove Housekeepers Association as Source Material for Folklife Studies." *Pennsylvania Folklife* XXI:1 (Autumn, 1971): 16–25.

Rollo, Vera A. Foster. *The Negro in Maryland: A Short History.* Baltimore: Maryland Historical Press, 1972.

Rorer, Sarah Tyson. *Philadelphia Cookbook.* Philadelphia: Arnold and Company, 1886.

Rundell, Maria. *A New System of Domestic Cookery*. Boston: William Andrews, 1807.

Rundell, Maria. *American Domestic Cookery*. Baltimore: Published by Fielding Lucas, Jr., 1819.

Rushmore, Jane P. *The Quaker Way*. Philadelphia: Philadelphia Yearly Meeting of Friends, n.d. [ca. 1951].

Scharf, J. Thomas. *History of Delaware 1609–1888*. Philadelphia: L. J. Richards & Co., 1888. 2 vols.

Scharf, J. Thomas. *History of Western Maryland*. 2 vols. Philadelphia: Louis H. Everts, 1882.

Schrijnen, Jos. *Nederlandsche Volkskunde*. 2 vols. Zutphen: W. J. Thieme et Cie., n.d.

Seebohm, Benjamin, ed. *Memoirs of William Forster*. 2 vols. London: Alfred W. Bennett, 1865.

Shoemaker, Alfred L. "About Apees." *Pennsylvania Dutchman* V:13 (Mar. 1, 1954): 5.

Smith, Eliza. *The Compleat Housewife; or, Accomplish'd Gentlewoman's Companion*. London: Printed for R. Ware, 1753.

Smith, Mary. *The Complete House-Keeper*. New Castle, England: S. Hodgson, and G.G. J. and J. Robinson, 1786.

Stabler, William. *A Memoir of the Life of Edward Stabler*. Philadelphia: John Richards, 1846.

Stallings, W. S. "Ice Cream and Water Ices in 17th and 18th Century England." *Petits Propos Culinaires 3—Supplement* (London, 1979).

Stearns, Samuel. *The American Herbal or Materia Medica*. Walpole, N.H.: David Carlisle, 1801.

Straron, Laura B. "Applebutter Making as Practiced by Our Ancestors." *Papers Read Before the Bucks County Historical Society* IV (1917).

Teuteberg, Hans-Jürgen and Günter Wiegelmann. *Der Wandel der Nahrungsgewohnheiten unter der Einfluss der Industrialisierung*. Göttingen: Vandenhoeck & Ruprecht, 1972.

Thomas, Lawrence Buckley. *The Thomas Book, Giving the Genealogies of Sir Rhys ap Thomas, K.G., the Thomas Family Descended from Him, and of Some Allied Families*. New York: Henry T. Thomas Co., 1896.

Thomson, James W. "Indian Corn. Experiments in Manufacturing Corn Meal." *Monthly Journal of Agriculture* II:1 (July, 1846): 40–41.

Thomson, Samuel. *New Guide to Health; or, Botanic Family Physician*. Boston: E. G. House, 1822.

Thomson, Samuel. *Neue Anweisung zur Gesundheit; oder, Botanischer Familien-Arzt*. Lancaster, Ohio: Johann Herman, 1828.

Thornton, R. H. "An American Glossary." *Dialect Notes*, VI, Parts 12–13 (1936): 528–76.

Tibbott, S. Minwell. "Traditional Foods in Wales at the Beginning of the 20th Century, with Particular Emphasis on the Diet of the Farming Community." *Kansatieteellinen Arkisto 26* (Helsinki, 1975), pp. 266–76.

Tibbott, S. Minwell. *Welsh Fare.* Cowbridge and Bridgend, Wales: Welsh Folk Museum, 1976.

Tracy, William W. "American Varieties of Garden Beans." *U.S. Department of Agriculture Bulletin No. 109.* Washington, D.C.: U.S. Government Printing Office, 1907.

Trall, R. T. *The New Hydropathic Cook-Book.* New York: Fowlers and Wells, 1854.

Turner and Fisher. *Turner's Improved House-Keeper's Almanac.* Philadelphia and New York: Turner & Fisher, 1846.

Turner and Fisher. *The Kitchen Companion, and House-Keeper's Own Book.* Philadelphia: Turner & Fisher, 1844.

Tyson, Martha Ellicott. *A Sketch of the Life of Benjamin Banneker; from Notes Taken in 1836.* Baltimore: J. D. Toy, 1854.

Tyson, Martha Ellicott. *A Brief Account of the Settlement of Ellicott's Mills.* Baltimore: John Murphy and Co., 1871.

The United States Magazine and Domestic Review (New York) XXVIII:156 (June, 1851).

van Winter, Johanna Maria. *Van Soeter Cokene: Recepten uit de Oudheid en Middeleeuwen.* Haarlem: Fibula-Van Dishoeck, 1976.

von Martens, Georg. *Die Gartenbohnen: Ihre Verbreitung, Cultur und Benützung.* Ravensburg: Eugen Ulmer, 1869.

Wallace, Paul A. W. *Indians in Pennsylvania.* Harrisburg, Pa.: Pennsylvania Historical and Museum Commission, 1970.

Waugh, F. A. *Iroquois Foods and Food Preparation.* Ottawa: Government Printing Bureau, 1916.

Weaver, William Woys. "Food Acculturation and the First Pennsylvania-German Cookbook." *Journal of American Culture* II:3 (Fall, 1979): 421–32.

Weaver, William Woys. "*Die Geschickte Hausfrau:* The First Ethnic Cookbook in the United States." *Food in Perspective* (Edinburgh, 1981), pp. 343–63.

Wharton, James. *Bounty of the Chesapeake.* Newport News, Va.: Mariner's Museum, 1957.

Widdifield, Hannah. *Widdifield's New Cook Book.* Philadelphia: T. B. Peterson, 1856.

Wiegelmann, Günter. *Alltags- und Festspeisen: Wandel und Gegenwärtige Stellung.* Marburg: N. G. Elwert, 1967.

Wissler, Clark. "Aboriginal Maize Culture as a Typical Culture-Complex." *American Journal of Sociology* XXII (1916): 656–60.

Wiswe, Hans. *Kulturgeschichte der Kochkunst.* Munich: Heinz Moos, 1970.

Witthoft, John, and Bonita Freeman-Witthoft. "Lenape Indian Fall Harvest." *Frontiers* (Fall, 1975): 9–13.

Wright, Joseph. *The English Dialect Dictionary.* 6 vols. London: Henry Frowde, 1904.

Wurmbach, Annemarie. "Kuchen-Fladen-Torte: Eine wort- und sachkundliche Untersuchung." *Zeitschrift für Volkskunde* LVI:1 (1960).

Yoder, Don. "Pennsylvanians Called It Mush," *Pennsylvania Folklife* XIII:2 (Winter, 1962).

Unpublished Sources

Anderson, Jay A. "Yeoman Foodways in Stuart England." Ph. D. dissertation, University of Pennsylvania, Philadelphia, 1972.

Maryland State Historic Sites Survey. *ACHS Summary Form, "Walnut Hill," 23/89.* Annapolis, Md.: Maryland Historic Trust, 1979.

Oliver, Elizabeth Lea. Letter to William Woys Weaver, Haverford, Pa., May 26, 1978.

Pierce, Joshua. *Day Book, 1822–1849.* Sandy Spring, Md. Collection of Martha Nesbitt, Sandy Spring, Md.

Sandy Spring Monthly Meeting (Society of Friends). *Record of Births, Deaths and Membership.* Sandy Spring, Md. 1730–1895. Collection of the Friends Historical Library, Swarthmore College, Swarthmore, Pa.

Thomas, Mary Larkin. Interview by William Woys Weaver. Oct. 5, 1977.

Thomas, Mary Larkin. "Interview." *Oral History Among Friends.* West Chester, Pa.: Chester County Library and Philadelphia Yearly Meeting, 1979.

Warder, Ann Aston. *Cookbook.* Chedioke, Ohio, 1844. Collection of William Woys Weaver.

Wilson, Deborah Iddings. Letter to William Woys Weaver, Columbia, Md., Sept. 15, 1980.

EDITOR'S NOTE

Aside from a few minor changes, *Domestic Cookery* is a faithful facsimile reproduction of the fifth edition of 1853. This facsimile is offered as a source and document for early American food research, not as a modern cooking guide. However, anyone with a flair for experimental cookery will soon discover that many of Elizabeth Lea's recipes can be reproduced without difficulty in kitchens today. Should snags develop over questions of weights and measures, kindly refer to Measurements in the glossary.

DOMESTIC COOKERY

DOMESTIC COOKERY,

USEFUL RECEIPTS,

AND

HINTS TO YOUNG HOUSEKEEPERS.

BY

ELIZABETH E. LEA

"The Source of Liberal Deeds is Wise Economy."

FIFTH EDITION.

BALTIMORE:
CUSHINGS AND BAILEY.
1853.

PREFACE

~~~~~~~~~~~

THIS WORK having passed through several editions, and having met with a very favorable reception, the Authoress has been induced to thoroughly revise and re-arrange the whole work. Numerous additions have also been made, particularly under the heads Miscellaneous Receipts and Hints to Young Housekeepers, which she hopes will be found to have enhanced its value.

INTRODUCTORY ADDRESS.

THE compiler of "Useful Receipts and Hints to Young Housekeepers" having entered early in life upon a train of duties, was frequently embarrassed by her ignorance of domestic affairs. For, whilst receipt books for elegant preparations were often seen, those connected with the ordinary, but far more useful part of household duties, were not easily procured; thus situated, she applied to persons of experience, and embodied the information collected in a book, to which, since years have matured her judgment, she has added much that is the result of her own experiments.

Familiar, then, with the difficulties a young house-keeper encounters, when she finds herself in reality the mistress of an establishment, the Authoress offers to her young countrywomen this Work, with the belief that, by attention to its contents, many of the cares attendant on a country or city life, may be materially lessened; and hoping that the directions are such as to be understood by the most inexperienced, it is respectfully dedicated to those who feel an interest in domestic affairs.

DOMESTIC COOKERY,

AND

USEFUL RECEIPTS.

~~~~~~~~~~~~~~~~~~~~~

MEATS AND POULTRY.

To Boil Fresh Meat.

In boiling fresh meat, care is necessary to have the water boiling all the time it is in the pot; if the pot is not well scummed, the appearance of the meat will be spoiled.

Mutton and beef are preferred, by some, a little rare; but pork and veal should always be well done. A round of beef that is stuffed, will take more than three hours to boil, and if not stuffed, two hours or more, according to the size; slow boiling is the best. A leg of mutton requires from two to three hours boiling, according to the size; a fore-quarter from an hour to an hour and a half; a quarter of lamb, unless very large, will boil in an hour. Veal and pork will take rather longer to boil than mutton.

All boiled fresh meat should have drawn butter poured over it, after it is dished, and be garnished with parsley.

The liquor that fresh meat, or poultry, is boiled in, should be saved, as an addition of vegetables, herbs, and dumplings make a nourishing soup of it.

A large turkey will take three hours to boil—a small one half that time; secure the legs to keep them from bursting out; turkeys should be blanched in warm milk and water; stuff them and rub their breasts with butter; flour a cloth and pin them in. A large chicken that is stuffed should boil an hour, and small ones half that time. The water should always boil before you put in your meat or poultry. When meat is frozen, soak it in cold water for several hours, and allow more time in the cooking.

To Boil a Turkey.

Have the turkey well cleaned and prepared for cooking, let it lay in salt and water a few minutes; fill it with bread and butter, seasoned with pepper, salt, parsley and thyme; secure the legs and wings; pin it up in a towel; have the water boiling, and put it in; put a little salt in the water; when half done, put in a little milk. A small turkey will boil in an hour and a quarter; a middle sized in two hours, and a large one in two and a half or three hours; they should boil moderately all the time; if fowls boil too fast, they break to pieces;—half an hour will cook the liver and gizzard, which should be put round the turkey; when it is dished, have drawn butter, with an egg chopped and put in it, and a little parsley; oyster sauce, and celery sauce are good, with boiled turkey or chicken.

To Boil Beef Tongue, Corned Beef, &c.

If the tongue is dry, let it soak for several hours; put it to boil in cold water, and keep it boiling slowly for two hours; but if it is just out of the pickle, the water should boil when it goes in.

Corned or pickled beef, or pork, requires longer boiling than that which is dry; you can tell when it is done by the bones coming out easily. Pour drawn butter over it when dished.

To Boil a Ham.

A large ham should boil three or four hours very slowly; it should be put in cold water, and be kept covered during the whole process; a small ham will boil in two hours. All bacon requires much the same management,—and if you boil cabbage or greens with it, skim all the grease off the pot before you put them in. Ham or dried beef, if very salt, should be soaked several hours before cooking, and should be boiled in plenty of water.

To Boil Calf's Head.

Cut the upper from the lower jaw, take out the brains and eyes, and clean the head well; let it soak in salt and water an hour or two; then put it in a gallon of boiling water, take off the scum as it rises, and when it is done, take out the bones; dish it, and pour over a sauce, made of butter and flour, stirred into half a pint of the water it was boiled in; put in a chopped egg, a little salt, pepper, and fine parsley, when it is nearly done. You can have soup of the liquor, with dumplings, if you wish.

To Boil Veal.

Have a piece of the fore-quarter nicely washed and rubbed with flour; let it boil fast; a piece of five pounds will boil in an hour and a half; dish it up with drawn butter.   Oyster sauce is an improvement to boiled veal.

Roasting Meat.

Roasting either meat or poultry requires more attention than boiling or stewing; it is very important to
baste it frequently; and if the meat has been frozen,
it should have time to thaw before cooking.   Beef,
veal, or mutton, that is roasted in a stove or oven,
requires more flour dredged on it than when cooked
before the fire in a tin kitchen.   There should be but
little water in the dripping pan, as that steams the
meat and prevents its browning; it is best to add more
as the water evaporates, and where there is plenty of
flour on the meat it incorporates with the gravy and
it requires no thickening; add a little seasoning before
you take up the gravy.   Meat that has been hanging
up some time should be roasted in preference to boiling, as the fire extracts any taste it may have acquired.
To rub fresh meat with salt and pepper will prevent
the flies from troubling it, and will make it keep
longer.

To Roast a Turkey—to make Gravy, &c.

A very large turkey will take three hours to roast,
and is best done before the fire in a tin oven.   Wash
the turkey very clean, and let it lay in salt and water
twenty minutes, but not longer, or it changes the
color; rub the inside with salt and pepper; have
ready a stuffing of bread and butter, seasoned with
salt, pepper, parsley, thyme, an onion, if agreeable,
and an egg; if the bread is dry, moisten it with boiling water; mix all well together, and fill the turkey;
if you have fresh sausage, put some in the craw;
have a pint of water in the bottom of the dripping

pan or oven, with some salt, and a spoonful of lard, or butter ; rub salt, pepper and butter over the breast; baste it often, and turn it so that each part will be next the fire.

Gravy may be made from the drippings in the oven by boiling it in a skillet, with thickening and seasoning. Hash gravy should be made by boiling the giblets and neck in a quart of water, which chop fine, then season and thicken ; have both the gravies on the table in separate tureens.

Cranberry and damson sauce are suitable to eat with roast poultry

To Roast a Goose.

Make a stuffing of bread, butter, salt, pepper, sage, thyme and onions ; it requires but little butter, as geese are generally fat; wash it well in salt and water, wipe it, and rub the inside with salt and pepper. A common sized goose will roast in an hour, and a small one in less time ; pour off nearly all the fat that drips from the goose, as it will make the gravy too rich. Make hash gravy of the giblets the same as for turkey.

Ducks.

Wild ducks are generally cooked without stuffing; and for those that like them rare, fifteen or twenty minutes will be long enough; for common ducks, a stuffing should be made the same as for a goose; they will roast in half an hour. Currant jelly and apple sauce should be eaten with ducks and geese.

Chickens.

A large fowl will roast in an hour, and a small one in half an hour; boil the livers and gizzards in a

2*

skillet with a pint of water; thicken and season for gravy. The breasts of the chickens should be rubbed with butter or lard to keep them from breaking. Tie the legs in, to keep them from bursting out. When butter is scarce, it is a good way to make rich short cake to stuff poultry with; it will require nothing added but pepper, parsley, &c.

To Roast Beef.

Season the beef with pepper and salt, and put it in the tin kitchen, well skewered to the spit, with a pint of water in the bottom; baste and turn it frequently, so that every part may have the fire. A very large piece of beef will take three hours to roast; when it is done, pour the gravy out into a skillet, let it boil, and thicken it with flour mixed with water; if it be too fat, skim off the top, which will be useful for other purposes.

To Roast Veal and Lamb.

Veal should be well seasoned, and rubbed with lard; when it begins to brown, baste it with salt and water; a large loin will take from two to three hours to roast, the thin part of the fore-quarter an hour; it should be well done; boil up and thicken the gravy. A leg of veal or mutton may be stuffed before baking.

Lamb and mutton do not require to be rubbed with lard, as they are generally fatter than veal; make the gravy as for veal. A quarter of lamb will roast in an hour; a loin of mutton in two hours.

To Roast a Pig—Hash Gravy, &c.

Have a pig of a suitable size, clean it well, and rub the inside with pepper and salt. Make a stuffing of bread, butter, parsley, sage and thyme; if the bread is stale, pour a little boiling water on it; mix altogether; fill the pig, and sew it up with strong thread; put in the skewers and spit, and tie the feet with twine; have a pint and a half of water in the bottom of the tin kitchen, with a spoonful of lard and a little salt, with this baste it; and turn it, so as each part will have the benefit of the fire. It should be basted until the skin begins to get stiff with the heat of the fire; then grease it all over with butter or lard, and continue to turn it before the fire, but baste no more, or the skin will blister. A pig will take from two to three hours to roast, according to the size; when it is done, pour the water out in a skillet; season it and thicken it with flour and water. To make hash gravy, put the liver and heart to boil in three pints of water; after they have boiled an hour, chop them very fine, put them back in the pot, and stir in a thickening of flour and water, with salt, pepper, parsley and thyme. Have the gravies in separate tureens on either side of the pig. Apple sauce and cold slaw are almost indispensable with pig.

To Roast Pork.

After washing the pork, cut the skin in squares or stripes; season it with salt and pepper, and baste it with salt and water; thicken, and boil up the gravy.

To Bake a Stuffed Leg of Veal.

Cut off the shank, and make holes round the bone for stuffing, which should be of bread and butter, the yelk of an egg, and seasoning; fill the holes with this, and spread it over the top, with little pieces of the fat of ham; dust salt and pepper over, put it in the dutch-oven, or dripping pan, and bake it brown; put a pint of water in the bottom, and if it should dry up, put in more; when it is done, dust in some flour for the gravy. If done carefully, meat is almost as good roasted in the stove as before the fire. If you let the gravy boil over in the stove, it makes an unpleasant smell through the house, and spoils the flavor of the meat. The ham of fresh pork is good, done in the same way.

To Bake a Pig's Head.

Have the head nicely cleaned, with the eyes taken out, and the ears cut off; season it with salt and pepper; rub crumbs of bread over, with a spoonful of lard; put it in the dutch-oven, or dripping pan, with a pint of water; bake it an hour; thicken and season the gravy.

To Cook Pigeons.

Pigeons should be roasted about fifteen minutes before a quick fire; as the meat is dry, they should have a rich stuffing, and be basted with butter.

You may bake them in a dutch-oven or stew them in a pot, with water enough to cover them, and some crumbs of bread or flour dusted over them; let them cook slowly half an hour; mix together flour and water, with salt, pepper, and parsley to season, and a lump of butter; stir this in and let it boil up; put them in a deep dish and pour the gravy over. Pigeons make a very nice pie in the same way as chickens.

To Bake a Ham.

Make a dressing of bread, seasoned with pepper and herbs, moisten it with about five eggs, instead of water. Take a ham that has been cut at the table, either fresh or salt, fill up the place where it has been cut, and cover the top with the dressing, bake it half an hour, and garnish it with parsley before sending it to the table.

To Bake Beef's Heart.

After washing the heart, make a rich stuffing with bread and suet, highly seasoned; fill it with this, and put it in a dutch-oven, or the dripping pan of a stove, with half a pint of water; let it bake an hour and a half; the gravy will not need any thickening, as some of the stuffing will fall out.   Put the gravy in the dish.

Beef Alamode.

Take part of a round of beef, bone it, and make holes for stuffing, which is made of bread, suet, thyme, parsley, chopped onions, mace, cloves, pepper, salt and a raw egg; stuff the meat, bind it with tape, and put it in a dutch-oven, with a plate in the bottom to keep it from burning; just cover it with water, and let it stew from three to four hours according to the size.

Make gravy with some of the water it was stewed in, seasoned with claret and butter, and thickened with flour.   If you wish it to taste of any other sort of wine, add a glass to the gravy.

Beef Steak.

Choose the tenderest part of beef, cut it an inch thick, broil it gently over good coals, covered with a plate; have butter, salt, pepper, and a little water in a dish; and when you turn the beef, dip it in this; be careful to have as much of the juice as you can.   When done, put it in a warm dish, and pour the basting over, with some more butter.

Mutton Chops.

Cut some pieces of mutton, either with or without bone, about an inch thick; have the gridiron hot, first rubbing it with a little suet; put on the chops, turning them frequently, and butter and season them with pepper and salt as you cook them; then dish them on a hot dish and add more butter.

Rabbits and Squirrels.

Rabbits and squirrels, or birds, may be fried as chickens, or stewed in a pot with a little water. If you make a pie of rabbits or squirrels, they should be stewed first to make them tender, and then made in the same way as chicken pie. Rabbits are very good cooked with chopped onions, in a pot with a little water, and thickening of milk and flour stirred in when they are nearly done. Squirrels make very good soup.

To Fry Ham.

Slice the ham, and if it is very salt, pour boiling water on it, and let it soak a while; then fry it with a small piece of lard; when done, dish it; mix together flour, milk, parsley and pepper, let it boil, and pour it over the ham.

To Fry Beef with Kidney.

Cut the kidney in small pieces; take out all the strings, and let it soak several hours in salt and water; wash and drain it; season some pieces of beef and kidney, and put them in a frying pan, with hot lard or drippings of any kind; dust a little flour over; when it is fried on both sides, take it up in a dish; mix a spoonful of flour in some water with salt and pepper, and pour in; when it has boiled, pour it over the beef.

To Fry Liver.

Liver should be cut across the grain in slices about half an inch thick; pour boiling water over it, drain and season it with pepper and salt; flour each piece and drop it in a frying-pan of hot bacon drippings; do not fry it any longer than it is done, or it will be hard; take it up in a dish, make gravy as for beef, and pour over it.

Veal Cutlets.

Cut the veal in slices near an inch thick; wash, drain, and season it; beat up an egg, and have ready some pounded crackers or bread crumbs; dip the slices first in the egg, and then in the bread, and fry them in hot lard; mix a gravy of flour and water, with salt, pepper and parsley; when the veal is taken up, pour it in; let it boil a few minutes and pour it over the dish, and grate a little nutmeg over.

To Fry Veal, Lamb or Pork.

Cut up the meat in thin slices, and season it; dip it in flour and drop it in a pan of hot lard; when brown, take it up, and make gravy with flour, milk, parsley, pepper and salt, which stir in.

To Stew Veal, Lamb or Pork.

Cut the meat small, season it, and put it in a pot with water enough to cover it; let it cook for half an hour; then pour in thickening of flour and milk, with parsley and thyme, and a piece of butter, (if the meat is not fat;) take it up in a deep dish.

Brains and Tongue.

Pour boiling water on the brains, and skin them; tie them tight in a cloth, and boil them and the tongue with the head; when done put them on a plate, chop three leaves of green sage fine, and beat up with the brains; spread them round a small dish, and after skining the tongue, place it in the middle.

Veal Hash.

Take the lights, heart, and some of the liver; boil them in a pint of water; when done, take them out and chop them fine; season it with salt, pepper and a little sweet marjoram; put it back in the pot, and thicken it with butter and flour; let it boil a few minutes, and dish it in a small tureen.

Brain Cakes.

When the head is cloven, take out the brains and clear them of strings, beat them up with the yelks of two eggs, some crumbs of bread, pepper, salt, fine parsley, a spoonful of cream, and a spoonful of flour; when they are well mixed, drop them with a spoon into a frying-pan with a little hot butter, and fry them of a light-brown color.

Force Meat Balls.

Take a pound of veal, half a pound of suet, two slices of ham, and some crumbs of bread, chop them very fine, and put in the yelks of two eggs; season it with parsley, thyme, mace, pepper and salt; roll it into small balls, and fry them brown.

They are nice to garnish hashes, roast veal or cutlets, and to put in soup.

To Fry Veal's Liver.

Cut the liver and heart across the grain, wash it well, pour boiling water on, and let it stand a few minutes, then drain and season it with salt and pepper, flour it and drop it in hot lard; when it is brown on both sides, dish it; dust a little flour in the pan, and pour in some water, let it boil a minute, stirring in a seasoning of parsley, thyme, or sweet marjoram; pour the gravy over the liver. This is a good breakfast dish.

To Fry Veal Sweet Breads.

Dip them in the yelk of an egg beaten, then in a mixture of grated bread, or flour and salt and pepper; fry them a nice brown.

To Stew Sweet Breads.

Stew them in a little water, with butter, flour, and a little cream; season with salt, pepper, parsley and thyme.

To Brown a Calf's Head with the Skin on.

After scalding and washing the head clean, take out the eyes, cut off the ears, and let it boil half an hour; when cold, cleave the upper from the lower jaw, take out the tongue, strike off the nose, score the part which has the skin on, rub it over with beaten egg, sprinkle it over with salt, parsley, cayenne and black pepper; lay pieces of butter over it, and put it in a dutch-oven to brown, basting it often; cut down the lower part in slices, skin the tongue and palate, and cut them up; put them in a pot with a little water; when done, thicken it with brown flour and butter, season it with pepper, salt, some pickled oysters, wine or brandy (if you like it,) and let it stew fifteen minutes. Lay the baked head in a dish and put the hash around it, and lay force meat balls or brain cakes round the edge of the dish.

3

Bacon Fraise.

Cut streaked bacon in small thin slices, make a batter of a pint of milk, two eggs, and two large spoonsful of flour; some salt and pepper; put some lard or dripping in a frying-pan, and when it is hot pour in half of the batter, and strew the bacon over it; then pour on the remainder of the batter; let it fry gently, and be careful in turning, that the bacon does not come to the pan.

Irish Stew.

Take five thick mutton chops, or two pounds of the neck or loin, two pounds of potatoes, peel them and cut them in halves, six onions or half a pound of onions, peel and slice them also. First put a layer of potatoes at the bottom of your stew-pan, then a couple of chops and some onions, then again potatoes, and so on till the pan is quite full; season with pepper and salt, and three gills of broth or gravy, and two teaspoonsful of mushroom catsup; cover it very close to prevent the escape of steam, and stew on a slow fire for an hour and a half; a slice of ham is an addition Great care should be taken not to let it brown.

To Brown Flour for Gravy, &c.

Put some flour in a dutch-oven and set it over some hot coals; keep stirring it until it is of a light-brown color; in this way several pounds can be done at once, and kept in a jar covered; and is very convenient to thicken brown soups and gravies with.

Drawn Butter.

Put half a pint of water in a skillet, rub a quarter of a pound of butter in a large spoonful of flour; when the water boils, stir it in and let it boil a few minutes; season it with parsley, chopped fine.

Stuffing or Dressing.

Stuffing for poultry is made of bread and butter, an egg, salt, pepper, chopped parsley or thyme, mixed together; if the bread is dry, it should have a little boiling water poured on it.

Egg Sauce.

This is made as drawn butter, with one or two eggs boiled hard and chopped into it, and a little salt.

Celery Sauce.

Take a large bunch of celery, cut it fine, and boil it till soft, in a pint of water; thicken it with butter and flour, and season it with salt, pepper, and mace.

Bacon Dumplings.

Cut slices of cooked bacon, and pepper them; roll out crust as for apple dumplings; slice some potatoes very thin, and put them in the crust with the meat; close them up, and let them boil fast an hour; when done, take them out carefully with a ladle.

Drop Dumplings.

These are good for almost any kind of soup, and may be made of a quart of flour, two eggs, a spoonful of butter, some salt and pepper, wet with milk and water; drop them in while it is boiling, and let them boil ten or fifteen minutes.

Vermicelli.

Beat three fresh eggs very light, make them into a stiff paste, with flour and water; knead it well, and roll it very thin, cut it in narrow strips, give them a twist, and dry them quickly, on tin sheets or dishes, in the sun or a moderate oven; soak them a few minutes in cold water, and put them in chicken soup. They are very good and convenient.

Hash made of Fowls.

Take the bones and pieces that have been left of roast or boiled fowls, either turkeys or chickens, crack the bones, cut off the meat, and chop it fine; put it in a small iron pot, or stew pan, cover it with water; put in the gravy that may be left from the fowls; season with pepper and salt, put in some chopped celery, crumbs of bread, a lump of butter, and if it requires it, dust in a little flour; if you like it you may slice in an onion.

Beef Steak Pudding.

Take two pounds of beef from the round or surloin, and after taking out the bone, season it according to fancy; some prefer a seasoning of pepper, salt, onions, thyme, marjoram or sage; others the pepper and salt alone. Then prepare a plain stiff crust, either with or without butter or lard; spread the crust over a deep dish or bowl, put in the beef, and if you like it, add some butter; cover it close with a crust which must be closely turned in to prevent the water from penetrating; tie it up tight in a cloth, put it in a pot of boiling water and let it boil quickly for an hour. The cloth should be dipped in hot water, and floured, as for other boiled puddings.

Beef Steak Pie.

Take some fine beef steaks, beat them well with a rolling-pin, and season them with pepper and salt, according to taste. Make a good crust; lay some in a deep dish or tin pan; lay in the beef, and fill the dish half full of water; put in a table-spoonful of butter and some chopped thyme and parsley, and cover the top with crust; bake it from one to two hours, according to the size of the pie, and eat it while hot.

Baked Beef Pudding.

Par-boil some tender pieces of beef, in water enough to barely cover it; grease a pan with lard, season the beef and lay it in; make a batter of eggs, milk and flour, with a little salt, and pour it over; bake it an hour in a stove or dutch-oven, and when done keep it hot till it is eaten. Save the water the beef was boiled in, add a little butter, flour, pepper, salt and chopped parsley, thyme or sweet marjoram, and boil it up; when you dish up the pudding pour this over, or put it in a gravy dish to be served hot at the table.

Pork Stew Pie.

Take small bones and pieces of pork that will not do for sausage; roll out some crust with but little shortening; lay in the meat and small pieces of crust alternately; sprinkle in flour and seasoning, cover it with water, and put on a crust.

Spiced Beef in the Irish Style.

To a round weighing from twenty to twenty-five pounds, take a pint of salt, one ounce of saltpetre, two ounces of pepper, two ounces of cloves, one ounce of allspice, four ounces of brown sugar, all well pulverized, and mixed together; rub the round well with it, and lay it in a small tub or vessel by itself. Turn and rub it once a day for ten days. It will

3*

not injure if it remain a week longer in the spices, if it should not be convenient to bake it. When you wish to have it cooked, strew over the top of the round a small handful of suet. Be particular to bind it tight round with a cord, or narrow strip of muslin, which must be wrapped several times round to keep it in shape; put it in a dutch-oven, and add three pints of water when it is first put down; keep water boiling in the tea-kettle, and add a little as it seems necessary, observing not to add too much. It will require a slow heat, and take four hours to bake.

This is a very fine standing dish, and will be good for three weeks after cooking. Keep the gravy that is left to pour over it to keep it moist.

To Bake Fowls.

Season and stuff them the same as for roasting; put them in a dutch-oven or stove, with a pint of water; when they are half done, put in the giblets; when these are done, chop them with a knife, and put in thickening and a lump of butter.

If chickens are young, split them down the back, and put them in a dutch-oven, with a plate in the bottom, and a pint of water; when they are done, stir in a spoonful of flour, mixed in half a pint of milk, a piece of butter, salt, pepper and parsley; let it boil up and dish them.

To Fry Chickens.

After cutting up the chickens, wash and drain them; season them with salt and pepper; rub each piece in flour, and drop them separately in a frying-pan or dutch-oven of hot lard; when brown, turn the other side to fry; make a thickening of rich milk, flour, a piece of butter, salt, and chopped parsley; take up the chicken on a dish; pour a little water in the pan to keep the gravy from being too thick; put in the thickening, stir it, and let it boil a few minutes; then pour it over the chicken.

Chickens Fried in Batter.

Make a batter of two eggs, a tea-cup of milk, a little salt, and thickened with flour; have the chickens cut up, washed and seasoned; dip the pieces in the batter separately, and fry them in hot lard; when brown on both sides, take them up on a dish, and make a gravy as for fried chickens.

Lard fries much nicer than butter, which is apt to burn.

Chickens in Paste.

Make a crust as for pies, and roll it out in cakes, large enough to cover a chicken. The chickens should be very nicely picked and washed, and the inside wiped dry; put in each a small lump of butter, a little salt, pepper, and parsley; have the pot boiling, close the chickens in the dough, pin them up in separate cloths, and boil them three-quarters of an hour; dish them, and pour drawn butter over. Pigeons can be cooked in the same manner.

To Fricassee Chickens.

Cut up the chickens, and put them in a pot with just water enough to cover them; let it boil half an hour; have ready some thickening made of milk, flour, and butter, seasoned with parsley, thyme, pepper, and salt; let it boil a few minutes longer, and when it is dished, grate a little nutmeg over, if you like it. This is one of the easiest, cheapest and best ways of cooking chickens.

Chicken Pie.

Cut up the chickens, and if they are old, boil them fifteen minutes in a little water, which save to put in the pie; make a paste like common pie crust, and put it round your pan, or dish; lay in the chicken, dust flour over, and put in butter, pepper, and salt; cover them with water, roll out the top crust quite thick, and close the pie round the edge; make an opening in the middle with a knife; let it bake rather more than an hour. If you warm a pie over for the next day, pour off the gravy and warm it separately, and add it to the pie.

Pot Pie.

Cut up two large chickens; grease your pot, or dutch-oven, with lard; roll out crust enough in two parts, to go round it, but not to cover the bottom, or it will burn before the pie is done. As you put in the pieces of chicken, strew in flour, salt, and pepper, some pieces of the crust rolled thin, and a few potatoes; cover this with water, and put on a covering of paste, with a slit cut in the middle; let it cook slowly for about two hours; have hot water in a tea kettle, and if it should dry up too much, pour some in; just before you dish it, add a little parsley and thyme.

Veal, lamb and pork pies, may be made in the same way. If you like more top crust, cook it in a dutch-oven; and when the first crust is done, take it off in a pan and set it near the fire, and cover the pie again with dough.

Giblet Pie and Soup.

If you can get livers and gizzards from market, you can have a very nice pie made, the same as chicken pie, or soup with dumplings made of milk, egg and flour, beaten together, and dropped in when the soup is nearly done, and season it with parsley, pepper, and salt.

Chicken Stewed with New Corn.

Cut up the chickens as for pies; season them well; have green corn cut off the cob; put a layer of chicken in the bottom of a stew pan, and a layer of corn, and so till you fill all in; sprinkle in salt, pepper and parsley, and put a piece of butter in; cover it with water, and put on a crust, with slits cut in it; let it boil an hour; when done, lay the crust in a deep dish; dip out the chicken and corn, and put it on the crust; stir in the gravy a thickening of milk and flour; when this boils up, pour it in with the corn and chicken. Chicken and corn boiled together in a pot, make very nice soup, with dumplings.

To Broil Chickens.

Split the chickens down the back; season them, and put them on the gridiron over clear coals; cover them over with a plate, (which will make them cook faster;) baste with melted butter: be careful not to let them burn. Make gravy of the giblets, boiled in water and chopped fine ; put in butter, thicken and season it; pour this in a dish, and put the chickens on the top.

Chicken Pudding.

Make a batter of six eggs, milk, flour and a little salt; par-boil the chickens; have each joint cut, grease a pan with lard, and lay the pieces in; put in some lumps of butter, and season it well with pepper and salt; then pour the batter over, and bake it an hour, in a stove or dutch-oven. Veal or beef makes a very nice pudding, done in the same way; but the batter

3*

need not be as rich as for chicken, and it requires no butter. Or it makes a good dish, if you cut slices of ham, after it will not do to appear on the table; make a batter, as for other pudding; put in a little butter and pepper, and bake it in a pan.

Cold Chicken with Vinegar.

Cut up the chicken in small pieces, and crack the bones; season it with salt and pepper, and put it in a deep baking plate, with a lump of butter and a table-spoonful of vinegar; cover it with hot water, put a plate over, and let it stew on a stove or hot embers.

Chicken Salad.

Cut up the white parts of a cold chicken, season it with oil, or drawn butter, mustard, pepper, salt, and celery, chopped very fine, and a little vinegar. Turkey salad is made in the same manner as above.

Stewed Chickens with Rice.

The rice must first be soaked in water, and very nicely washed, or it will not be white; two tea-cups-ful of rice are sufficient to serve with one chicken, and must be boiled in a quart of water, which should be boiling when you put the rice in; add a dessert-spoonful of salt; generally half an hour is long enough to boil rice, and it must not be too long in the water after it is done, or it is less wholesome. Drain the water off, if the rice has not absorbed it, and place it in the bottom of the dish; the chicken must be in preparation at the same time with the rice, and should be cut up at the joints, as for fried or fricasseed chicken, and salted and seasoned; boil it in a little more water than sufficient to cover it; and when it is done, take it out, and lay it over the rice on the dish; then rub a small piece of butter with sufficient flour to thicken it, and stir both together in the liquor, which must remain over the fire for about two minutes; and just before it is taken up, add the yelk of an egg well beaten, and some chopped parsley; it must then be immediately poured over the chicken. In preparing this dish, take care that it does not get smoked.

SOUPS.

In making soup, allow yourself plenty of time. Dumplings should be put in about half an hour before the soup is done, and herbs a quarter of an hour:— vegetables, about an hour,—rice, twenty minutes. If herbs are put in too soon, the flavor will fly off and be lost.

Chicken Soup.

Cut up the chicken; cut each joint, and let it boil an hour; make dumplings of a pint of milk, an egg, a little salt and flour, stirred in till quite stiff; drop this in, a spoonful at a time, while it is boiling; stir in a little thickening, with enough pepper, salt and parsley, to season the whole; let it boil a few minutes longer, and take it up in a tureen. Chopped celery is a great improvement to chicken soup; and new corn, cut off the cob, and put in when it is half done, gives it a very nice flavor.

Brown Calf's Head Soup.

Scald and clean the head, and put it to boil with two gallons of water, a shank of veal, three onions, two carrots, a little bacon, and a bunch of sweet herbs. When they have boiled half an hour, take out the head and shank of veal, and cut all the meat off the bones into pieces of two inches square; let the soup boil half an hour longer, when strain it, and put in the meat; season it with salt, cayenne and black pepper, and cloves, if you like; thicken it with butter and browned flour, and let it boil nearly an hour; put some fried force meat balls in the tureen; and just before you pour out the soup, stir into it a table-spoonful of sugar, browned in a frying-pan, and half a pint of wine. This resembles turtle soup.

Beef Shin Soup, Mutton Soup, &c.

Crack the shin in several pieces, and wash it through three waters; put it in a pot of water four hours before dinner; when it begins to boil, take off the scum as it rises, and keep it covered; an hour before it is done, skim off all the fat, and put in pota-toes, onions, turnips, carrots, and cut cabbage, if you like it; either beat up dumplings with eggs and milk, or roll them out of dough made as pie crust; a few minutes before it is done, stir in thickening with pars-ley, thyme, pepper and salt, and tomatoes, if they are in season; then dish it for dinner.

A shin will make a good dinner for a large family, and will do to warm up, if any is left. To eat pickles with it, or pour a little vinegar in your plate, is an improvement.

Soup made of mutton, veal and lamb, does not re-quire many vegetables; carrots and potatoes are the most suitable. A shank of veal or mutton will make a small pot of very good soup. Celery, cut fine, is very nice seasoning.

Gumbo Soup.

Take two pounds fresh beef; put this in a dinner-pot, with two gallons of water; after boiling two hours, throw in a quarter of a peck of ocra, cut into small slices, and about a quart of ripe tomatoes, peeled and cut up; slice four or five large onions; fry them brown, and dust in while they are frying from your dredge-box, several spoonsful of flour; add these, with pepper, salt and parsley, or other herbs, to your taste, about an hour before the soup is finished; it will require six hours moderate boiling.

ANOTHER WAY.

Cut up a large fat chicken; boil it in two gallons of water, adding at the time you put in the chicken the same quantity of ocra, two large onions cut fine; season with pepper, salt, thyme and parsley; and when nearly done, drop in dumplings made of one egg, half a pint of rich milk, and flour sufficient to make them so that they will drop from a spoon. This soup requires from four to five hours moderate boiling. Just before serving, take up the chicken, and after taking out all the bones, return the chicken into the soup, and dish it up.

Pea Soup.

Leave a pint of peas in the pot, with the water they were boiled in; make a thickening of flour, milk and butter, seasoned with salt, pepper, parsley and thyme; toast two or three slices of bread; cut it up in the tureen; and when the soup has boiled about ten minutes, pour it over.

Children are mostly fond of pea soup, and it seldom disagrees with them. A few slices of fat ham will supply the place of butter.

4

Soup of Dried White Beans, &c.

Dried beans or peas should be soaked before boiling; they make very good soup with a small piece of bacon or salt pork boiled with them; put them to boil in plenty of water, and after they have boiled an hour, pour it off, and put in cold water—and the meat or bones, and let them boil an hour longer; stir in a little thickening, with pepper, salt, parsley and thyme; mix up some dumplings, and drop in half an hour before the soup is done. Where you have a large family, you should always be provided with dried beans for winter use.

A Vegetable Soup.

Take an onion, a turnip, two pared potatoes, a carrot, a head of celery; boil them in three pints of water till the vegetables are cooked; add a little salt; have a slice of bread toasted and buttered, put it into a bowl, and pour the soup over it. Tomatoes when in season form an agreeable addition.

FISH, OYSTERS, &c.

To Bake a Rock Fish.

Rub the fish with salt, black pepper, and a dust of cayenne, inside and out; prepare a stuffing of bread and butter, seasoned with pepper, salt, parsley and thyme; mix an egg in it, fill the fish with this, and sew it up or tie a string round it; put it in a deep pan, or oval oven and bake it as you would a fowl. To a large fish add half a pint of water; you can add more for the gravy if necessary; dust flour over and baste it with butter. Any other fresh fish can be baked in the same way. A large one will bake slowly in an hour and a half, small ones in half an hour.

To Stew a Rock Fish,

Rub the fish with salt and pepper, and a little cayenne on the inside; put it in an oval stew-pan. To a fish that weighs six pounds, put a pint of water; when it is about half done, season it well with salt and pepper, and a little mace or cloves; rub a quarter of a pound of butter in a half a tea-cup of flour, with a little parsley and thyme; stir this in with a pint of oysters. Serve it with the gravy in the dish. A large fish should be allowed an hour, small ones half an hour.

To Broil Shad,

Soak a salt shad a day or night previous to cooking; it is best to drain an hour before you put it to the fire; if it hangs long exposed to the air, it loses its flavor: grease the gridiron to keep it from sticking; have good coals, and put the inside down first. Fresh shad is better to be sprinkled with salt, an hour before it is put to broil; put a plate over the top to keep the heat in. In broiling shad or other fresh fish you should dust them with corn meal before you put them down.

To Bake a Fresh Shad,

Make a stuffing of bread, butter, salt, pepper and parsley; fill a large shad with this, and bake it in a stove or oven.

To Fry Fresh Fish,

Have the fish well scalded, washed and drained; cut slits in the sides of each; season them with salt and

pepper, and roll them in corn flour; have in your frying-pan hot lard or bacon drippings; if the fish have
been kept several days, dip them in egg before rolling
them in corn flour, to keep them from breaking; fry
them light brown on both sides.

To Fry Clams.

After opening them as oysters, wash them in their
own liquor and drain then; make a batter of an egg,
flour and pepper; dip them in this, and fry them in
butter.

To Stew Clams.

Strain the liquor and stew them in it for about
twenty minutes; make a thickening of flour, water and
pepper; stir this in and let it boil up; have some
bread toasted and buttered in a deep dish, and pour
the clams over.

Clam soup may be made by putting an equal quantity of water with the liquor, and putting in toasted
bread, crackers or dumplings.

To Pot Fresh Herring.

Scale and wash them well; cut off the heads and
fins, and season them with salt, pepper and cloves;
pack them neatly in a large jar, and pour on enough
cold vinegar to cover them ; put a plate over the top
of the jar, and set it in a moderately warm oven, or
on the top of a stove, in a pan of hot water, for five
or six hours; they will keep in a cool place several
weeks, and are an excellent relish. The jar or pan
should be of stone ware, or fire-proof yellow ware.

To Boil Salt Cod.

Put your fish to soak over night; change the water
in the morning, and let it stay till you put it on, which

should be two hours before dinner; keep it at scalding heat all the time, but do not let it boil, or it will get hard; eat it with egg sauce or drawn butter. If you have any cod fish left from dinner, mix it with mashed potatoes, and enough flour to stick them together; season with pepper; make it into little cakes, and fry them in ham drippings.

To Boil Salt Shad, Mackerel or Herring.

Wash the fish from the pickle; put it in a frying-pan; cover it with water, and let it boil fifteen minutes; take it up and drain it between two plates; put a little butter over and send it hot to the table: or, after boiling, you can flour, and fry it in drippings of any kind.

To Boil Salt Salmon.

Let salmon soak over night, and boil it slowly for two hours; eat it with drawn butter. To pickle salmon after it has been boiled, heat vinegar scalding hot, with whole peppers and cloves; cut the fish in small square pieces; put it in a jar, and pour the vinegar over. Shad may be done in the same way.

To Boil Fresh Fish.

After being well cleaned, rub the fish with salt, and pin it in a towel; put it in a pot of boiling water, and keep it boiling fast;—a large fish will take from half to three-quarters of an hour—a small one, from fifteen to twenty minutes. A fat shad is very nice boiled, although rock and bass are preferred generally; when done, take it up on a fish dish, and cover it with egg sauce or drawn butter and parsley. Pickled mushrooms and walnuts, and mushroom catsup, are good with boiled fish.

4*

To Stew Terrapins.

Wash four terrapins in warm water; then throw
them in a pot of boiling water, which will kill them
instantly; let them boil till the shells crack; then take
them out, and take off the bottom shell; cut each
quarter separate; take the gall from the liver; take
out the eggs; put the pieces in a stew-pan, pour in
all the liquor, and cover them with water; put in salt,
cayenne, and black pepper, and a little mace; put in a
lump of butter the size of an egg, and let them stew
for half an hour; make a thickening of flour and
water, which stir in a few minutes before you take it
up, with two glasses of wine; serve it in a deep covered dish; put in the eggs just as you dish it.

Oyster Soup.

Strain the liquor from the oysters, and put it on to
boil, with an equal quantity of water; take off the
scum as it rises; put in pepper, salt, parsley, thyme
and butter; stir in a thickening of flour and water;
throw in the oysters, and let them scald. If you
have cream, put in half a pint just before you take
them up.

ANOTHER WAY.

Strain the liquor from a gallon of oysters, and add to
it an equal quantity of water; put it on the fire, and
boil and skim it before you add the seasoning; then put
in six large blades of mace, a little cayenne, and black
or white pepper; (the latter, on account of the color,
is preferable, as it is desirable to have the soup as
white as possible;) afterwards, permit all to boil together about five minutes; then pour in the oysters
and a quarter of a pound of butter, into which a

dessert-spoonful of wheat flour has been rubbed fine; keep this at boiling heat until the oysters begin to look plump—when it is ready for the table, and must be served up very hot. If you can procure a pint of good cream, half the amount of butter will answer;— if you believe the cream to be rather old, even if it seems to be sweet, add before it goes into the soup, half a small teaspoonful of soda, well mixed with it; after you put in the cream, permit it to remain on the fire long enough to arrive at boiling heat again, when it must be taken up, or it may curdle; throw into the tureen a little finely cut parsley.

Scolloped Oysters,

Toast several slices of bread quite brown, and butter them on both sides; take a baking dish, and put the toast around the sides, instead of a crust.

Pour your oysters into the dish, and season, to your taste, with butter, pepper and salt, adding mace or cloves.

Crumb bread on the top of the oysters, and bake it with a quick heat about fifteen minutes.

To Fry Oysters,

Pick out the largest oysters and drain them; sprinkle them with pepper and salt; beat up an egg, and dip them first in it, and then in pounded crackers, and fry them in butter. It is a plainer way to dip them in corn meal.

Oyster Fritters,

Make a thick batter with two eggs, some crumbs of bread and flour, and a little milk; season this well with pepper and salt; have in a frying-pan equal parts of lard and butter; drop in a spoonful of the batter and put into it one large oyster, or two small ones; let them brown slowly, so as not to burn; turn them carefully. This is a good way to have oysters at breakfast.

To Stew Oysters.

Open them and throw them in a stew-pan, with a lump of butter; make a thickening of flour and water, salt and pepper, and stir it in just as the oysters boil: when they are done, take them up in a deep covered dish, with buttered toast in the bottom.

A Rich Oyster Pie.

Strain off the liquor from the oysters, and put it on to boil, with some butter, mace, nutmeg, pepper and salt; just as it boils, stir in a thickening of milk and flour; put in the oysters, and stir them till they are sufficiently stewed; then take them off, and put in the yelks of two eggs, well beaten; do not put this in while it is boiling, or it will curdle. Line a dish, not very deep, with puff paste; fill it with white paper, or a clean napkin, to keep the top paste from falling in; put on a lid of paste, and bake it. When done, take off the lid carefully; take out the paper or napkin, and pour in the oysters. Send it hot to table.

A Baltimore Oyster Pie.

Make a crust after the directions given for puff paste; grease the bottom of a deep dish, cover it with paste; then season two quarts of raw oysters, (without the liquor,) with spices to your taste, (some preferring nutmeg, mace, cayenne pepper,—others, black pepper alone,) add butter and a heaped tea-cup of grated bread; put all together in the dish; then cover it with your paste, cut in strips, and crossed, or ornamented as your fancy dictates; a pound of butter to two quarts of oysters makes a rich pie; if the oysters are fine, less butter will answer.

A pie of this size will bake in three-quarters of an hour, if the oven is in good order; if the heat is not quick allow it an hour.

If in baking, the crust is likely to become too brown, put a piece of paper doubled over it, and the light color will be retained; when taken from the oven, if it should look dry, pour some of the liquor that was drained from the oysters in the dish, having previously strained and boiled it.

As paste always looks more beautiful when just from the oven, arrange your dinner so that the pie may be placed on the table immediately it is done.

Plain Oyster Pie.

Take from the shell as many oysters as you want to put in the pie; strain the liquor, put it with them over the fire and give them one boil; take off the scum, put in, if you wish to make a small pie, a quarter of a pound of butter, as much flour mixed in water as will thicken it when boiled, and mace, pepper, and salt to your taste; lay a paste in a deep dish, put in the oysters and cover them with paste; cut a hole in the middle, ornament it any way you please, and bake it. A shallow pie will bake in three-quarters of an hour.

Oyster Sauce.

Plump the oysters for a few minutes over the fire; take them out and stir into the liquor some flour and butter mixed together, with a little mace and whole pepper, and salt to your taste; when it has boiled long enough, throw in the oysters, and add a glass of white wine, just as you take it up.　This is a suitable sauce for boiled fowls.

To Pickle 100 Oysters.

Drain off the liquor from the oysters, wash them and put to them a table-spoonful of salt, and a tea-cup of vinegar; let them simmer over the fire about ten minutes, taking off the scum as it rises; then take out the oysters, and put to their own liquor a table-spoon-ful of whole black pepper, and a tea-spoonful of mace and cloves; let it boil five minutes, skim, and pour it over the oysters in a jar.

Oysters Pickled another way.

Wash and drain the oysters, and put them in salt and water, that will bear an egg; let them scald till plump, and put them in a glass jar, with some cloves and whole peppers, and when cold cover them with vinegar.

To Brown Oysters in their own Juice.

Take a quart of large oysters, wash them in their own juice, drain and dip them in the yelk of eggs; heat butter in a frying-pan, and after seasoning them with pepper and salt, put them in separately; when they are brown on both sides, draw them to one side of the pan; strain the liquor, and put it in with a piece of butter and flour enough to thicken it.

A Dish of Poached Eggs.

Have ready a kettle of boiling water, pour it in a pan or speeder, which is set on coals; have the eggs at hand; put a little salt in the water, and break them in, one at a time, till you get all in; let them remain till the white is set, and take them out with an egg-spoon, and put on a dish that has buttered toast on it.

Fried Eggs.

Slice and fry any kind of bacon, dish it; have the eggs ready in a dish, and pour them into the gravy; when done, take them up and lay them on the meat.

Fried Eggs another way.

Have your lard or butter boiling hot; break in one egg at a time; throw the hot fat over them with an egg slice, until white on the top; slip the slice under and take them out whole, and lay them on the dish or meat without breaking; season with salt.

Omelet.

Beat six or eight eggs, with some chopped parsley and a little salt; have the pan or speeder nicely washed; put in a quarter of a pound of butter, when it is hot, pour in the eggs; stir it with a spoon till it begins to form; when it is of a light-brown on the under side it is done; turn it out on a plate, and send to table immediately. Grated bread, soaked in cream, put in the omelet, some think an improvement. The dripping of a nice ham, some persons use for omelet instead of butter.

To Boil Eggs.

Have the water boiling, and look at your watch as you put them in; two minutes and a half will cook them to please most persons; if you want them very soft, two minutes will be sufficient, or if less soft three minutes. If you wish them hard, as for lettuce, let them boil ten minutes. Spoons that have been used in eating eggs should be put in water immediately, as the egg tarnishes them.

VEGETABLES.

To Boil Green Corn.

Pick out ears near the same size, and have the water boiling when you put them in; half an hour is long enough for young corn; that which is old and hard will take an hour or more; if young corn is boiled too long, it becomes hard and indigestible.

To Fricassee Corn.

Cut green corn off the cob; put it in a pot, and just cover it with water; let it boil half an hour; mix a spoonful of flour with half a pint of rich milk, pepper, salt, parsley, thyme and a piece of butter; let it boil a few minutes, and take it up in a deep dish. Corn will do to cook in this way when too old to boil on the cob.

To Keep Corn for Winter.

When boiled, cut the corn off the cob, and spread it on dishes; set these in the oven to dry after the bread comes out. If you have no oven, it can be dried in a stove of moderate heat, or round a fire. When perfectly dry, tie it up in muslin bags, and hang them in a dry place; when you use it, boil it till soft in water; mix flour, milk, butter, pepper and salt together, and stir in.

Corn Fritters.

Cut the corn through the grain, and with a knife scrape the pulp from the cob, or grate it with a coarse grater, and to about a quart of the pulp, add two eggs beaten, two table-spoonsful of flour, a little salt and pepper, and a small portion of thin cream, or new milk;

beat the the whole together; have the butter or lard hot in the pan, and put a large spoonful in at a time, and fry brown, turning each fritter separately; this makes an agreeable relish for breakfast, or a good side dish at dinner.

Hominy.

Large hominy, after it is washed, must be put to soak over night; if you wish to have it for dinner, put it to boil early in the morning, or it will not be done in time; eat it as a vegetable.

Small hominy will boil in an hour; it is very good at breakfast or supper to eat with milk or butter, or to fry for dinner.

Both large and small hominy will keep good in a cool place several days. Be careful that the vessel it is cooked in, is perfectly clean, or it will darken the hominy.

To Fry Hominy.

Put a little lard in your frying-pan, and make it hot; mash and salt the hominy; put it in, and cover it over with a plate; let it cook slowly for half an hour, or longer if you like it very brown; when done, turn it out in a plate. If you do not like it fried, mash it well, with a little water, salt, and butter, and warm it in a frying-pan.

To Boil Potatoes.

When the potatoes are old, pare them, put them in plenty of boiling water, and boil them till you can run a fork through easily; if you wish to have them whole, pour off all the water, throw in some salt, and let them stand a few minutes over coals, to let the steam go off; they will then be white and mealy.

It is a mistaken notion to boil potatoes in but little

5

water, as they are sure to turn dark and taste strong. In cold weather they may be kept pared several days in a pan of water, by changing the water every day, and will be whiter. If you like mashed potatoes, take them up when barely done, sprinkle them with salt, and mash them; put in a spoonful of cream and a small lump of butter; keep them hot till they are taken to table.

In the summer when potatoes are young, put them in a small tub, with a little water, and rub them with a piece of brick, to break the skin; you can then peel enough for dinner with a knife in a few minutes. When they are older, boil them with the skins on, and squeeze them separately in a cloth to make them mealy. New potatoes are nice with cream and butter over them.

In boiling old potatoes, some persons cut them round without paring, which allows the moisture to escape; this is an improvement; you can then either peel them or send them to table without peeling.

To Stew Potatoes.

Chop or slice cold potatoes; season with pepper and salt; stew them with a little butter and milk, and a dust of flour; when nearly done, stir in a yelk of egg, with some chopped parsley—they will cook in a few minutes, and may be sliced over night if you wish an early breakfast.

Sweet Potatoes.

To boil sweet potatoes, put them in a pot with plenty of water; let them boil fast till you can run a fork through the largest; then pour off the water, and leave them in the pot a quarter of an hour; you can then peel the skin off or leave it on. Some prefer them baked in a dutch-oven; they should have a quick heat; large potatoes will take an hour to bake. It has been found a good way to boil them, till nearly done; then peel and bake them—they are drier and nicer.

To Fry Potatoes.

Cold potatoes are very good fried for breakfast with scraps of bacon; if they have been mashed, make them out in cakes with a little flour, and fry them brown, or slice them.

Tomatoes.

If you wish to bake tomatoes in the oven with bread, pour boiling water on, and skin them; cut them in small pieces; season with salt and pepper, and put them in a pan with crumbs of bread and butter; cover the pan with a plate, and bake three-quarters of an hour; when done, mash them and take them out on a dish.

To Fry Tomatoes.

Slice them, season with pepper and salt, and fry in hot butter; if they are green, dip them in flour after being seasoned.

Tomato Omelet.

Pour boiling water on the tomatoes, skin and cut them fine; to one quart of this, put two chopped onions and a lump of butter the size of an egg; let them boil half an hour, then mash them; put in grated bread, pepper, salt, and the yelks of two eggs.

To Stew Tomatoes.

Wash and pour boiling water over them; peel off the skins, and cut them up; season them with pepper and salt; put in a lump of butter, and boil them in their own juice for half an hour; stir in enough crumbs of bread to thicken them; let them cook slowly ten minutes longer; be careful that the bread does not burn.

To Bake Tomatoes.

Take out the inside of large tomatoes, make a stuffing of bread, butter, pepper, salt and an egg; fill them with this, and set them in a deep pie-plate; let them bake slowly half an hour.

Tomato Jelly, to eat with Roast Meat.

Wash the tomatoes, and put them in a bell-metal kettle, with a little water; let them boil thirty minutes; take them out and strain them through a sieve, till you get all the pulp; let it settle and pour off the top; put the thick part in deep plates, and set them in the oven after the bread is drawn; season it with pepper and salt to your taste, and put it away in a jar It can either be eaten cold, or warmed up with crumbs of bread and butter. Some persons slice tomatoes, and dry them on dishes in an oven.

To Fricassee Tomatoes.

Wash and cut them in two, if large; if small, leave them whole, but do not peel them or they go too much to pieces; have a broad speeder or stove-pan; put in a half spoonful of butter; season the tomatoes with pepper and salt, and flour them; cover them with a plate; they will cook in ten minutes, stirring them once; pour in half a tea-cup of cream just as they are done; let them boil up and dish them while hot; this dish is much liked either for breakfast, dinner or tea.

To Broil Tomatoes for Breakfast.

Take large round tomatoes, wash and wipe them, and put them on the gridiron over lively coals—the stem side down; when this is brown, turn them and let them cook till quite hot through; place them on a hot dish and send them quickly to table, where each one may season for himself with pepper, salt and butter.

To Bake Tomatoes for Breakfast.

Season them with pepper and salt; flour and bake them in a stove, in a deep plate with a little butter over them.

Tomatoes sliced with Onions.

Pick the best tomatoes; let them stand a little while in cold water, then peel and slice them. To about six tomatoes, you may add two red onions, also sliced; season with pepper, plenty of salt, and a small portion of vinegar.

To put up Tomatoes for Winter.

Gather a quantity of tomatoes, wash, scald, skin and cut them up; season them highly with pepper and salt, and put them in a large stone jar; set this in the oven with your bread, and leave it till it is cold; stir them, and set them in the oven every time you bake for several weeks; when the juice is nearly dried up, put a piece of white paper over the jar, melt some lard and pour on it. When you use them, stew them with bread, butter and water.

Baked Egg Plant.

Boil them ten minutes; then cut them in half and take out the seeds; fill them with a stuffing of crumbs

5*

of bread, seasoned with butter, pepper, salt, the yelk of an egg, and if you choose, the juice of a tomato; close them and tie each one with a string; put a little water in the dutch-oven, and lay them in with some of the stuffing on the top; let them cook slowly half an hour, basting them with butter; take them out, thicken the gravy, and pour it over them on the dish.

To Fry Egg Plant.

Cut them in slices half an inch thick; sprinkle them with salt, and let them stand a few minutes to extract the bitter taste; wash them in cold water, and wipe them dry; season with salt and pepper; dip them in flour, and fry them in butter.

Another way of cooking them is to cut them in thin slices, and bake them on a bake-iron that is hot enough to bake cakes.

Salsify, or Oyster Plant.

Scrape the roots, and boil them till soft; mash them, and put in butter pepper, salt, and egg and flour enough to stick them together; make this in cakes as large as an oyster, and fry them in butter; or after boiling, you can cut them in slices and stew them in water; then butter and season, and thicken with a little flour and cream.

To Stew or Fry Mushrooms.

Be careful in gathering mushrooms that you have the right kind; they are pink underneath, and white on the top, and the skin will peel off easily, but it sticks to the poisonous ones.

After you have peeled them, sprinkle them with salt and pepper, and put them in a stew pan, with a little water, and a lump of butter; let them boil fast ten minutes, and stir in a thickening of flour and cream. They may be fried in butter, or broiled on a gridiron. They are sometimes very abundant in the fall, on ground that has not been ploughed for several years; they appear after a warm rain; they may be peeled, salted, and allowed to stand some hours before cooking.

Cucumbers, to Fry or Slice.

To fry cucumbers, take off the rinds in long pieces, a quarter of an inch thick; season them with pepper and salt; dip them in flour, and fry them in butter.

Many persons think cucumbers unwholesome, and they certainly are if kept for several days before they are eaten; but if sliced thin, with onions, pepper, salt and good vinegar, they may generally be eaten without danger.

Lettuce.

Persons that are fond of lettuce may have it nearly all the year, by sowing the different kinds, and keeping it covered through the winter; the most approved way of dressing it is to cut it fine, and season with oil, mustard, pepper, salt, vinegar, and a hard egg chopped. The essence of ham is also very good to season lettuce.

Where there is a large family, it is a good and economical way to cut the fat of ham in small pieces, fry it, and make a gravy with flour, water and pepper, to eat with lettuce. To cook lettuce you must fry a little ham; put a spoonful of vinegar into the gravy; cut the lettuce, put it in the pan; give it a stir, and then dish it.

Cold Slaw.

Cut hard white cabbage across the leaves, and put it in a deep plate, scald two large spoonsful of vinegar with a piece of butter, some pepper and salt; pour this

over the slaw; have an egg boiled hard; chop it fine,
and spread it over the top. Some persons like it
heated in a pan with vinegar and water, and the yelk
of a raw egg mixed through it.

Cauliflowers, &c.

Have a pot with half milk, and the rest water; when
this boils, put in the cauliflowers, and let them boil till
tender; put in some salt just before you take them up;
have ready drawn butter with parsley, to pour over
them, or a sauce of cream and butter. Good heads
of yellow Savoy cabbage, cooked in this way, resemble cauliflowers. Brocoli is a delightful vegetable,
and may be cooked in the same manner.

To Boil Cabbage.

In summer, you should allow a large head of cabbage an hour to boil, but when it has been tendered
by the frost, it will boil in half that time. Most
persons prefer cabbage boiled with ham; the pot
should be well skimmed before it goes in or the grease
will penetrate the cabbage, and make it unwholesome;
take it up before it boils to pieces. It is very good
boiled with corned beef or pork, or with milk and
water, with a little salt added. Some like it with a
little salæratus thrown in while boiling, as that tenders
it and makes it of a more lively green.

To Boil Greens and Poke.

After skimming the pot that the bacon has been
boiled in, put in cabbage sprouts, and let them boil till
the stalks are tender; all greens are best boiled in a
net. Spinach cooks in a few minutes; some persons
prefer it when boiled in salt and water; you should

have drawn butter or hard eggs to eat with it when done in this way. There are several kinds of wild greens to be found in the country in the spring, as wild mustard, poke and lambs-quarter, which are very good cooked as cabbage sprouts. Pour boiling water on poke, after tying it in bunches, as asparagus, let it stand a few minutes; pour off the water; boil it with a little salt in the water, and if you choose a little sal-æratus; dress it with butter, and dish it as asparagus.

String Beans.

String beans, if boiled in salt and water, will require fully two hours; but if boiled in a net, in a pot with bacon, they will not take so long; if they are cooked in the same pot with cabbage, it will injure the flavor. It is a good way to boil a very small piece of pork or bacon, or a ham-bone in the pot with beans; when they are done, season them with cream, butter, salt and pepper.

Lima Beans.

Shell them, and wash them in cold water; let them boil about an hour; when done, dip them from the water, and season with salt, pepper, cream or butter; keep them hot till they are sent to table.

Dried Lima beans should be soaked over night, and boiled two hours or longer, if they are not soft.

Peas.

Early peas require about half an hour to boil, and the later kinds rather longer; the water should boil when they are put in; when they are tough and yellow, they may be made tender and green, by putting in a little pearl-ash, or ashes tied up in a rag, just before they are taken up; this will tender all green vegetables, but do not put too much;—when done, dip them out; drain and season them with butter, pepper and salt; put a bunch of parsley in the middle of the dish.

To Keep Green Beans for Winter.

Boil salt and water to make a strong pickle; string the beans, and put them in a tight wooden firkin; sprinkle them with salt as they go in; when the pickle is cold, pour it on, and put on a weight to keep the beans under; they will keep in the cellar till the next spring. They should soak several hours in cold water before they are boiled.

Asparagus.

All persons that have a garden should have an asparagus-bed; it is valuable as being one of the first vegetables in the spring. Put the stalks of the same length in bunches together, and tie them with strings; boil it three-quarters of an hour in clear water; (if you put salt in, it turns it dark;) have buttered toast in the bottom of a deep dish; untie the strings, and put the asparagus in; sprinkle it over with pepper and salt, and put butter on. Asparagus is also agreeable in chicken soup.

Cymlings, or Squashes.

In cultivating this vegetable, the small bunch cymling is the best, as it takes so little room in the garden, and comes soon to maturity; if they are so hard that a pin will not run in easily, they are unfit for use. Boil the cymlings till soft; cut them open, and take out the seeds; put them in a colander, and mash them; when the water is drained off, put them in a small pot, and stew them with cream and butter for ten minutes; just as you dish them, season with pepper and salt. If boiled with salt meat, they require but little seasoning.

Pumpkins.

Young pumpkins resemble cymlings, when cooked in the same way. When they are ripe, they should be pared and cut up, and boiled till soft in a good deal of water; take them up as soon as they are done, or they will soak up the water; mash them and season them with salt, pepper and butter. They are good to eat with roast or boiled beef.

To Bake Pumpkins.

The long striped pumpkin, with a thick long neck, called by some potato pumpkin, is the best for baking; cut it up in slices, leaving on the rind; put it in a dutch-oven or dripping-pan, and let it bake an hour with a quick heat. Where sweet potatoes cannot be had, pumpkins make a very good substitute. If you put ripe pumpkins that have not been frosted, in a dry place, they will keep to make puddings till spring.

To Dry Pumpkins.

Pare them, and cut them in thin slices; have a strong thread, and string them on it with a needle; hang them out in the sun till dry, taking them in at night; tie them up in a muslin bag, and hang them in a dry place. Soak them before they are stewed, and they are nearly as good for puddings as when in season. Some dry them, as apples, by spreading on boards.

Parsnips.

Scrape and split them, and boil until quite soft, either in salt and water, or with meat; they are very good served up in this way, with plenty of butter. They may, when boiled, either be baked with a few slices of salt meat, and require no seasoning but pepper, or made into small round cakes, seasoned with butter, pepper and salt, and fried.

Carrots.

Carrots should be scraped, and boiled till soft, in plenty of water; when they are done, take them up, and slice them thin; season them with salt, pepper and butter. They are suitable to eat with boiled meat or fowls.

Turnips.

Pare and quarter the turnips, and put them in a pot of clear water, or with fresh meat; boil them half an hour; drain, and season them with butter, pepper and salt; mash them.

Onions.

After they are peeled, boil them in milk and water; if small, they will cook in half an hour; when they are done, pour off the water; put in cream, butter and salt, and let them stew a few minutes. Small onions are much better for cooking, as they are not so strong.

Beets.

Wash the beets; cut the tops off, and put them in boiling water; the early turnip beet is best for summer, and will boil in less than an hour; the long winter beet should be boiled two hours;—when they are done, drop them in cold water for a minute; peel and slice them; season with butter, pepper and salt; send them hot to table.

To pickle beets, put them in a jar after they have been boiled; fill it up with weak vinegar; put in salt, cayenne and black pepper.

To Boil Rice.

Pick a pint of rice, wash it clean—put it in three pints of boiling water: it should boil fast, and by the time the water evaporates, the rice will be sufficiently cooked; set it where it will keep hot, until you are ready to dish it.

To Keep Vegetables in Winter.

Beets, parsnips, carrots and salsify should be dug up before the frost is severe; those wanted for use in the winter should be put in barrels, and covered with sand; what you do not want till spring should be buried in the garden, with sods on the top. Celery may be dug in November, and set in a large box covered with sand, in the cellar, with the roots down; it will keep till the frost is out of the ground. Or it may be left in the ground all winter, and dug as you want it for use.

BREAD, &c.

As bread is the most important article of food, great care is necessary in making it, and much judgment, as the weather changes so often.

In warm weather, the rising should be mixed with water nearly cold; if there should be a spell of damp weather in the summer, have it slightly warm and set it to rise on a table in the kitchen.

In winter it should be mixed with warm water, and left on the warm hearth all night. If the yeast is fresh, a small quantity will do; if several weeks old,

6

it will take more. If you use dry yeast, let it soak fifteen minutes, and put in a tea-spoonful of salæratus to prevent it from getting sour.

Light Bread, Baking in a Stove, &c.

For two loaves of bread, thicken a quart of water with flour, till it will just pour easily; put in a table-spoonful of salt and half a tea-cup of yeast; this should be done in the evening. If the weather is cold, set it where it will be warm all night; but, if warm, it will rise on a table in the kitchen. (If it should not be light in the morning, and the water settles on the top, stir in a little more yeast, and set it in a pan of hot water for a few minutes;) knead in flour till it is nearly as stiff as pie crust, and let it rise again. Have your baking pans greased, and when it is light, mould out the bread, and put it in them; set it by the fire, covered with a cloth, till it begins to crack on the top—when it is light enough to bake. To bake in a stove requires care to turn it frequently; if it browns too fast at first, leave the door open a little while; a thick loaf will bake in an hour, and a small one in less time. In trying the heat of a stove, drop a few drops of water on the top, if it boils gently it is in good order, and the heat should be kept at this point.

To Bake a Dutch-oven Loaf.

If you wish to make a large loaf, it will take three pints of water, more than half a tea-cup of yeast, and two spoonsful of salt; when the rising is light, knead it up, have the dutch-oven greased; put it in, and set it near the fire, but not so near that it will scald. When it rises so as to crack on the top, set the oven on coals; have the lid hot, cut the loaf slightly across the top, dividing it in four; stick it with a fork and put the lid on; when it is on a few minutes, see that it does not bake too fast; it should have but little heat at the bottom, and the coals on the top should be renewed frequently; turn the oven round occasionally.

If baked slowly, it will take an hour and a half; when done, wrap it in a large cloth till it gets cold.

To Bake in a Brick Oven.

If you have a large family, or board the laborers of a farm, it is necessary to have a brick oven, so as to bake but twice a week; and to persons that understand the management of them, it is much the easiest way.

If you arrange every thing with judgment, half a dozen loaves of bread, as many pies or puddings, rusk, rolls or biscuit may be baked at the same time. Some persons knead up their bread over night in winter; to do this, the sponge should be made up at four o'clock in the afternoon. If you wish to put corn flour in your bread, scald one quart of it to six loaves, and work it in the flour that you are going to stir in the rising; to make six loaves of bread, you should have three quarts of water and a tea-cup of yeast.

Scalded corn flour, or boiled mashed potatoes, assists bread to rise very much in cold weather. Have a quart of potatoes well boiled and rolled fine with a rolling-pin on your cake board; mix them well in the rising after it is light; if the oven is not ready, move the bread to a cool place. If the bread is sour before you mould it out, mix a heaped tea-spoonful of salæratus in a little water; spread out the bread on the board, dust a little flour on it, and spread the salæratus and water over, and work it well through. This quite takes away the sour taste, but if the bread is made of good lively yeast, it seldom requires it; let it rise in the pans about half an hour. Many persons that make their own bread, are in the constant practice of using salæratus, putting in the rising for six loaves a heaped tea-spoonful, dissolved in a little warm water; in this there is no disadvantage, and it insures sweet bread, and will also answer in making rolls or light cakes.

Common sized loaves will bake in an hour in the brick oven. If they slip easily in the pans, and, upon breaking a little piece from the side, it rises from the pressure of the finger, it is done; but if it should not rise, put it back again; when the bread is taken out of the oven, wrap it in a cloth till quite cold.

You should have a large tin vessel with holes in the top, to keep bread in; in this way, it will be moist at the end of the week in cool weather.

Coarse brown flour or middlings makes very sweet light bread, by putting in scalded corn meal, say, to two loaves, half a pint, and is also good to use for breakfast made as buckwheat cakes.

Directions for Heating a Brick Oven, &c.

It is very important to have good oven-wood split fine, and the oven filled with it as soon as the baking is out; by this precaution it is always ready and dry. Early in the morning, take out half of the wood, and spread the remainder over the oven, in such a way as it will take fire easily; light a few sticks in the fire, and put them in; when it burns well, turn the wood about, and occasionally add more till it is all in; when it is burnt to coals, stir them about well with a long-handled shovel made for the purpose.

When it looks bright on the top and sides, it is hot enough; let the coals lay all over the bottom till near the time of putting in the bread, when draw them to the mouth, as it is apt to get cool the quickest. If you have biscuit to bake, put some of the coals on one side near the front, as they require a quick heat, and should be put in immediately after the coals are taken out; they will bake in fifteen or twenty minutes.

When all the coals are taken out, if the bottom of the oven sparkles, it is very hot, and should wait a few minutes; but if not, you may put in the bread first, and then the pies; if you have a plain rice pudding to bake, it should be put in the middle of the front, and have two or three shovels of coals put round it, if the oven is rather cool. Close the oven with a wooden stopper made to fit it; after they have been in a few minutes, see that they do not brown too fast; if so, keep the stopper down a little while. Pies made of green fruit will bake in three-quarters of an hour; but if the fruit has been stewed, half an hour will be long enough.

Rusk, or rolls, take about half an hour to bake in a brick oven; if you should have to open the oven very often before the bread is done, put in a few shovels of coals and shut it up.

When all is taken out, fill the oven with wood ready for the next baking.

There is nothing in any department of cooking that gives more satisfaction to a young housekeeper than to have accomplished what is called a good baking.

Graham Bread.

Take six quarts of unbolted flour, one tea-cup of good yeast, and six spoonsful of molasses; mix them with a pint of milk, warm water, and a tea-spoonful of salæratus; make a hole in the flour and stir this mixture in it, till it is like batter; then proceed as with

6*

fine flour. Mould it, when light, into four loaves. Have your oven hotter than for other bread, and bake it fully one hour and a half. It is an excellent article of diet for dyspeptic and sedentary persons.

Dyspepsy Bread.

This is three-fourths unbolted flour, and the remaining fourth common flour, and is risen and made as other light bread, but should be baked rather more.

Yeast.

It is important to those that make their own bread, to make their own yeast, or they cannot judge of its strength. The best is the old-fashioned hop yeast, which will keep for six weeks in winter.

Put a pint of hops in a pot, with a quart of water; cover it tightly, and let it boil slowly for half an hour; strain it while boiling hot on a pint of flour, and a heaped table-spoonful of salt; stir it well, and let it stand till nearly cool; when put in a tea-cupful of good yeast; if it is not sweet, put in a little salæratus, just as you stir it in; keep it in a warm place till it rises, when put it in a stone jug, and cork it tightly. Keep it in a cool place in summer, but do not let it freeze in winter; shake it before you use any.

When your yeast jug is empty, fill it with water, and let it soak; wash it well, and if it should smell sour, rinse it with salæratus water. If you have a garden, raise your own hops by all means; pick them by the first of September, or they will lose their strength; dry them on sheets spread on the garret floor.

If you buy hops, choose light green ones, with the yellow dust about them. Brown hops have generally stayed too long on the vines.

ANOTHER METHOD.

Put two handsful of hops into three pints of water; let it boil to one quart; when cold, strain it on to a pint of best flour, a table-spoonful of salt, half a pint of sugar-house molasses, and a tea-cup of good yeast: as it rises, skim off the top several times, when the yeast looks white, bottle it up tight and it will keep for several weeks.

Corn Flour Dry Yeast.

Put a large handful of good hops in a quart of water; cover it close, and let it boil nearly half away, when strain it over corn flour; it must all be wet, but not so soft as for bread; put in a large spoonful of salt, and mix it well; when about milk warm, put in two table-spoonsful of yeast, (observe that the yeast is lively,) rub it through with your hands; it must be so stiff as just to stick together; set it in a warm place to rise, which it should do in a few hours. When light, rub in more corn flour, and scatter it in dishes, very thin, (or put it on a cloth on a large waiter, spread thinly.) It should be dried quickly, or it may turn sour, either in the sun, (which is best,) or a warm stove room; stir it over frequently; when perfectly dry, cover it close, either in a jar or wooden box, and keep it in a dry closet. Select a sunny day, and begin early in the morning, as by this method you may have your yeast dry by night. Half a tea-cupful is enough for two loaves of wheat bread, (it should be soaked in water some minutes before using it,) and it is generally best to put in half a tea-spoonful of salæratus, as dry yeast is more apt to turn sour than the liquid yeast.

Some good housekeepers use this yeast where hops are scarce, and it answers very well. It will keep good six weeks or two months.

Potato Yeast.

Boil four large potatoes with a tea-cupful of hops tied loosely in a bag; mash the potatoes in a pan, with a spoonful of salt, and four of flour; pour the hop-water on it, and mix all together; when nearly cold, put in two table-spoonsful of yeast; put it in a quart jar, and let it rise; it will do to use in five or six hours. This yeast is much weaker than the first receipt; but it has this advantage,—that with a pint of it you may knead up four loaves of bread at night without making rising. It is best to make this yeast once a week, always being careful to have the jar sweet before you put it in.

Potato Yeast with Sugar.

To about a quart of potatoes, boiled and made thin enough with warm water to pass through a sieve, add, when cold, a tea-cupful of sugar, a table-spoonful of salt, and a gill of common yeast. This is a quick yeast, but will not keep so long as those before mentioned.

Dry Yeast.

Put a pint of hops in half a gallon of water; cover it close and boil it down to one half; strain it over flour enough to make a thick batter; when nearly cold, put in a tea-cup of yeast, and three table-spoonsful of salt; when well risen, work in as much corn meal as will make it as stiff as biscuit dough; add a spoonful of sugar and one of ginger; when it rises again, make it out into little cakes, which must be dried in the shade, and turned twice a day. If made in dry weather, this yeast will keep for several months, and is useful when hops are scarce; it should be kept in a tight box, or a bag hung up in a dry place.

Milk Yeast.

If you have no yeast, you may make some with milk, to rise with. Take a pint of new milk and stir in it two tea-spoonsful of salt, and half a tea-cup of flour; keep it moderately warm by the fire, and it will lighten in about an hour; stir in flour enough to make a large loaf of bread, with more milk or water. This yeast should be used immediately, and will do to lighten hop yeast. To thicken half a gallon of water with a quarter of a pound of sugar, a little salt and flour, makes very good yeast when you cannot get hops. It will do to use in a day.

Superior Boiled Milk Rolls.

Boil a quart of new milk; pour it on a quart of flour, while boiling hot, and stir it well; when nearly cold, add two tea-spoonsful of salt, two table-spoonsful of lard, and half a tea-cup of good yeast; set it in a warm place to rise for about two hours; when light, work flour in it on the cake-board, and, when quite smooth, mould it out into rolls, and put them in a baking-pan, which has been rubbed with lard or butter; set them in a warm place to rise again;—if the weather is warm, on a table in the kitchen, but if cold, set them by the fire. When light, put them in a cool place till you are ready to bake; they should have a moderate heat, and will bake in half an hour. In winter they may be moulded out and placed in the bake-pan over night for breakfast, or some hours before wanted for tea, and kept in a cool place till half an hour before baking, when set them near the stove to rise up. With the addition of nutmeg and sugar, you may make nice rusk.

Egg Rolls.

Boil a quart of new milk with a quarter of a pound of butter, the same of lard, and a little salt; beat up two eggs, and pour the boiling milk on them, stirring all the time; when nearly cold, add a tea-cup of yeast, and as much wheat flour as will make it a thick batter; when quite light knead it up as bread, and let it lighten before moulding out; grease the pans, and bake them with a moderate heat. A little sugar and water rubbed on just before baking rolls makes them glossy.

Soft Rolls.

Rub two ounces of butter into two pounds of flour; stir in as much boiling milk as will make a soft dough; when cold enough, add half a tea-cup of yeast, and a little salt; beat it well with a spoon, and let it rise as long as bread; mould them out in pans, and bake as other rolls.

Water Rolls.

Make a rising of a quart of warm water, a little salt, a tea-cup of yeast, two spoonsful of butter and flour; let this rise, and knead it with as much flour as will make a soft dough, and work it well; when it has risen again, mould it out, and bake half an hour.

A nice griddle cake may be made by rolling this out, and baking it on the griddle or dripping-pan of a stove.

Potato Rolls.

Boil potatoes enough to make a quart when mashed, which should be done with a rolling-pin on a cake-board; mix these with a gallon of flour, a spoonful of butter, one of lard, and some salt; stir in water sufficient to make dough, not quite so stiff as for light bread, and a tea-cup of yeast; knead it for half an hour, and set it to rise; when it is light, set it away in a cold place, and as you require it, cut off a piece; mould it in little cakes, and let them rise an hour before baking. These rolls will keep several days in cold weather. If the dough should get sour, mix in some salæratus.

Boil a quart of pared potatoes—pour off the water, mash them, add half a pint of sweet milk, warmed, and a small table-spoonful of salt; stir well, and pour it scalding hot into a quart of flour; add cold milk enough to make it the right consistence for rising; stir in half a tea-cup of yeast, and set it by to rise; it will soon be light, and is then to be made into dough, with shortened flour, as other rolls, and made out into cakes; and after standing in a warm place to become light again, which should not take long, bake with rather a quick heat. These rolls may be eaten warmed over.

Mush Rolls without Milk or Eggs.

When milk is scarce, (or for a change,) you can make good rolls with mush. Take a pint of corn meal, pour on it three pints of boiling water—stirring it as you pour; put in three ounces of lard, a table-spoonful of salt, and when milk warm, put in two table-spoonsful of yeast, then mix in wheat flour, and make it a soft dough; cover the pan close, set it in a warm place till it begins to rise; as soon as light, set it in a cold place; mould them out an hour before you bake them, and allow them to rise in the dripping-pan. It will do to bake in a large cake rolled out.

Twist Rolls.

Boil a pint of milk, put in a small lump of butter and a little salt; beat up an egg and put in, when nearly cold, with a spoonful of yeast and some flour; when light, knead in more flour to make it quite stiff; work it well, and let it rise again; grease a dutch-oven or spider, flour your hands, and roll it out in rings, or round several times, a little higher in the middle. They will be nearly all crust, and suit delicate persons that cannot eat other warm bread.

French Rolls.

To one quart of sweet milk, boiled and cooled, half a pound of butter, half a tea-cup of yeast, a little salt, and flour enough to make a soft dough; beat up the milk, butter and yeast in the middle of the flour; let it stand till light, in a warm place; then work it up with the whites of two eggs, beaten light; let it rise again, then mould out into long rolls; let them stand on the board or table, to lighten, an hour or two; then grease your pans and bake in an oven or stove.

Bread Rolls.

In the morning, when your bread is light, take as much as would make one loaf; pour boiling water on half a pint of corn meal—stir it well—add a little salt, spread open the dough and work in the mush, with the addition of a table-spoonful of lard or butter, and a little flour; work well and mould out, placing them in your pans, and set them in a moderately warm place to lighten for tea; bake in a stove, if the weather is cold. This dough will keep two days, and may be baked as you need them.

Maryland Biscuit.

Rub half a pound of lard into three pounds of flour; put in a spoonful of salt, a tea-cup of cream, and water sufficient to make it into a stiff dough; divide it into two parts, and work each well till it will break off short, and is smooth; (some pound it with an iron hammer, or axe;) cut it up in small pieces, and work them into little round cakes; give them a slight roll with the rolling-pin, and stick them; bake them in a dutch-oven, brick-oven, or dripping-pan of a stove, with a quick heat. These biscuits are very nice for tea, either hot or cold.

Light Biscuit.

Boil a quart of milk, and when nearly cold, stir it in the middle of your pan of flour, with two spoonsful of yeast, and one of butter and salt; let it lighten for two or three hours; knead the flour in it, and let it rise again: a little while before you bake, roll it out, and cut it with the top of your dredging-box. Let them rise a few minutes in the dripping-pan.

Salæratus Biscuit.

Warm a quart of sweet milk, and put in it half a tea-spoonful of salæratus, and a heaped spoonful of lard or butter, and half a spoonful of salt; pour this in as much flour as will make a stiff dough; work it a quarter of an hour; mould and bake them as other biscuit.

Quick Biscuit.

Rub a small table-spoonful of lard into a quart of flour, and mix in two tea-spoonsful of finely powdered cream of tartar, with a tea-spoonful of salt; put a tea-

7

spoonful of super carbonate of soda in a pint of warm milk,—work it in and make the paste of ordinary consistence for biscuit or pie crust, adding flour or milk, if either is needed; make it out in biscuit form, or roll it about half an inch thick, and cut in shapes;— bake them about twenty minutes.

Tea Biscuit.

Melt half a pound of butter in a quart of warm milk; add a spoonful of salt, sift two pounds of flour, make a hole in the centre, put in three table-spoonsful of yeast, add the milk and butter; make a stiff paste; when quite light, knead it well, roll it out an inch thick, cut it with a tumbler, prick them with a fork, bake in buttered pans, with a quick heat; split and butter before sending them to table.

Dyspepsy Biscuit.

Make them as Maryland biscuit, except that, instead of either lard or butter, you must use a portion of rich cream; beat or work them well, and roll them moderately thin.

Salæratus Cake.

Warm a pint of butter-milk, put in it a tea-spoonful of powdered salæratus, and a piece of lard the size of an egg; stir it into flour till it is a soft dough; roll it out, and bake it on the griddle, or in the dripping-pan of a stove. If you have no sour milk, put a table-spoonful of vinegar in sweet milk.

Wafer Cakes.

Rub half a pound of lard into two pounds and a half of flour; add a little salt and water sufficient to make a stiff dough: work it well for half an hour, make it in small round lumps, and roll these until they are as thin as possible; bake them with a slow heat and they will look almost white. These are nice cakes for tea, either hot or cold.

Short Cake.

To three quarts of flour take three-quarters of a pound of lard, and a spoonful of salt; rub the lard in the flour, and put in cold water, sufficient to make a stiff dough; roll it out without working in thin cakes; have the bake-iron hot, flour it, and bake with a quick heat; when one side is brown, turn and bake the other; when baked in the dripping-pan of a stove, they do without turning;—you may cut them in round cakes, if you choose. Some use half milk and half water; in that case, less lard is required.

Cold Water Muffins.

Sift a quart of flour, add to it a little salt, a large spoonful of yeast, beat the white of a fresh egg to a froth; after mixing the flour up with cold water into a soft dough, add the egg; set it in a moderately warm place. Next morning beat it well with a spoon, put it on the bake-iron in round cakes; when one side is nicely brown, turn them; keep them hot till sent to table, split and butter them. If you wish to have muffins for tea, they should be made up early in the morning.

Smith Muffins.

Boil a quart of new milk, have three pounds of flour, three eggs well beaten, a quarter of a pound of lard, a table-spoonful of salt; rub the lard in the flour and while the milk is still warm, (but not hot,) stir it in the flour, put in the eggs, and a tea-cup of good yeast; beat all well, and set them in a warm place to rise; when light they should be set in a cool place till you are ready to bake them, which should be in rings, or round cakes on the bake-iron, in a dutch-oven, or the dripping-pan of a stove; butter just as you send them to table. If the batter is kept in a cold place it will keep good for two days in winter. Before baking muffins, or any kind of light cakes, taste the batter, and if at all sour, put in a small portion of salæratus, (previously dissolved in hot water.)—In this way superior muffins may be made.

Mansfield Muffins.

Take a quart of milk, three eggs, quarter of a pound of butter or lard, a tea-cup of yeast, and flour to make a soft dough; beat the whites of the eggs alone, the yelks with the milk; melt the butter and stir it in after all is mixed; bake them in rings, or in round cakes on the griddle: split and butter before sending them to table.

Rice Muffins.

Pour a quart of milk on four heaped spoonsful of rice flour, stir it well, and put in a little salt and wheat flour, to make it a proper thickness, two eggs and two spoonsful of yeast; allow it four hours to rise, and bake in rings, or thin it and bake as batter cakes.

Muffins.

Warm a pint of milk, and stir into it a pound and a quarter of flour, (a quart of flour is about equal to a pound and a quarter,) and two eggs, the yelks beaten with the batter, the whites alone; mix with these two spoonsful of lively yeast and a little salt; let them rise, and when you are nearly ready to bake them, stir in a large spoonful of melted butter; butter the rings and bake on a griddle, or in the dripping-pan of a stove. Split and butter before sending them to table.

Mush Muffins.

Make a quart of mush, put into it a lump of butter or lard, the size of two eggs, and a little salt; previously to making the mush, have ready a pint of light rising, stir into it a pint of new milk, and the mush, with as much wheat flour as will make it a very thick batter; let it rise four or five hours, and when light, set it in a cold place, till you are ready to bake; dip a spoon in water each time, and put the batter on the griddle in small cakes, or bake in rings. You may make it a little stiffer, and roll it out to bake in large cakes. If it should sour, put in a little salæratus. If you have no milk, water will do instead. They will be nice toasted.

A Loaf of Muffin Batter.

Stir into a pint of mush a small lump of butter, a little salt, a pint of milk, and wheat flour to make a thick batter; stir into it half a tea-cup of yeast, and let it rise; when it is light, butter a pan, pour it in and bake; eat it hot, at breakfast or supper. It will bake in a shallow pan in half an hour; if in a deep vessel, allow more time.

Boiled Milk Muffins.

Boil a quart of new milk, and pour it boiling hot, on as much flour as will make a thick batter; put in a table-spoonful of butter, and the same of lard, two tea-

7*

spoonsful of salt, half a tea-cup of yeast, one egg
beaten; allow time to rise from six to eight hours;
when perfectly light, set them in a cool place, till you
are ready to bake, when you may use rings, or not, as
you please—but be sure to butter the rings.

Cream Muffins.

Take a quart of sour cream, and two eggs well
beaten, a tea-spoonful of salt; stir the eggs into the
cream, gradually; add sifted flour enough to make a
thick batter, dissolve a tea-spoonful of salæratus in as
much vinegar as will cover it, and stir it in at the last;
bake in small cakes on the griddle, or in muffin rings
in the dripping-pan of a stove.

Waffles.

Make a batter of a pound and a half of flour, quarter
of a pound of melted butter, and two large spoonsful
of yeast; put in three eggs, the whites and yelks beaten
separately; mix it with a quart of milk, and put in the
butter just before you bake; allow it four hours to rise;
grease the waffle-irons, fill them with the batter—bake
them on a bed of coals. When they have been on the
fire two or three minutes, turn the waffle-irons over,—
when brown on both sides, they are sufficiently baked.
The waffle-irons should be well greased with lard, and
very hot before each one is put in. The waffles
should be buttered as soon as cooked. Serve them up
with powdered white sugar and cinnamon,

Quick Waffles.

Take a pint of milk, and beat into it three eggs, and
enough wheat flour to make a thick batter; add a
table-spoonful of melted butter, and a little salt; bake

them immediately. Some persons add two table-spoonsful of sugar, and a little cinnamon; others dust loaf-sugar and cinnamon, or nutmeg over each waffle, as it is baked.

Rice Waffles.

To six spoonsful of soft boiled rice, add two tea-cups of water or milk, and some salt; stir in three tea-cups of ground rice, and bake as other waffles.

Flannel Cakes.

Warm a quart of milk, put in a spoonful of butter, a little salt, and two eggs well beaten; stir in flour till it is a thin batter, and two spoonsful of yeast; beat all well together, adding the eggs at the last; allow it five hours to rise, and bake it on the griddle in cakes, the size of a breakfast plate. Do not butter them till you send them to the table.

Mush Flannel Cakes.

Mix a pint of corn mush with two of wheat flour, a spoonful of butter or lard, two eggs and half a tea-cup of yeast; make it in a batter with water or milk, and bake like buckwheat cakes.

Bread Batter Cakes.

Soak slices of stale bread in cold sweet milk for half an hour; then put it over the fire, and let it come to a boil, and mash it well; when nearly cool, add wheat flour enough to make a stiff batter; beat this together with two eggs, a tea-spoonful of salt, and a table-spoonful of good yeast; let it rise and bake as buckwheat cakes; if light before you are ready, set them in a cold place.

Butter-milk Cakes.

You may make a very good batter cake without eggs. To a quart of butter-milk, put a piece of lard, the size of an egg; warm them together, and stir in a tea-spoonful of salæratus; make it in a thin batter with flour; beat it a few minutes, and bake it as other cakes.

Buckwheat Cakes.

Take quart of buckwheat flour, half a pint of wheat flour, and a spoonful of salt; make them into a thick batter, with milk-warm water; put in a half tea-cup of yeast, and beat it well; set it by the fire to rise, and if it should be light before you are ready to bake, put a tea-cup of cold water on the top, to prevent it from running over; if it should get sour, pour in a tea-spoonful of salæratus, dissolved in hot water, just before you bake.

It is best to make them up quite thick, and thin them with a little warm water before you bake; butter them just as you send them to table. If you can get brewers' yeast, it is much better for buckwheat cakes. In very cold weather, they may be kept made up for several days, and baked as required.

Sally Lunn.

Warm a quart of milk with a quarter of a pound of butter, and a heaped spoonful of sugar; beat up three eggs, and put in, with a little salt, and flour enough to make it stiffer than pound-cake; beat it well; put in a tea-cup of yeast, and let it rise; butter a fluted pan and pour it in; bake it in a quick oven, slice and butter it. If you wish tea at six o'clock, set it to rise at ten in the morning. Bake it an hour.

Butter-milk Batter Cakes.

Soak pieces of dry stale bread in a quart of butter-milk, until soft; break in two eggs, add a little butter or lard, and salt and flour enough to make it stick together; beat it well, add a tea-spoonful of salæratus, dissolved in warm water; thin it with a little sweet milk, and bake as other batter cakes. They may be prepared in a short time.

Toast.

Cut your bread (which is better to be stale) in tolerably thick slices, brown it slowly before the fire on each side; you may either butter it dry, or mix butter in water, with a little salt added, and after making it boiling hot, pour over each slice as you send it to table.

A Dish of Milk Toast for Breakfast.

Boil a quart of rich milk, take it off, and stir in half a pound of fresh butter, mixed with a small spoonful of flour: let it again come to a boil; have ready a dish of toast, pour it from a spoon over each piece, and what remains, pour over the whole; keep it covered and hot, till you send to table.

General Remarks on making Bread of Indian Corn Meal.

A wooden spoon with a long handle, is the best for stirring and mixing the bread or cakes. It requires more salt than other bread, and should be well mixed or beaten. If it is mixed over night, it should generally be done with cold water, and set in the cellar or some cool place in summer; in winter it requires rather a warmer place to stand. It sours more easily than

bread made of other flour. In the morning, if you find
that it is at all acid, dissolve half a tea-spoonful of salæratus in warm water, and stir it just before it is put
to bake. Where milk is used, it should be baked immediately, and the richer the milk, the more palatable
it is. Whatever you bake this bread in, should be well
greased first, as it is more apt to adhere to the oven
than some other kinds of flour. It should bake with a
quick heat.

When you buy salæratus, pound it fine, put it in a
wide-mouthed bottle, and cork it tight. Some persons
keep it dissolved in water, but you cannot judge of the
strength of it so well.

Corn Meal Porridge.

Put on to boil in a saucepan a quart of milk, mix a
small tea-cup of corn meal with half a pint of cold
water, (let it settle, and pour off what swims on the
top,) then stir it in well to keep it from being lumpy;
let it boil *only* a few minutes; add salt to the taste.
This makes a good breakfast for children, and is a light
diet for an invalid. It can be seasoned with sugar.

Mush, Mush Cakes, and Fried Mush.

Mush will keep for several days in cool weather; the
best way of making it is to have a pot of boiling water,
and stir in corn meal, mixed with water, and salt
enough to season the whole; let it boil, and if it is not
thick enough you can add more meal; keep stirring all
the time to prevent it from being lumpy. It should
boil an hour.

To make the cakes, take a quart of cold mush, mix
in it half a pint of wheat flour, and a little butter or
lard, make it out in little cakes with your hands; flour

them and bake them on a griddle or in a dripping-pan. Fried mush is a good plain dessert, eaten with sugar and cream. Cut the cold mush in slices, half an inch thick, or make them into small cakes, dip them in flour, and fry them in hot lard.

Journey Cake.

Pour boiling water on a quart of meal, put in a little lard and salt, and mix it well; have an oak board with a rim of iron at the bottom, and an iron handle fastened to it that will prop it up to the fire; put some of the dough on it, dip your hand in cold water and smooth it over; score it with a knife, and set it before coals to bake.

Corn Batter Cakes.

Take a quart of good milk, three eggs, a little salt, and as much sifted corn meal as will make a thin batter; beat all well together, with a spoonful of wheat flour to keep them from breaking; bake in small cakes, keep them hot, and butter just as you send to table.

Another way to make corn batter cakes, is to take a quart of corn meal, two eggs, a small lump of butter or lard, and mix it up with milk, or half water, if milk is scarce, and bake them either thin or thick.

Rice Cakes.

Take a pint of soft boiled rice, a pint of milk, a little salt, and as much corn meal as will make a thin batter with two eggs; beat all together, and bake as corn batter cakes, or make it thicker and bake it in a pan.

Corn Bannock.

To one quart of sour milk, put a tea-spoonful of salæratus, dissolved in water; warm the milk slightly, beat up an egg, and put in corn meal enough to make it as thick as pudding batter, and some salt; grease a pan and bake it, or you may put it in six or eight saucers.

Virginia Pone.

Beat three eggs, and stir them in a quart of milk, with a little salt, a spoonful of melted butter, and as much sifted corn meal as will make it as thick as corn batter cakes; grease the pans and bake quick.

Lightened Pone.

Take half a gallon of corn meal, and pour boiling water on one-third of it; mix it together with warm water till it is a thick batter; put in two table-spoonsful of lively yeast, and one of salt; stir it well and set it by the fire to rise; when it begins to open on the top, grease the dutch-oven and put it to bake, or bake it in a pan in a stove.

Cold Water Pone.

Make a stiff batter with a quart of Indian meal, cold water and a little salt; work it well with the hand; grease a pan or oven, and bake it three-quarters of an hour. Eat it hot at dinner, or with milk at supper.

Indian Bread with Butter-milk.

To one quart of butter-milk, slightly warmed, put a tea-spoonful of salæratus, dissolved in water, two eggs, well beaten, a table-spoonful of melted butter or lard, a little salt; stir in with a spoon as much Indian meal as will make a thick batter; beat it for a few minutes, grease your pans, and bake quickly. If you bake this quantity in two pans, a half hour will be sufficient, or if in one, it will take an hour. Look at it often while baking, as it is liable to burn. An excellent recipe.

Little Indian Cakes.

Put a spoonful of lard in a quart of meal, and two tea-spoonsful of salt; pour boiling water on half the meal, stir it; then add as much cold water as will enable you to make it out in cakes of a convenient size; bake on the bake-iron over the fire.

Maryland Corn Cakes.

Mix a pint of corn meal with rich milk, a little salt, and an egg; it should be well beaten with a spoon, and made thin enough to pour on the iron; bake in cakes the size of a breakfast plate; butter and send them hot to table.

A Virginia Hoe Cake.

Pour warm water on a quart of Indian meal; stir in a spoonful of lard or butter, some salt, make it stiff, and work it for ten minutes; have a board about the size of a barrel head, (or the middle piece of the head will answer,) wet the board with water, and spread on the dough with your hand; place it before the fire; prop it aslant with a flat-iron, bake it slowly; when one side is nicely brown, take it up and turn it, by running a thread between the cake and the board, then put it back, and let the other side brown. These cakes used to be baked in Virginia on a large iron hoe, from whence they derive their name.

Batter Bread with Yeast.

Rub a piece of butter the size of an egg, into a quart of corn meal; add a little salt; make it in a batter with two eggs and some new milk; add a spoonful of yeast, set it by the fire an hour to rise; butter little pans, and bake with a quick heat.

8

Carolina Corn Rolls.

Take a pint of corn meal; pour over it sufficient boiling water to make a very stiff dough, then add a table-spoonful of salt, and permit it to stand until about milk-warm; work it well with the hand, then make out the rolls, of an oblong shape, and bake them from half to three-quarters of an hour, according to their size. The addition of a small lump of butter or lard is an improvement. If they are rightly made, they will split on the top in baking, and can be eaten by those who cannot partake of other preparations made of corn flour.

Mixed Bread.

Put a little salt, and a spoonful of yeast, into a quart of flour; make it sufficiently soft with corn meal gruel; let it rise; bake in a mould.

New England Hasty Pudding, or Stir-about.

Boil three quarts of water in an iron pot; mix a pint of Indian meal in cold water, and make it thin enough to pour easily; when the water boils, pour it in; stir well with a wooden stick kept for the purpose; it takes about an hour to boil; salt to your taste; stir in dry meal to make it thick enough, beating it all the time. Eat it with milk or molasses, or butter and sugar. This is said to be a wholesome diet for dyspeptic patients, and makes a good meal for children.

Corn Muffins.

Warm three pints of milk, and stir into it as much corn meal as will make it as thick as pudding batter; add two handsful of wheat flour, two tea-spoonsful of salt, three eggs, and a tea-cup of yeast. Beat the whole well together, and let it rise about six hours, when bake as other muffins.

Soaked Crackers for Tea.

Pour boiling water on crackers, put in some butter and a little salt; cover them close and keep them warm till tea is ready; if you have milk, boil it, and pour over instead of water. This is easily prepared.

PIES, PUDDINGS, CAKES, &c.

To Make Common Pies.

ONE pound of lard to a gallon of flour will make very good common pies. Work the lard in the flour, put in some salt, and wet it with water; make it so that it can just be rolled out; when you have put in the fruit, wet the crust with water, put on the top and close it up; stick it with a fork on the top.

To Stew Fruit for Pies.

All fruits that are not fully ripe should be stewed and sweetened. To boil a gallon of molasses at a time, and keep it to sweeten pies, is cheaper than sugar, and answers a very good purpose, where there is a large family. When fruit is fully ripe it does very well to bake in pies, without being stewed.

After washing the dried fruit, put it on to stew in a bell-metal kettle over the fire, or in a tin pan in a stove, let it have plenty of water, as it swells very much, and if it seems dry, put in more water. Apples take longer to stew than peaches, and should have more water. Fruit stewed in this way is very good to

put on the table to eat with meat. Do not stir the
fruit while it is stewing, or it will burn. Dried
cherries and damsons may be stewed in the same
manner, adding the sugar before they are quite done.

Pie Crust.

Sift a pound and a half of flour, and take out a
quarter for rolling; cut in it a quarter of a pound of
lard, mix it with water, and roll it out; cut half a
pound of butter, and put it in at two rollings with the
flour that was left out.

For making the bottom crust of pies, cut half a
pound of lard into a pound of flour, with a little salt;
mix it stiff, and grease the plates before you make
pies; always make your paste in a cold place, and
bake it soon.

Some persons prefer mixing crust with milk instead
of water.

Paste for Puddings.

Sift a pound of flour, have half a pound of butter
and quarter of a pound of lard, save out a quarter of
the flour for rolling, cut the lard into the remainder,
and mix it with water; roll it out, and flake in half
of the butter; dust over it some of the flour, close it
up; roll it again, and put in the rest of the butter.
This quantity will make crust for five or six puddings.

ANOTHER WAY.

To three and a half pounds of sifted flour, put two
pounds of lard, and a piece of volatile salts (as large
as a full sized nutmeg) dissolved in a little water;—
make a pretty stiff paste; then roll in three-quarters of
a pound of butter. This will make about eight pies
and twelve shells.

Puff Paste.

Sift a pound of flour, and take out a quarter for rolling; divide a pound of butter into four parts, cut one part of the butter into the flour with a knife; make it a stiff dough with water, roll it out, and flake it with part of the butter; do this three times till it is all in; handle it as little as possible, and keep it in a cool place. This quantity will make crust sufficient for three puddings and ten puffs. They should bake with a quick heat, but do not let them burn; they will take from ten to fifteen minutes to bake, according to the number of layers of paste. Do not put on the preserves till a short time before they are eaten.

Rich Mince Pies.

Take four pounds of beef, boiled and chopped fine; pick and chop three pounds of suet, wash two pounds of currants, and one of raisins; grate the peel of two lemons, and put in the juice; pound a spoonful of dried orange peel, slice an ounce of citron, and chop twelve large apples; mix these together with three pounds of sugar, half a pint of wine, and the same of brandy—and sweet cider to make it a proper thickness; put in mace and nutmeg to your taste. If the cider is not sweet, you must put in more sugar before the pies are baked; cut several places in the top of each with a pair of scissors.

Mince Pies not so Rich.

Take four pounds of beef after it has been boiled and chopped, one of suet, two of sugar, two of raisins, and four of chopped apples; mix these together with a pint of wine and cider, to make it thin enough; season

8*

to your taste with mace, nutmeg and orange peel; if it is not sweet enough, put in more sugar. Warm the pies before they are eaten. Where persons are not fond of suet, put butter instead, and stew the apples instead of so much cider.

Farmers' Mince Pies.

When you kill a beef, save the head for pies; it is some trouble to prepare it, but it is very nice for the purpose. Split the head, take out the brains and eyes, wash it well in cold water, and soak it all night with two hog's heads that have been cleaned; in the morning, boil them till you can take out the bones easily; skim off the froth as it rises, or it will stick to the meat; pick out the bones, and chop it fine, with three pounds of suet. This should be done the day before you want to bake.

Mix to this quantity of meat, two gallons of chopped apples, four pounds of raisins, half a gallon of boiled molasses, a pint of currant wine, a tea-cup of rose brandy, an ounce of cinnamon, orange peel and mace, from two to four nutmegs, and sweet cider enough to make it the right thickness; if the cider is not sweet, put in more molasses; when all is mixed, it is best to bake a small pie, as you can alter the seasoning, if it is not to your taste. If you have not raisins, dried cherries or small grapes, that have been preserved in molasses, are very good, or stewed dried apples, instead of green; and where you have no cider, stew the apples in plenty of water, so as to have them very soft; a little good vinegar, sweetened and mixed with water, also does instead of cider, but is not so good.

This will make about forty pies, and if you have a convenient way of keeping them, you may bake all at once, as they will keep for two months very readily when the weather is cold. If you do not bake all at once, put what is left in a jar, cover the top with melted suet, and over this put a piece of white paper, with a tea-cup of spirits poured on the top; tie it up and keep it where it will not freeze. Where persons have a large family, and workmen on a farm, these pies are very useful.

Rhubarb Pie.

Peel the stalks, cut them in small pieces, and stew them till very soft in a little water; when done, mash, and sweeten with sugar; set it away to cool; make a puff paste, and bake as other pies. Some prefer it without stewing, cutting the stems in small pieces, and strewing sugar over them before the crust is put on. These pies will lose their fine flavor after the first day. They take less sugar than gooseberries.

Peach Pie.

Take mellow cling-stone peaches, pare, but do not cut them; put them in a deep pie plate lined with crust, sugar them well, put in a table-spoonful of water, and sprinkle a little flour over the peaches; cover with a thick crust, in which make a cut in the centre, and bake from three-quarters to one hour.

Sweet Potato Pie.

Boil the potatoes, skin and slice them; put a layer of potatoes and a layer of good apples sliced thin in a deep dish; put potatoes and apples alternately till the dish is filled, mix together wine, water, sugar, butter and nutmeg, and pour over, cover it with crust, and bake as oyster pie.

Pork Mince Pies.

Take pieces of fresh pork that have been left from sausage meat, or any trimmings of the hams or shoulders; boil them, then chop. Have two heads nicely washed and cleaned, boil, pick out the bones and chop them; mix with the other meat, and season as you do other mince pies, they do not require any suet. The lower crust of mince pies need not be so rich as the top; always cut several places in the top crust with scissors, to keep the juice from wasting. When you warm mince pies, do it gradually, and do not have the crust scorched. Some prefer them cold. When the pies are very plain, a little preserve syrup, and a glass of wine added is an improvement.

Currant Pie.

After stemming green currants, scald them, and allow them to stand awhile; pour off the water; have the crust in your plates; put in the currants, sweeten them well; put in a little water, a dust of flour and a little orange peel. Gooseberries are prepared in the same way, but require more sugar. Cherries should not be scalded.

Pumpkin Pudding.

Choose a yellow pumpkin, with a fine grain, pare and cut it in small pieces, boil it in plenty of water, and take it up as soon as it is done, or it will soak up the water; to a gallon of pumpkin, stewed and mashed, put two quarts of milk, eight eggs, half a pound of butter, half a tea-cup of lemon or rose brandy; nutmeg and sugar to your taste; bake it in deep plates, with a bottom crust.

Apple Pudding.

Take three pints of stewed apples, well mashed, melt a pound of butter, beat ten eggs with two pounds of sugar, and mix all together with a glass of brandy and wine; put in nutmeg to your taste, and bake in puff paste.

Quince Pudding

Take six quinces, pare them, cut them in quarters, and stew them in a little water with lemon peel; cover them and let them cook gently till soft, when mash, or rub them through a sieve; mix them with sugar till very sweet, season with mace and nutmeg; beat up four eggs and stir in with a pint of cream; bake it in paste.

Potato Pudding.

Take a pound and a half of well mashed potatoes; while they are warm put in three-quarters of a pound of butter; beat six eggs with three-quarters of a pound of sugar, rolled fine, mix all well together, and put in a glass of brandy; season with nutmeg, mace or essence of lemon, and bake in paste.

Cocoanut Pudding.

Take three-quarters of a pound of grated cocoanut, with the brown skin taken off, half a pound of sugar, the same of butter, the whites of six eggs, beaten light, half a pint of cream, a glass of brandy, or rose-water, and a quarter of a pound of crackers, pounded fine, beat them together and bake in paste. If you wish the pudding rich, take a pound of butter, the same quantity of cocoanut, of sugar and whites of eggs, omitting the crackers and cream. Season as above. This quantity will fill six dessert plates of large size.

Sweet Potato Pudding.

Boil the potatoes, take off the skin, mash and strain them while warm; to a pound of potatoes put half a pound of butter; beat six eggs with half a pound of loaf-sugar, add a little mace or nutmeg; mix all together, and bake with or without paste.

Lemon Pudding.

Grate the rind of six fresh lemons, squeeze the juice from three, and strain it; beat the yelks of sixteen eggs very light, put to them sixteen table-spoonsful of powdered sugar, not heaped, with four crackers finely powdered; beat it till light; put a puff paste in your dish and bake in a moderate oven.

ANOTHER WAY.

Take one pound of potatoes strained through a sieve, half a pound of butter, the same of rolled sugar, the juice of two lemons and the peel of one; beat five eggs, and mix all together with a glass of wine and a nutmeg.

A Preserve Pudding.

Take a deep dish, butter it well and spread a layer of preserves, without syrup—either quinces, citron, apples or peaches; rub together a pound of fresh butter, and the same of powdered loaf-sugar, and add the yelks of sixteen eggs well beaten; pour this on the preserves, bake it in a quick oven for half an hour; it may be set by till the next day; beat the whites of the eggs as for island, seasoning with currant jelly, and spread it over the pudding cold, just as it goes to table. This makes a rich dish and is eaten without sauce. This quantity will bake in four ordinary pie plates.

Arrow Root Pudding.

Take four table-spoonsful of arrow root, mixed in a little cold milk; pour on this a quart of boiling milk, beat six eggs with three table-spoonsful of sugar, and stir all together with a spoonful of butter; bake it twenty minutes in paste.

Rice Pudding.

Pour a quart of boiling milk on a pint of rice flour, stir it well, and put in six spoonsful of sugar, one of butter, and four eggs; beat all together, and bake in deep plates, with or without crust.

ANOTHER WAY.

Boil half a pound of rice till soft; when nearly cold stir in half a pound of white sugar, a quarter of a pound of butter, and three eggs well beaten; grate in half a nutmeg, stir in a pint of rich milk; pour all in a yellow dish and bake half an hour; then put a thick coating of loaf sugar on the top, and eat hot, with or without cream.

Pudding of whole Rice.

Boil a pint of washed rice in milk or water, till soft; put in a lump of butter, five eggs, and sugar to your taste; season with essence of lemon, or lemon peel, and mix in cream to make it thin enough to pour; bake it in paste, in deep plates.

A Pudding of Corn Meal.

Pour three pints of boiling milk on nearly half a pint of sifted corn meal, stir in half a pound of butter, add four eggs, a little nutmeg, rose brandy, and the grated peel of a lemon; sweeten it, and bake it in paste.

Corn Pudding in Paste.

To two pounds of mush moderately warm, put three-quarters of a pound of butter, the yelks of six eggs, the rind of one lemon, and juice of two; sugar and nutmeg to your taste, and bake in paste as potato puddings. This is much admired.

Richmond Pudding.

Take one pound of raisins, stoned and chopped, half a pound of currants rubbed in flour, a pound and a half of grated bread, a pound of suet shred fine, eight eggs, two glasses of brandy, and two of wine; beat them all together, adding the eggs at the last; dip your bag or cloth in boiling water and flour it well; pour in the pudding and tie it up, leaving room for it to swell; allow it four hours to boil; eat it with white sauce.

Suet Pudding.

Take half a pound of suet chopped fine, four tea-cups of flour, and five eggs; beat these together with a quart of milk, and half a spoonful of salt; put in three tea-cups of raisins just before you tie it up; they should be rubbed in flour to prevent them from sinking; dried cherries, or pared dried peaches, are very good instead of raisins; scald the cloth and flour it; leave room for the pudding to swell. If you put one-fourth corn meal, you can do with fewer eggs.

Cheese Cakes.

Take one quart of curd, after the whey has been strained off, mix with it half a pound of fresh butter, an ounce of pounded blanched almonds, the whites of three eggs, a tea-cup of currants; season with sugar and rose water to your taste, and bake in plates with paste.

Baked Apples.

Wash and core your apples, and in the vacancy left by the core, put brown sugar, and bake them in a stove or oven.

Batter Pudding with Green Fruit.

Make a batter as for suet pudding. If you have small fruit, put it in whole; if apples, chop them fine; boil it three hours.

Custard Bread and Butter Pudding.

Fill a pan with slices of buttered bread, with raisins, grated nutmeg and sugar over each slice; beat six eggs with a tea-cup of sugar; add two quarts of rich milk, and pour it over the bread and butter; bake it in a stove or oven.

Balloon Puddings.

Mix a pint of rich milk with a pound and a quarter of flour; break nine eggs; beat the yelks with the batter, the whites alone; when they are mixed, stir in three-quarters of a pound of melted butter; grease cups or bowls with butter; pour in the batter, and bake them half an hour; if in a dutch-oven, put some water in the bottom; eat them with white sauce.

Plain Rice Pudding.

Put two quarts of good milk in a tin pan, with a tea-cup of whole rice, the same of stemmed raisins, and a little nutmeg or cinnamon, and sugar to your taste. If you bake it in a dutch-oven, it is best to put a little water in the bottom before you set it in; bake it till the rice is soft, and there is a brown crust on the top.

9

A Rice Dish with Fruit.

Put a tea-cup of rice in a quart of milk, and boil it very slowly to keep it from burning; when done, add a little salt, a tea-cup of cream, and sugar enough to sweeten it; have ready, in a deep dish, any fruit that is in season,—cherries, blackberries or apricots, apples, or peaches, cut up and well sweetened, but uncooked; spread the rice roughly over, and bake it slowly two hours. It may be eaten with cream and nutmeg, and is quite as good cold as warm.

Bread Pudding.

Bread pudding is made out of bread that is too dry to use; cut it fine, boil it in milk, and mash it well; beat four eggs and put in, with half a pound of raisins; boil it an hour and a half, or bake it.

Bread and Apple Pudding.
To be eaten with Sauce.

Put a layer of buttered bread in the bottom of a well buttered dish, with chopped apples, sugar, grated bread and butter, and a little pounded cinnamon; fill up the dish with alternate layers of these articles, observing that it is better to have the inner layer of bread thinner than that of the top and bottom. This is a nice dish for those who cannot partake of pastry.

Custard Hasty Pudding.

Put a quart of new milk on to boil; then mix a tea-cup of rice flour with a little milk, two eggs, and three spoonsful of sugar; beat it, and when your milk boils, stir it in; let it boil five minutes—when pour it out on some buttered toast, in a bowl or dish, and grate nutmeg over it.

Elkridge Huckleberry Pudding.

One pound of flour, one of light-brown sugar, eight eggs—beat as sponge cake, and add one quart of berries, nicely picked, washed, and allowed to dry; bake as sponge cake. This may be served with sauce, either hot or cold.

Huckleberry Pudding.

Make a batter of five eggs to a quart of milk, and a little butter; pick, wash, and rub in flour a pint or more of huckleberries; put them in, and bake as long as other puddings, or boil it in a bag.

Green Corn Pudding.

Cut the green corn through the grain, and scrape it off the cob with the back of a knife; prepare a batter made of a quart of rich milk, two eggs, and wheat flour, and a little salt; then add the corn, and beat it well for a few minutes: it should be of a consistence to pour easily; grease the pan, and pour it in; bake with quick heat in a stove or spider, about half an hour. Six ears of corn will be enough for a quart of milk, or you may double the quantity; eat it with butter, sugar and cream, molasses, or any sauce that is convenient.

Baked Pudding.

Boil a quart of milk, and stir into it half a pint of corn meal and a tea-spoonful of salt—mix this well together; beat two eggs, stir in when nearly cold; add a tea-cup of chopped suet, two table-spoonsful of sugar, a little spice—grease a pan, and pour it in; bake three-quarters of an hour. Eat it with sugar and cream, or molasses sauce.

A Boiled Indian Pudding.

Boil a quart of milk, and stir in meal to make it a thick batter; put in a tea-spoonful of salt, a tea-cup of suet, a spoonful of sugar; mix these well together, add two eggs, well beaten. If you have dried peaches, soak them; sprinkle them with dry flour, and put them in, or put in raisins, previously rubbed with wheat flour—beat it well; have your pot boiling, scald the bag, flour it, and put in the pudding;—it will boil in two hours. Eat with sugar and cream, molasses, or any kind of pudding sauce.

Boiled Bread Pudding.

Take a loaf of stale light bread, tie it in a cloth, boil it an hour, and eat it with sauce.

A Bird's Nest Pudding.

Pare and core some apples, enough to fill a deep dish; they should be ripe, and such as will cook easily. Make a custard of five eggs, to a quart of milk, and sugar and nutmeg to taste; pour this over, and bake half an hour.

Little Puddings in Pans.

Beat four eggs very light; make a batter of two tea-cups of flour, three of milk, and one of cream; pour in the eggs, and beat all well together; put in a spoonful of melted butter; grease your shallow pans or cups, and bake from twenty to thirty minutes; eat them with sauce, or sugar, cream and nutmeg.

Switzerland Pudding.

Make a batter of five eggs, a quart of milk and flour; pare and core enough good apples to cover the bottom of your pan; fill the holes where the cores came out with sugar; grease the pan, lay them in, and pour the batter over; bake it an hour and a half, and make wine sauce to eat with it.

Boiling Puddings.

In boiling puddings, you must observe to have plenty of water in the pot; the pudding should be turned frequently; have the water boiling when it goes in, and do not let it stop; have a tea-kettle of water by the fire to pour in as it evaporates. When the pudding is done, it should be dipped in a pan of cold water, to prevent its adhering to the cloth.

Screw Dumplings.

Roll out some paste thin, in a long strip; lay in preserves of any kind, or stewed fruit, well sweetened; roll it up and close it tight; pin it up in a towel, and boil it an hour; eat it with butter, sugar and cream, or sauce.

Large Dumplings.

Take green fruit of any kind—peaches, apples, cherries, blackberries, or huckleberries; make crust as for pies, roll it out, put in the fruit, and pin it in a cloth; boil it two hours.

Peach and Apple Dumplings.

Make crust as for plain pies; cut it in as many pieces as you want dumplings; pare and core the apples, roll out the crust, and close them up; have the water boiling when they go in, and let them boil three-quarters of an hour. Peaches pared and stoned make very good dumplings; eat them with sauce of any kind, or sugar, cream and butter.

9*

Light Bread Dumplings.

Take as much lightened dough as will make a loaf of bread, work into it half a pound of stemmed raisins, tie it up in a cloth, and boil it an hour and a half.

Rice Dumplings.

Wash and pick a pint of rice, boil it in water till it is soft; have some apples pared and cored whole, fill the holes with sugar, cover them over with the rice, and tie each one separately in a cloth; boil them till the apples are done.

Indian Suet Dumplings.

Chop beef suet fine, and to a pint of Indian meal, take a table-spoonful of the suet and a little salt; pour on boiling water enough to make a stiff dough, work it well, make into round cakes, and boil in clear water. These are good when vegetables are scarce, to eat with meat, or as a dessert with sugar or molasses.

Corn Dumplings.

When you boil corned beef, new bacon, or pork, you can make dumplings, by taking some grease out of the pot, with some of the water, and pouring it hot on a quart of Indian meal, mix and work it well, (it will not require salt,) make it into little round cakes; (they should be stiff, or they will boil to pieces;) take out the meat when it is done, and boil the dumplings in the same water for half an hour. They may be eaten with molasses, and make a good common dessert.

Pan Cakes.

Take five eggs to a quart of milk, make a thin batter with flour, have a little hot lard in the frying-pan, and pour in enough batter to cover the bottom; turn and fry the other side; if eggs are scarce, a tea-spoonful of salæratus will supply the place of two. Eat them with wine and sugar.

Water Pan Cakes—a cheap Dessert.

Stir a quart of warm water in sufficient flour to make a batter of moderate thickness; dissolve a tea-spoonful of salæratus, with a little salt, into a tea-cupful of butter-milk, or sour cream; beat it well; put a little lard in a frying-pan, and when it is hot, fry them. They are much better to be eaten hot, with sauce, sugar and cream, or any thing you may fancy. This is a very cheap dessert, and has been thought nearly equal to pan cakes made with milk and eggs.

Apple Fritters.

Allow four eggs to a quart of milk; make a thick batter with flour, and beat it well; stir in a quart of apples, chopped fine; have a frying-pan with hot lard, and drop a spoonful in a place; fry them light-brown on both sides, and eat with sugar and wine, or sweet cider.

Rice Fritters.

To a pint of rice flour add a tea-spoonful of salt and a pint of boiling water; beat four eggs and stir them in, have hot lard in a frying-pan, and fry them as other fritters.

Indian Meal Fritters.

Take a quart of butter-milk, (in which dissolve a tea-spoonful of salæratus,) stir in meal to make a batter of suitable thickness, a tea-spoonful of salt and two eggs; beat all well together, and fry in hot lard, as other

fritters.   If you like, you can put in chopped apples.
Eat with sugar or molasses.

Snow Fritters.

Take of light new fallen snow, three table-spoonsful
for every egg you would otherwise use—that is, if you
would wish the quantity that three eggs would make
in the usual way, take nine table-spoonsful of snow,
and stir in a quart of rich milk that has been setting in
a very cold place, so that it will not melt the snow,
and destroy its lightness; put in a tea-spoonful of salt,
and enough wheat flour to make a stiff batter; have
ready a frying-pan with boiling lard, and drop a spoonful in a place as with other fritters, and set the remainder in a cold place till the first are done.   Eat
them with wine sauce, or sugar, butter and cream, or
any thing you fancy.

Rice Flummery.

Rice that is ground coarse, in a hand-mill, is much
better for making flummery than the flour you buy: put
three pints of milk to boil, mix with water two tea-cups
of ground rice, and stir it in the milk when it boils;
while the milk is cold, put in it two dozen peach kernels, blanched, and rolled with a bottle; wet your
moulds with cold cream or water; keep stirring the
rice till it is thick, when pour it out in the moulds;
just before dinner turn them out on dishes, have cream,
sugar and nutmeg mixed, to eat with it.

Rice Milk.

Take a tea-cupful of rice, boil it till about half done,
and let all the water be evaporated; then add the milk,
and beat an egg with some flour, and stir in; let it boil
a few minutes, and season with sugar and nutmeg.

Wine Sauce for Puddings.

Mix a spoonful of flour in a tea-cup of water, with two-spoonsful of sugar and one of butter; stir this in half a pint of boiling water; let it boil a few minutes, when add a glass of wine and some nutmeg.

White Sauce.

Take half a pound of powdered white sugar, and quarter of a pound of butter, beat them well together with a glass of wine, and grate in half a nutmeg. A little currant jelly is preferred by some in this sauce instead of wine.

Cream Sauce.

Boil half a pint of cream, thicken it a very little, and put in a lump of butter; sweeten it to your taste, and after it gets cold add a glass of white wine; this is good to eat with boiled rice, plain pudding, or apple dumplings.

Molasses Sauce.

Put half a pint of molasses to boil in a skillet, with a piece of butter the size of an egg; when it has boiled a few minutes, pour in a tea-cup of cream, and grate in half a nutmeg; this is the most economical way of making sauce.

Egg Sauce.

Take the whites of three eggs and the yelks of two, beat them till very light, and add a large table-spoonful of butter ready creamed, with sugar and nutmeg to your taste; boil three glasses of wine, and pour over the other ingredients, put it over the fire, and let it boil two minutes, stirring all the time. This is nice sauce for any kind of pudding.

Cherry Toast.

Stone and stew a quart of ripe cherries, sweeten them, place some slices of buttered toast in a deep dish, and put the stewed cherries over them. A little powdered cinnamon or grated nutmeg may be put on the toast.

Apple Custard.

Lay a crust in your pie plates, slice apples thin and half fill the plates, pour over a custard made of four eggs to a quart of milk, sweeten and season it; bake it slowly.

Custard baked in Cups.

Beat up five eggs with two heaped spoonsful of sugar, mix these with a quart of rich milk and a little nutmeg; fill the cups, pour water in the bottom of a dutch-oven or dripping-pan, and set them in and bake them till thick.

Boiled Custard.

Put on to boil a quart of new milk; have ready a dozen peach kernels, scalded, peeled, and rubbed fine with a bottle; beat five or six eggs, with some sugar, and when the milk boils stir them in with the kernels; keep stirring till it thickens, but do not let it boil, or it will curdle; then take it off the fire, pour it in a pitcher, and continue to stir till it is nearly cold, when pour it into your cups, and grate nutmeg over the top of each. If you wish to have it flavored with lemon, boil some peel with the milk. This custard may be put in a glass bowl, and an island on the top.

Cold Custard.

Sweeten half a gallon of milk, put into it a tablespoonful of rennet wine, and let it stand in a warm place till it begins to come, when it should be set in cold water till dinner time; just as you take it to table, pour some cream on it, and grate nutmeg over the top.

Cream Custard.

To a pint of thin cream, take one egg, and beat and season as other custard; bake it in a plate with paste; this quantity is sufficient for one large plate, and is more delicate than custard made in the usual way.

Ice Custard with Vanilla.

Boil three pints of rich milk with as much vanilla as will give it a good flavor; sweeten it to your taste; have ready four eggs well beaten, pour the boiling milk on them, and keep stirring till cool; when put it to freeze.

Custard with Raisins.

Stone and cut a tea-cup of raisins, put them in a quart of milk; when it boils stir in five eggs well beaten, with two table-spoonsful of sugar, and a little lemon peel; keep stirring till it boils again, then take it off the fire, and stir till nearly cold; when put it in cups, or in a large bowl; beat the whites of three eggs with sugar, and when quite cold put them on the top of the custard.

To Boil Custard in Water.

Beat the eggs, sugar and seasoning together, and put it in a pitcher or nice stone jar; put in the milk and stir it well together; set the pitcher in a pot of boiling water, and stir till it is cooked, when take the pitcher out and stir till nearly cool. Custard should never be boiled or baked two much—a minute too long will sometimes spoil it.

Whips.

Grate the peel of a lemon in a pint of cream, sweeten it with loaf sugar, and whip it well; beat the whites of three eggs and mix with it; put apple jelly, seasoned with lemon, in the bottom of your glasses, and as the froth rises put it on the top of the jelly.

Trifle.

Put slices of sponge cake or Naples biscuit in the bottom of a deep glass dish; on this put slices of pre-served citron, or apples preserved with lemon; pour over this a boiled custard, and on the top put a whip made by the foregoing receipt.

Floating Island.

Beat the whites of five eggs till the beater will stand up in them; then add, a little at a time, four spoonsful of powdered loaf-sugar, and currant jelly, or preserved syrup of any kind; put rich milk in the bottom of a glass, or china bowl, and put the island on the top. In making floating island, you should allow the whites of six eggs to six persons. You can have very good custards at the same time with the yelks of the eggs.

Apple Float.

To a quart of apples, slightly stewed and well mash-ed, put the whites of three eggs, well beaten, and four table-spoons heaping full of loaf sugar, beat them to-gether for fifteen minutes, and eat with rich milk and nutmeg.

Carrageen or Irish Moss Blancmange.

Wash in three waters half an ounce of Carrageen moss; drain and put it in two quarts of new milk, let it boil for a few minutes, strain it in a pitcher, wet the moulds, and pour it in while hot; let it stand till it becomes thick, when it may be eaten with sugar and cream, seasoned with peach or rose water, or with a lemon rolled in the sugar. Some prefer seasoning the blancmange before putting it in the moulds. It will keep in a cool place two days, and is better to be made the day before it is eaten.

To Keep Suet for several Months.

Chop the suet you wish to preserve until summer as fine as for mince pies or puddings, then add a table-spoonful of salt to three table-spoonsful of suet; mix all well together, and put it in jars. Keep it tied up close, as exposure to the air makes it strong. It should be soaked an hour before you wish to use it, to remove the salt taste.

Skim Curds.

Put to boil a gallon of sweet milk; when it fairly boils, pour in a quart of butter-milk; in a few minutes the curd will rise, which skim off and set by, to cool for dessert; season it as you help to it at table, with cream and sugar to the taste.

Whey Skim Curds.

Boil the whey, and put in a pint of sour butter-milk; when the curds rise to the top take them off, and set them in a cold place; they make a nice dessert to eat with sugar, cream and nutmeg.

Cheese Curds.

Put to boil a gallon of skim milk, stir into it two spoonsful of rennet wine; when it turns, dip up the

10

curds and set them away to cool; eat them with sweet-ened cream and nutmeg.

Rennet Wine for cold Custards or Curds.

Rub the salt from a nicely dried rennet, and cut it up; put it in a bottle, and fill it up with good wine. If care is taken to keep it filled up, it will last for several years, to make cold custard and cheese curds.

To Preserve Milk to use at Sea.

To every quart of new milk put a pound of loaf-sugar; let it boil very slowly in an iron pot, over clear coals, till it is as thick as thin cream—stirring it all the time; pour it out in a pitcher, and stir till it is cold; put in bottles, cork it tight, and put sealing wax over the corks; it must be shaken before it is used.

SYRUPS, ICES, &c.

Lemon Syrup.

CLARIFY a pound of loaf or Havana sugar, or if you wish to make a large quantity, allow half a pint of water to every pound of sugar, and boil it, skimming it when the scum arises, until it is of the consistency of honey; then to every pound of sugar, add an ounce of tartaric acid. If you do not find it sour enough, after it has stood two or three days, add more of the acid. If you like the taste of oil of lemon, add a few drops. A small quantity of the syrup prepared in this way, poured into cold water, makes a refreshing drink in warm weather.

Lemon Syrup for Seasoning.

Pare the lemons very thin, and put the peel to boil in a quart of water; cover it, to keep in the flavor; put two pounds of loaf sugar to the peel of a dozen lemons, and boil it till it becomes a rich syrup; keep it corked up in a bottle, to season ice cream.

Syrup of Lemon Juice.

Dissolve three pounds of loaf-sugar in three quarts of water, squeeze and strain lemons enough to make a quart of juice; boil it slowly with the water and sugar, and take off the scum as it rises; when it is quite clear, strain and bottle it. It will supply the place of fresh lemons when they cannot be had.

Pine Apple Syrup.

Pare the pine apples, cut them in pieces, and to three pounds of pine apple put a quart of water; cover it and let it boil till very soft, when mash and strain it; to a pint of this juice put a pound of sugar, boil it till it is a rich syrup, and keep it corked up in bottles to season ice cream.

Almond Cream.

Take a pound of blanched almonds, and roll them fine with a bottle; mix them with a few drops of rose-water, and stir them into a quart of cream; sweeten it with loaf-sugar, put it in a pot over the fire, and stir it till it thickens.

Tincture of Vanilla.

Vanilla beans, well bruised, half an ounce; French brandy, one gill; let it stand one week, and it will be fit for use. Keep it corked tight. This article will keep any length of time, and is very convenient for seasoning ices.

Superior Receipt for Ice Cream.

One gallon of cream, two pounds rolled loaf-sugar, one tea-spoonful of oil of lemon.   If for vanilla cream, use a table-spoonful of tincture of vanilla, two eggs beaten; mix well and freeze in the usual way.   The seasoning should be well mixed with the sugar, before it is added to the cream; by this means, it will be all flavored alike.   This has been much admired.

Coloring for ice cream, may be made in this way: take of powdered cochineal, cream of tartar and powdered alum, each two drachms; of salts of tartar, ten grains; pour upon the powders half a pint of boiling water; let it stand for two hours to settle, or filter through paper.   Use as much of this infusion as will give the desired shade.   This produces a brilliant pink color.

Freezing Ice Cream.

Take a bucket of ice and pound it fine; mix with it two quarts of salt; put your cream in a freezer; cover it close, and immerse it in the bucket; draw the ice round it, so as to touch every part; after it has been in a few minutes, put in a spoon, and stir it from the edge to the centre.   When the cream is put in a mould, close it and move it in the ice, as you cannot use a spoon without waste.

Ice Cream with Lemon.

Roll two fresh lemons, in as much powdered loaf-sugar as will sweeten a quart of cream; if you wish the juice, you can put some in with more sugar; freeze it.   A good plan is to rub the lemon on a large lump of sugar, and then use the sugar in sweetening the cream.

Ice Cream with Fruit.

Mix the juice of the fruit with as much sugar as will be wanted before you add the cream, which need not be very rich.

Pokeberry Juice to Stain Ices.

Mash and strain ripe pokeberries; to each pint of juice put a pound of sugar; boil them together till it becomes a jelly; when cold put it in a jar and tie it close; use a small quantity of this to stain ice cream or jelly.

Isinglass Jelly.

To one ounce of shaved isinglass, put a quart of water; boil it down to a pint, and strain it through a flannel bag; add some sugar and wine; stir it and put it in glasses.

Blancmange.

Shave an ounce of isinglass, and dissolve it in boiling water; then boil it in a quart of new milk; strain it and sweeten it to your taste; season as you prefer, with rose water, cinnamon, or vanilla.

Blancmange of Jelly,

To one pint of calf's foot jelly, add a pint of cream, a little mace, and a quarter of a pound of loaf-sugar; boil it fifteen minutes, stirring it constantly; strain it through a flannel bag, and when nearly cold put in a glass of white wine; wet your moulds with cold cream before putting it in.

Calf's Foot Jelly.

Split the feet, and soak them in cold water, four or five hours; wash them clean, and put them to boil in six quarts of water; when it has boiled down to one-

10*

half, strain it through a colander, and skim off all the fat that is on the top; set it away to cool, and when the jelly is quite stiff, wipe it with a towel, to take off any grease that should remain; cut it in pieces, and pare of the discolored parts; put it in your preserving kettle, with half a pint of wine, the juice and peel of two lemons, mace and sugar to your taste, and the whites and shells of six eggs; after it has boiled twenty minutes, pour in a little cold water, to make it settle; if any scum arises, take it off; let it boil five minutes longer, and take it off the fire; keep it covered for about an hour, when strain it through a bag that has been dipped in hot water, and put it in your glasses.

When eggs are used in calf's foot and other jellies, care should be taken to have the ingredients cool. If the jelly is hot when the eggs are added, it cannot be clarified so well—they should only cook by heating the jelly after they have been diffused, by stirring them through it.

Raisins in Syrup.

Make a syrup of half a pound of sugar to a pint of water, boil and skim it; put in five bunches of raisins, and let them boil twenty minutes; if you prefer, you can pick off the stems.

To Blanch Almonds and Peach Kernels.

Pour boiling water on them, which will make them peel easily; either roll them with a bottle on the cake board or pound in a mortar, with a little loaf-sugar; they should not be pounded too much or they will be oily; peach kernels make a fine flavoring for custard, but as they contain prussic acid, do not use too many.

Snow Cream.

Take the richest cream you can procure, season it with a few drops of essence of lemon, or syrup of lemon peel, and powdered white sugar, and if you choose a spoonful of preserve syrup, and just as you send it to table, stir in light newly fallen snow till it is nearly as stiff as ice cream.

Kisses.

Beat the whites of eight eggs till they will stand alone; put with them, a little at a time, a pound of powdered sugar; roll a lemon in some of the sugar till the flavor is extracted. After it is beaten very well, drop it in heaps about the size of half an egg on a sheet of paper; smooth them over with a spoon, and let them be of a regular shape; bake them in an oven that has been moderately heated, till they are of a pale brown color; do not have the oven too cool, or they will run together; take them from the papers carefully, and stick two together.

CAKES.

Remarks on Making and Baking Cake.

The materials for making cake should be of the best quality, as your success very much depends on it. Flour should be dried and sifted, sugar rolled fine, spices pounded and sifted. Where brown sugar is used, it should be spread on a dish and dried before rolling it. I have known very good pound cake made with brown sugar; also jumbles, &c. Persons that make their own butter sometimes use it fresh from the churn, which prevents the necessity of washing the salt out of it for cake, and it mixes more readily than hard butter. Currants should be picked over, washed and dried; raisins should be stemmed and stoned. When these preparations are made the day before, it is a great assistance. Eggs should be fresh, or they will not beat light: in beating the whites, take a broad flat dish, and beat them until you can hold the dish upside down;—this is a test of their lightness. A large bowl is best for mixing and beating cake. You must use your hand for mixing the sugar and butter, and as you add the other ingredients, you may take a large wooden spoon; beat it some time after all is mixed. The oven should be ready to bake immediately, as standing makes cake heavy. A brick oven is the most certain,—and over your pans of cake, you should spread several layers of newspaper, to prevent its browning too suddenly. Cake requires more time than bread: a large cake should stay in the oven from an hour and a half to two hours, turning and looking at it from time to time; when you think it is sufficiently baked, stick a broad bright knife in the centre; if it is dry and free from dough when drawn out, the cake is likely to be done, though sometimes this is not a certain test, and you will have to draw a little from the centre of the cake with the knife. A broom straw will sometimes answer in a small cake instead of a knife. A large stone pan, with a cover, is the best for keeping cake, or a large covered bowl.

Icing for Cake.

Roll and sift a pound of loaf-sugar; whip the whites of three eggs; put in the sugar gradually, and beat it for half an hour; if it is so thick that it will not run, put in some rose water; let the cake be nearly cool; dry it in an oven that is nearly cool.

ANOTHER WAY.

Put the white of one egg and a little rose water into half a pound of pulverized sugar, and beat them together till they stand; when it is nearly light enough, add a few drops of lemon juice, or a small portion of tartaric acid, dissolved in a *little* water. It must be beaten in a bowl which has never had any thing greasy in it, (either cream or butter.) The cake must have a little flour sifted over it, and wiped off with a towel, then cover it with a thin coat of the icing, set it under the stove or in a place that is a little warm, and let it harden; then add the second coat thicker; this will be perfectly white, but the first is always dark and has crumbs through it.

A Rich Fruit Cake.

Have the following articles prepared before you begin the cake: dry and sift four pounds of flour, four pounds of butter with the salt washed out, two pounds of loaf-sugar pounded, one ounce of nutmegs grated, an ounce of mace pounded; wash four pounds of currants; dry, pick, and rub them in flour; stone and cut two pounds of raisins; slice two pounds of citron, blanch a pound of sweet almonds and cut them in very thin slices; break thirty eggs, separate the whites and yelks, and beat them till very light; work the butter with your hand till it is soft as cream; put in alternately the flour, sugar and eggs. When all are mixed in, and the cake looks very light, add the spice, fruit, almonds, and half a pint of brandy; set it in a well heated oven to bake; when it has risen, and the top is beginning to brown, cover it with paper; let it bake four hours, and when it is nearly cool, ice it. This will keep a long time in a stone pan, covered close.

A cheaper Fruit Cake.

Take four pounds of flour, three of butter, three of sugar, two of raisins, one of currants, two dozen eggs, an ounce of mace, three nutmegs, and a half pint of brandy; if you want it dark, put in a little molasses; mix the ingredients together, as the above fruit cake, and bake it from two to three hours.

Fruit or Plum Cake.

Dry and sift a pound of flour, roll a pound of sugar, and beat it with a pound of butter, and the yelks of ten eggs well beaten; wash and dry a pound of currants and rub them in flour; stone and cut half a pound of raisins, and mix in with a glass of rose brandy, and a grated nutmeg, or mace; when all the rest are well mixed together, beat up the whites of the eggs, and add them; bake it an hour and a half.

Pound Cake.

Wash the salt from a pound of butter, and beat it with a pound of loaf sugar till it is as soft as cream; have a pound of flour sifted, and beat ten eggs, the whites and yelks separately; put alternately into the butter and sugar the flour and eggs; continue to beat till they are all in, and the cake looks light; add some grated lemon peel, a nutmeg, and half a wine-glass of brandy; butter the pan, and bake it an hour; when it is nearly cold, ice it. If you want a very large cake, double the quantity. You can tell when a cake is done by running in a broom-straw, or the blade of a bright knife; if it comes out without sticking, it is done, but if not, set it back. You can keep a cake a great while in a stone pan that has a lid to fit tight.

White Cake.

Beat the whites of twenty eggs; wash the salt out of a pound of butter; sift a pound of flour, roll a pound of loaf-sugar, blanch a pound of almonds; roll them fine with a bottle, and mix them with rose water.

Work the butter, sugar and almonds together till they look like cream; have the eggs beaten very light, and add them and the flour alternately till you get all in; beat the whole together till it is very light; have a pan buttered, and put it in a heated oven to bake; when it begins to brown, put white paper over the top; bake it about three hours; when it is nearly cold, prepare an icing, flavored with rose water; put it on the top and sides.

Washington Cake.

Take a pound and three-quarters of sugar, the same of flour, three-quarters of a pound of butter, eight eggs, a pint of milk, and mix them as a pound-cake; just as it is ready to bake, dissolve a tea-spoonful of salæratus in a little sour cream, and stir in; season with nutmeg and rose brandy, or essence of lemon; bake it as pound cake.

Some persons put in a tea-spoonful of lemon juice just before baking.

Madison Cake.

Take a pound and a quarter of flour, and the same of sugar and butter; five eggs, a pound of raisins, and one of currants; two glasses of wine or brandy;

mace, nutmeg, and a tea-spoonful of salæratus, dissolved in a pint of new milk; bake it as pound cake.

Indian Pound Cake.

Take three-quarters of a pound of Indian meal sifted, and one-quarter of wheat flour; roll a pound of sugar, work into it three-quarters of a pound of butter; season with nutmeg and rose brandy; add four eggs beaten light; mix and bake as other pound cake.

Rice Flour Pound Cake.

Take seven eggs, a pound of rice flour, one of sugar, and half a pound of butter; season it with rose water and nutmeg; mix and bake it as other pound cake, and ice it.

Sponge Cake.

Balance twelve fresh eggs with sugar, and six with flour; beat the eggs very light, the whites and yelks separately; mix alternately the sugar and eggs, and add the grated peel of a lemon; butter a large pan, or several small ones; add the flour just as it is put in the oven, stirring it just sufficiently to mix. Beating it after the flour is added makes it heavy; pour it in, and put it to bake as soon as possible. This makes a good pudding, with white sauce. One-half rice flour is an improvement.

Rice Sponge Cake.

Take three-quarters of a pound of rice flour, one pound of white sugar, finely powdered, and ten eggs; beat the yelks with the sugar, the whites alone; add them and the flour to the yelks and sugar, a little at a time; season it with rose brandy and nutmeg, and bake it in shallow pans.

Sponge Cake, in Small Pans.

Take twelve eggs, with the weight of them in sugar, and the weight of six of them in flour; beat the yelks with the sugar, the whites alone; season with nutmeg or grated lemon peel; put all together, adding the flour the last; stir it quickly after the flour is added, as it will make it heavy to beat it much; grease several small pans and pour it in, bake with a quick heat, and they will be done in half an hour, or less, according to the size. They are pretty iced.

Lemon Sponge Cake.

Take ten eggs, separate them, a pound of loaf-sugar, half a pound of flour, the grated peel of two lemons and the juice of one; beat the yelks with the sugar, the whites alone, when add them and sift in the flour by degrees; beat well, have your pan buttered, and bake with a quick heat either in a stove or dutch-oven, or a brick oven, the heat should not be quite so great as for light bread—it will bake in about an hour.

Cup Cake.

Take four cups of flour, three of sugar, one of melted butter, one of sour cream, with a tea-spoonful of salæratus dissolved in it, and three eggs; season it with brandy and nutmeg; mix and bake it as pound cake.

Loaf Cake.

Take about a pound of risen bread dough, work into it a tea-cup of butter, three eggs beaten, a pound of sugar, a nutmeg grated and a glass of brandy or wine; a pound of raisins, stoned and chopped, should be added after it is well beaten; half a pint of cream

11

slightly warmed, with a table-spoonful of vinegar, and a tea-spoonful of dissolved salæratus should be stirred in just as you are ready to bake it; also sifted flour enough to make it the proper consistence; bake in a large pan, in a brick oven or stove, and it will require an hour and a quarter.

Queen Cake.

Mix a pound of dried flour, the same of sifted sugar, and currants; wash a pound of butter, add rose water— beat it well—a tea-cup of cream; then mix with it eight eggs, yelks and whites beaten separately; add the dry ingredients by degrees; beat the whole an hour, bake in little tins, or saucers, filling only half.

Rich Jumbles.

Rub a pound of butter into a pound and a quarter of flour; beat four eggs with a pound and a quarter of sugar; when very light, mix them with the butter and flour; mix in a glass of rose water, and a nutmeg ; roll them in rings, and bake them slowly; sift powdered sugar over after they are baked.

Common Jumbles.

Take a pound of flour, half a pound of butter, and three-quarters of sugar, three eggs, a little nutmeg and rose brandy; mix the butter and sugar together, and add the flour and eggs; mould them in rings, and bake them slowly.

Molasses Jumbles.

Beat three-quarters of a pound of sugar, the same of butter, and three eggs together; stir in half a pint of molasses; add rose brandy and nutmeg, and enough flour to make a soft dough; roll it in rings, and bake as other jumbles. By the addition of half a pint of molasses and a tea-spoonful of salæratus, you will have a common black cake, which may be baked in one large pan.

Jumbles for Delicate Persons.

Roll a heaped pint of light-brown sugar, and rub it in two pints of flour, half a pound of butter, and a dessert spoonful of cinnamon; beat an egg, and mix it with half a tea-cup of rich milk (in which a very small lump of salæratus has been dissolved;) stir all together with a wine glass of rose brandy; work it well, roll thin and cut them out—bake with moderate heat.

Cup Jumbles.

Five tea-cups of flour, three of sugar, one heaped of butter, one of sweet cream, three eggs and the peel of one lemon grated, or nutmeg, or mace if you like; roll them thin, and bake in a quick oven.

Jackson Jumbles.

Three tea-cups of sugar, one of butter, five of flour, one tea-spoonful of salæratus in a cup of sour cream and two eggs; bake in a quick oven; season them with the peel of a fresh lemon grated, and half a wine-glass of brandy.

Macaroons.

Blanch a pound of almonds, beat them in a mortar, and put with them a little rose water to keep them from oiling, the white of an egg, and a large spoonful of flour; roll a pound of loaf-sugar, and beat the whites of four eggs; beat them all together; shape them on white paper with a spoon, and bake them on tin plates in a slow oven; let them be quite cold before you remove them from the paper.

Naples Biscuit.

Beat twelve eggs till light; add to them a pound of dried flour and one of powdered sugar; beat all together till perfectly light; put in some rose water and nutmeg, and bake it in small shallow pans in a moderately heated oven.

New Year Cake.

Mix together three pounds of flour, a pound and a half of sugar, and three-quarters of a pound of butter; dissolve a tea-spoonful of salæratus in enough new milk to wet the flour; mix them together; grate in a nutmeg, or the peel of a lemon; roll them out, cut them in shapes, and bake.

Cider Cake.

Take a pound and a half of flour, three-quarters of sugar, and a quarter of a pound of butter; dissolve a tea-spoonful of salæratus in as much cider as will make it a soft dough, and bake it in shallow pans; season it with spice to your taste.

Dover Cake.

One pound of flour, one of sugar, half a pound of butter, six eggs, half a nutmeg, a spoonful of rose brandy; beat the butter and sugar together, adding the other ingredients, the whites of the eggs beaten separately; bake as pound cake.

Jelly Cake.

This cake can be made by the sponge, cup, or Dover cake recipe; have shallow tin pans or plates of the same size, butter them, and pour in the batter so as to be about half an inch thick when baked; they take but a few minutes to bake of a light-brown; and as you take them from the oven, put them on a china plate, with a layer of jelly between each cake, till you have four or five layers; cut the cake in slices before hand ing it. Currant jelly is to be preferred, but quince will answer, or peach marmalade.

Almond Cake.

Ten eggs, one pound of loaf-sugar, half a pound of almonds, half a pound of flour, one nutmeg; beat the yelks first, then put in the sugar, beating them very light; blanch the almonds and pound them in a mortar, with rose water or the juice of a lemon; add them alternately with the flour, and the whites of the eggs well beaten. If you bake in one large cake, it will require an hour and a half in a slow oven; in small pans, it will take less time, and in either case, will require watching.

Raised Plum Cake.

Take three pounds of flour, and mix to it as much new milk as will make a thick batter, and a tea-cup of yeast; when it is light, beat together a pound of butter, a pound of sugar, and four eggs ; mix this in with a pound of raisins, stoned and cut, half a pound of currants, a grated nutmeg, and a glass of rose brandy; bake it two hours.

Black Cake.

Rub a pound and a half of softened butter in three pounds of flour, add a pound of brown sugar, rolled fine, a pint of molasses, a table-spoonful of rose brandy, a nutmeg or some mace, four eggs well beaten, a pound of raisins stoned and chopped; mix the whole well, and before baking add a tea-cup of sour cream with a tea-

11*

spoonful of soda dissolved in it—beat it up again, have the pans well buttered, and put in about three parts full; this quantity will make about six cakes, in bread pans; bake as bread and if it brown too much, put paper on it, if it seems too stiff, add a little more molasses or cream.   It will keep several weeks in cold weather.

Bunns.

Take a pound and a quarter of flour, half a pound of butter, and three-quarters of a pound of sugar, six eggs, half a pound of currants, half a nutmeg, a glass of brandy, and a pint of new milk; mix all well together, and put in half a tea-cup of yeast; let it rise, and when light, bake it in shallow pans.

Butter-milk Cakes.

One pound of sugar, a quarter of a pound of butter, three eggs, a tea-cup of butter-milk, nutmeg or cinnamon to taste; add as much flour as will make a dough that will roll out; cut in round cakes and bake with a quick heat.

A Composition Cake.

One pound of sugar, one of flour, half a pound of butter, six eggs, two and a half wine-glasses of milk, one tea-spoonful of soda and one of tartaric acid; warm the milk and butter; add the sugar, then the yelks of the eggs beaten light, then the whites and the flour alternately, then the soda, (to be dissolved in half a wine-glass of water;) season with nutmeg, mace, or a little essence of lemon, and add lastly, the tartaric acid, dissolved in half a wine-glass of water.   Bake it one hour in an oven, as hot as is usual for bread; when brown at the top, cover it with paper.   A pound of dried currants is an agreeable addition.

Ginger Cup-cake.

Three cups of flour, one of sugar, one of molasses, one of butter, a table-spoonful of ginger, one tea-spoonful of salæratus, and three eggs; bake in pans. A pound of stoned and chopped raisins is an improvement.

Light Ginger-bread.

Take three cups of molasses, five of flour, one of sugar, three eggs, and a tea-spoonful of salæratus, dissolved in a cup of sour cream; work the sugar with a quarter of a pound of butter; beat two dozen cloves, and put in with two table-spoonsful of ginger; mix all together, and bake in shallow pans or cups.

Crisp Ginger-cake.

Take three pounds of flour, one of sugar, and one of butter; mix these together with three table-spoonsful of ginger, some cloves and aniseed, and wet it with molasses; roll it thin; cut it in shapes, and bake with a quick heat.

Ginger-bread Nuts.

Take a pound and a half of flour, three-quarters of a pound of sugar, the same of butter, some cloves and cinnamon pounded fine, and an ounce of ginger; mix these well together, and make it into a stiff dough, with molasses; roll it thin, and cut it in small cakes.

Crullers.

Take two pounds of flour, three-quarters of a pound of sugar, half a pound of butter, six eggs, and some mace or nutmeg; mix the flour, sugar and butter together, and wet it with the eggs; if too stiff, put in some cream, roll the dough thin; cut it in shapes, and fry them in boiling lard. The more lard there is, the less they will soak it up.

Rusk.

Take a quart of milk, a tea-cup of cream, half a pound of lard, quarter of a pound of butter, a spoonful of salt, and boil them together; beat well two eggs with a pound of sugar, and pour the boiling milk on them gradually, stirring all the time; when nearly cold, add a tea-cup of yeast, and flour sufficient to make a stiff batter; when quite light, knead it up as bread, and let it lighten again before moulding out; when they are moulded out, wet them over with sugar and cream, and let them rise a few minutes and bake them; grate a little sugar over when they come out of the oven.

Rusk for Drying.

Boil a quart of milk, and put in it half a pound of butter, and a little salt; when nearly cold, stir in a tea-cup of yeast, a pound of sugar, and flour to make a batter; when it is light, knead it up with flour, and let it rise again; grease your pans, and make it out in cakes, about the size of a tea-cup, and an inch thick; put two layers in each pan, and bake them three-quarters of an hour; when take them out, break them apart, and put the top ones in other pans, and let them dry slowly in the oven for an hour or more.

This rusk will keep for months, and is very useful in sickness, to make panada; it is also good for delicate persons that rich cake disagrees with, or to take on a journey. Nutmeg or mace to your taste.

If you like it richer, two eggs may be put in.

Bread Rusk,

Take as much lightened dough, as would make a loaf of bread, spread it open, and put in a tea-cup of sugar, some nutmeg and a piece of butter; work it well, mould it out, and bake it with your bread; wet the top with sugar and cream before it goes in the oven.

Dough-nuts.

Boil a quart of new milk and melt in it half a pound of butter; beat three eggs with two pounds of sugar, and pour on them the boiling milk, stirring all the time; when it is nearly cold, stir in a tea-cup of yeast, a spoonful of salt, and flour enough to make a stiff batter; when this is quite light, knead in flour to make a soft dough, two grated nutmegs and a little mace; let it rise again till it is very light; roll it out thin, cut it in shapes, and fry them in hot lard; dust over cinnamon and loaf-sugar, pounded fine, while they are hot.

Common Dough-nuts.

Pour a pint of boiling water into a pint of new milk, put in a quarter of a pound of lard, and a table-spoon-ful of salt; stir in a tea-cup of yeast and flour to make a stiff batter; let it rise, and when very light put in two pounds of light-brown sugar, two nutmegs, and enough flour to make a soft dough; work it well and let it rise again till it is very light; roll out and fry as other dough-nuts.

PRESERVES, JELLIES, &c.

To Clarify Sugar.

To every four pounds of sugar put a quart of water and the whites of two eggs; if you put in the egg after it gets hot, it will cook before it has the desired effect; when it comes to a boil, and the scum rises, pour in a little cold water; let it boil up; take it off to settle, and skim it well; let it boil up, and skim it three times, when it will be fit to preserve with. You should always clarify white Havana sugar.

Apples.

Apples should be preserved in November, and they will keep till June. Take firm pippins, pare them and take out the cores, leaving them whole; or after you have cored them, cut them across in two pieces, they will then be in rings; put them in cold water as fast as they are pared, to keep them from turning dark; make a syrup of a pound of loaf-sugar, and half a pint of water to each pound of apples; wipe the apples, and put in as many as will go in, without one laying on another; let them boil swiftly till they look clear, then take them up carefully on dishes, and put in some more; when all are done, if the syrup should seem too thin, boil it up after the apples are taken out; cut the peel of several lemons in thin rings, boil them in a little water till they are soft, and throw them in the syrup after the apples are taken out; put the syrup in a bowl, and set all away till the next day, when put the apples in glass jars or large bowls, spread the lemon peel about them and put the syrup on the top; paste several thicknesses of paper over, and set them in a dry cool closet.

If you only want the apples to keep a few weeks, they may be done with half a pound of sugar to a pound of apples, and will look and taste quite as well.

Apples with Brown Sugar.

Pare and halve your apples, either pippins, red-streaks or wine-saps; make a syrup of light-brown sugar, allowing half a pound to a pound of the fruit; after boiling and clarifying the syrup, pour it over the fruit, and set it by for two days, then cook them, and seasoned with green ginger root they are excellent; they will not require much cooking, and should be of a light-brown color.

Crab Apples.

Put the crab apples in a kettle with grape leaves in and around them, with some alum; keep them at scalding heat for an hour, take them out, skin them, and take out the seeds with a small knife, leaving on the stems; put them in cold water, make a syrup of a pound of sugar to a pound of apples; wipe the apples and put them in; let them stew gently till they look clear; take them out, and let the syrup boil longer.

Currants.

Make a syrup of one pint of currant juice to three pounds of sugar; if it is brown sugar, put in the white of an egg to clarify it; let it boil and skim it; have three pounds of currants picked and stemmed; put them in the syrup, and let them boil slowly, about twenty minutes; take them up and let the syrup boil longer.

Pine Apples.

Pare and slice the pine apples, and make a syrup of a pound of sugar and half a pint of water to a pound of fruit; clarify and skim it, then put in the apples and let them cook gently for half an hour; if you do not want to keep them long, much less sugar will do.

Blackberries.

Allow a pint of currant juice and a pint of water to six pounds of blackberries; give them their weight in brown sugar; let them boil till they appear to be done, and the syrup is rich. Blackberry jelly can be made as currant jelly, and is good for sick children, mixed with water.

Blackberry Flummery.

Stew three pints of blackberries with one pint of sugar—soak a tea-cup full of ground rice—and when the berries have been stewing about fifteen minutes, stir in the rice, and stir the whole time until it becomes thick. This should be eaten cold with cream, and will keep two days.

Cherries.

To preserve four pounds of cherries, take one pint of currant juice, into which put five pounds of sugar; when this boils up, take off any scum that rises, and put in half of the cherries, with part of each stem on; when they look so clear that you can see the stone, they are done; take these up on a dish and put in the rest, and let them do slowly the same length of time; take them up and let the syrup boil a few minutes longer; do not put them in the jars till they are quite cold. Glass jars are the best to keep all early fruits in, as you can then see if they begin to ferment; if they do, you must boil them over; always put them in a window where they will be exposed to the sun.

Common Cherries.

Stone the light-colored common cherries, and to every pound of fruit, allow a pound of sugar, which boil up with the juice; after you have skimmed it, throw in the cherries, and let them boil till the syrup is rich.

Cherries for Common Use.

Stone twelve pounds of morel cherries; allow half a pound of brown sugar to each pound of fruit, after it is stoned; let them cook slowly for two hours; examine them through the summer, and if they show any signs of fermentation, set them in a brick-oven, after the bread is done, or in a dutch-oven of hot water, which keep at boiling heat for an hour.

It is a good plan to know the weight of your preserving kettle, as you can then weigh the fruit in it, with a pair of steelyards.

Apricots.

Pour boiling water on the apricots and wipe them dry; then cut them in half and take out the stone; make a syrup of their weight in sugar, and a little water; when this has boiled, put in the fruit, and let it cook slowly till it is clear, and the syrup is rich.

Ginger.

Scrape the outside from the green ginger, and boil it in a little water, till it is soft; then take it out, and scrape off any spots that are on it; make a syrup of half a pint of water to a pound of sugar and a pound of

12

ginger; let it boil slowly about half an hour; take it up
and boil the syrup a little longer.

Green Gage Plums.

Take an equal quantity of fruit and sugar, pour boiling water on the plums, and wipe them dry; stick them
over with a pin; make a syrup of the sugar and some
water, and when it boils, put in half of the plums; let
them do slowly till they are clear, then take them out
and put in the rest; if the syrup should be thin, let it
boil longer. Do not put them in the jars till the next
day. Egg plums may be done in the same way.

Green Lemons.

Take the young lemons, cut them in half, scrape
them, and take out the pulp; cut them in such shapes
as you please; put them in a preserving kettle and
cover them with water; put in a little alum to green
them, and let them boil till they are transparent, then
take them out and drain them on a cloth; give the
kettle another cleansing, and put them in with their
weight in sugar; let them stew gently, but be careful
that they do not boil; let them cook till the syrup is
rich.

Raspberries.

Boil three pounds of raspberries in a pint of currant
juice, for ten minutes; put in four pounds of sugar, and
let them boil half an hour, or until it is a jelly. Paste
paper over the jar.

Citron Melon.

Pare the melon and cut it in slices half an inch thick,
without the seeds; let it lay in salt and water for an
hour, then wash the salt off, and boil it in strong

ginger tea; make a thin syrup and boil it again, then make a syrup of a pound of loaf-sugar to a pound of citron, and boil it in this till it is clear; season it with mace and lemon peel.

Water-melon Rinds.

Cut the rinds in any form you please; put them in strong salt and water, with cabbage leaves over and around them, and set them in a warm place till they become yellow; then wash them, and put them in a kettle with alum and water, and grape or cabbage leaves over and through them; set them on the fire, and keep it at scalding heat for two hours—but do not let them boil. If they are not of a fine green color, change the water and leaves; when they are green enough, put them in cold soft water for three days, changing the water twice a day; then make a syrup of rather more than a pound of sugar to a pound of melon, some sliced ginger, the peel of a lemon, and a little mace; let them boil slowly fifteen minutes, take them up, and boil them again at the end of a week.

Cantelopes, Cucumbers, or Melons.

Take young water-melons, cucumbers or cantelopes; scrape the melons, and cut the rinds in shapes—leave the cucumbers whole; put them in a preserving kettle with alum and water; cover them, and let them boil till they are transparent; take them out, wash them in cold water, and wipe each piece separately; have your kettle nicely cleaned, and give them rather more than their weight in sugar; put a layer of sugar, and a layer of melon, some slices of green ginger, and the rind and juice of a lemon; let them stew over the fire till the syrup is rich; take them up, and stew them over again in about a week.

Cranberries,

To preserve cranberries, allow them their weight in sugar; make a syrup of the proportions of half a pint of water to two pounds of the sugar; boil and skim it before you put the fruit in; then let them boil until clear.   To make sauce to eat with roast fowls, put three-quarters of a pound of sugar to a pound of fruit.

Gooseberries,

Take the large gooseberries, pick off the stems and blossoms, give them their weight in sugar; put them in the kettle alternately, with the sugar, and pour over them a pint of water to four pounds of fruit; let them boil gently till the scum arises; when this is taken off, let them cook faster; when clear, take them up on dishes, and boil the syrup longer.

Peaches,

Have sweet, white clingstone peaches—pare and stone them; to each pound, take a pound of sugar made in a syrup, put the peaches in, and when they look clear, take them up on dishes; let the syrup boil longer.

A New Mode of Preserving Peaches,

Pare, halve and weigh the peaches; put them in a preserving kettle of boiling water, and to six pounds of peaches, put a tea-spoonful of soda or pearl-ash; let them boil one minute; then take them out, and throw them in cold water; scrape off the black scum which adheres to the peaches; wipe and lay them on a dish; have the kettle cleaned, and put the peaches in layers, with half their weight in sugar; they will not require any water; let them cook slowly at first, then boil till clear—when take them out, and let the syrup boil till it becomes rich. The flavor of the peach is retained, and they are not so sweet as in the old way.

Damsons.

Weigh out as much sugar as you have fruit; if it is brown you must clarify it; put a pint of water to three pounds of sugar, make a syrup, wash the damsons, put them in and let them cook slowly for half an hour; then take them out on dishes, and let them dry in the sun for two days, taking them in the house at night; boil the syrup half an hour after the fruit is taken out; when done in this way they will be whole and clear. You can make a jam by boiling them slowly for two hours; or a jelly as currants.

To Preserve Strawberries.

Gather the strawberries in the mid-day, pick out the largest and best, stem them, and to each pound of strawberries put a pound of loaf-sugar and a glass of white wine; let them stand four or five hours; take off the syrup so as not to mash the fruit, and clarify it; then put in the strawberries, and to each pound put as much fine alum as will lay on the blade of a pen-knife; let them boil up several times, and shake them round in the kettle, but do not stir them with a spoon, as that will mash them; a few minutes boiling is suffi-cient; after you take out the fruit, let the syrup boil up, and when it is nearly cold pour it over them in the jar; put a piece of white paper over the top, and pour a spoonful of brandy on it; paste several thicknesses of paper over the jar.

12*

If you like your preserved strawberries, cherries, or peaches, to have a fine *pale* color, allow them to boil half the time recommended in the receipt, then spread the fruit thin on dishes, with but little syrup, pour the rest of the syrup also on dishes, and set them daily in the sun; if the weather be clear and the sun hot, four days will be sufficient. Preserves done in this manner do not ferment. You should spread a piece of gauze or netting over them to keep out insects or dust.

ANOTHER WAY.

To each pound of the fruit take a pound of crushed sugar; put them in the preserving kettle, a layer of sugar and a layer of fruit; let them stand a little while to make syrup before putting them over the fire; they should boil fast for twenty minutes; watch them all the time, taking off the scum as it rises; stir them gently without mashing the berries; put them in jars, put brandy papers over them and paste or tie them close. Preserves should never be put in jars that have had pickles in them.

Tomatoes.

Take solid round tomatoes, scald and peel them; give them their weight in sugar; put a layer of sugar and of tomatoes alternately; let them boil slowly till the syrup forms, then boil faster, till clear, and the syrup is rich; season with lemon peel, ginger or mace; some prefer the yellow tomato for preserving.

Quinces.

Pick out the finest quinces, pare them, and cut them in halves, or in rings; take the best of the parings and the seed, and boil them in water till they are very soft; strain the liquor, and have the kettle cleaned again;

wash and weigh the quinces, and give them their weight in sugar; put the sugar in the water the parings were boiled in—skim it, and put in the quinces; let them boil very slowly till clear; take them up on dishes, and boil the syrup longer.

Green Peppers.

Get peppers that have a sweet taste; take out the seeds, leaving on the stems; lay them in salt and water for three days, changing the water each day; then put them in a kettle with leaves around them, and a small piece of alum; let them scald, but not boil, for two hours; take them out, and let them lay in water three days, changing it twice each day; then boil them in sugar and water fifteen minutes; then make a syrup, allowing them their weight in sugar, and boil them gently in it half an hour; take them out and boil the syrup longer.

Pumpkin.

Choose a fine-grained, high-colored pumpkin, fully ripe; cut it in thin slices, about four inches long and two wide; to two pounds of pumpkin, put two pounds of sugar in a bowl; cut the peel of two lemons in rings, and squeeze the juice over the pumpkin; let it stand all night; the next day put it on to preserve with two tea-cups of water; let it cook gently till the pumpkin seems clear and crisp; take it up, scald the lemon peel, and boil it in the syrup; cool it on dishes, and put it in a jar.

Green Fox-grape Jelly.

Fill a kettle with grapes, and let them boil with a pint of water till the skins burst; mash and strain them; put a pound of sugar to a pint of juice, and let it boil half an hour. Ripe fox-grapes may be made into very

nice jelly in the same way, and is very good to drink
in sickness, mixed with water.

Pears.

Pare and core the fruit, but leave the stems on; put
them in a syrup of a pound of sugar, and a half a pint
of water to a pound of pears, with some green ginger
or lemon peel; boil the syrup half an hour after they
are done.

Ripe Fox-grape Jam.

To two quarts of grapes, allow three pounds of brown
sugar, and a pint of water; have the grapes picked
over and washed; put them all together and let them
boil more than an hour; take them up on shallow
dishes, and pick out as many seeds as you can with a
spoon. This makes a good common preserve when
other fruits are scarce; they are also very good for
pies.

Currant Jelly.

Pick the leaves from the currants and fill your kettle
with them; put a tea-cup of water to keep them from
sticking; cover them with a plate and let them boil
slowly half an hour; take them out, and strain them
through a flannel bag; to every pint of juice put a
pound of loaf-sugar; let it boil till it is a thick jelly,
which will be in about fifteen minutes, and put it in
tumblers or jars.

Lemon Butter or French Honey.

Take half a pound of butter, melt it in an earthen
dish and squeeze in the juice of six lemons; beat
twelve eggs with two pounds of brown sugar, stir
it in with the rind of two lemons grated, mix it all

together, and let it boil twenty minutes, when it will be about the consistence of honey; the flavor is agreeable, and it may be eaten on bread, or as a sauce for boiled pudding.

Currant Syrup.

Prepare the currants as for jelly; to every pint of juice put a pint of water and a pound of sugar; let it boil half an hour and skim it well; if the flavor of the raspberry is preferred, it may be added in the proportion of one pint of it, to four of currant juice. It is a very pleasant drink mixed with water in warm weather.

Quince Jelly.

Wash and wipe the quinces; cut them in small pieces, and take out the seeds carefully; have your kettle cleaned and half full of water; throw the quinces and seeds in till you get it full; cover them over, and let them boil till very soft; mash them well and strain them; to every pint of juice put a pound of sugar; clean the kettle again, pour in the juice and sugar, and let it boil till it forms a jelly; it should be put into tea-cups, if you want it to turn out whole, with brandy papers on the top, and pasted over. It is a nice jelly to use with whips or trifle.

Apple Jelly.

Pare and quarter a preserving kettle full of pippin apples; cover them with water, and lay a plate close over them; let them boil until perfectly soft, taking the plate off to skim them; spread a coarse thin cloth over a large bowl; pour the apples on the cloth, and let the juice run through, without sqeezing; hold the towel by the corners, and move it gently; take three-quarters of a pound of loaf-sugar to a pint of the juice, and boil it fast, skimming it, until it becomes jelly, which will be in from ten to fifteen minutes; pour it in tumblers or glass jars, and when quite cold, paste them over: this will keep a year. Red-streak apples make a fine red jelly, boiled with the skins on them. If you have currant or grape jelly that has candied, they can be restored by making some apple syrup, and mixing it hot; it will not require any more sugar—about one-third apple juice; let it boil a few minutes. Very sweet preserves that have candied can be improved by this process.

Apple Marmalade.

Apples make a very good marmalade when other fruits are scarce, and can be done at any time through the fall, or winter; pare the apples, cut them up, and put them to boil, with some water and green ginger scraped, and tied up in a bag; after they have boiled an hour, take out the ginger, and put in half a pound of sugar to one of fruit; let it cook an hour longer.

Peach Marmalade.

Take soft yellow peaches, pare them, and cut them in quarters; give them their weight in sugar; put the peaches in the preserving kettle with a pint of water, without the sugar, and let them boil till they are well cooked, covered over with a plate; when done, mash them in the kettle till very fine, and stir in the sugar; let them cook slowly an hour, or they may be finished in a stone jar in the oven, or set in a stove boiler, and the water kept boiling all the time; they are not then so likely to burn as when finished over the fire; they will do with less sugar, if they are dried in the sun two days previous to preserving.

Pare and quarter the peaches, and to eight pounds of peaches, allow five pounds of sugar; put them on, sugar and peaches at once, mixing them through; let them stew slowly until a syrup forms, when they may cook pretty fast for several hours, without once stirring; then take them up, and mash them well; if the marmalade is not thick enough, spread it on dishes, and dry in your oven after the bread is taken out. Quinces and apples may be done in the same way.

Quince Marmalade.

Pare the quinces and cut them up fine; put the parings and cores to boil; then strain them; put in the quinces, and let them boil till soft—when mash them fine, and put in three-quarters of a pound of sugar to a pound of fruit; let them cook gently for two hours, and take them up in pint bowls; when cold, put brandy papers on the top of each, and paste them over; they will turn out whole to put on table.

Marmalade of Mixed Fruits.

Pare equal quantities of peaches, apples, pears and quinces; cut them fine, and put them to boil with a pint of water to six pounds of fruit; let them cook thoroughly, but do not let them burn; take them out, and mash them well; clean the kettle, and put them back, with half their weight in sugar; let them cook very slowly for two hours.

Lemon Marmalade.

Soak the peel of lemons that have been left after making lemonade, changing the water twice a day for three days, to extract the bitter; boil them till soft, then mash and put in enough sugar to make it pleasant to the taste; stew it a short time after the sugar is put in; put it in a bowl, and when cold, cut it in slices for the table; it will keep several weeks.

To Conserve Pears.

Have the nicest pears you can get, pare them, and leave on the stems ; take half a pound of loaf-sugar to a pound of pears; put them in the kettle together, with water enough to moisten the sugar; if the pears are very juicy, they will not need any; cover them over with a plate, and let them boil very gently for two hours; take them out on dishes, and boil the syrup to jelly, and put it away by itself; set the pears in the sun, or in a moderately heated oven; when quite dry, sprinkle them with loaf-sugar, and put them away in glass jars.

Peaches in Cider.

Scald and wipe the peaches; cut them from the stone, and dry them in the sun two days; boil a gallon of sweet cider half away; put in the peaches, and let them stew slowly till done; they will keep without any sugar, but you can put some in, if you wish them sweeter.

Pears can be kept in the same way.

Peaches, &c. in Brandy.

Take fresh yellow peaches, or large clingstones, pour boiling water on them, and wipe off the down; make a syrup of half a pound of sugar to a pound of fruit, and boil and skim it; put in the peaches, and let them cook for fifteen minutes; take them up without any syrup, and cool them on dishes; boil the syrup down to half, and put an equal quantity of peach or French brandy; pour this over the peaches after they are in jars.

Plums or cherries may be done in the same way.

Grapes in Brandy.

Put some close bunches of grapes, not too ripe, in a jar, and prick each one with a needle; strew over them half their weight in pounded rock candy, and fill up the jar with brandy.

To Conserve Peaches.

Take the yellow peaches, pare them, and cut them from the stone in one piece; to six pounds of peaches have two pounds of sugar; make a syrup of three-quarters of a pound of sugar, and a little water; put them in, and let them stay till they are quite clear; then take them up carefully on a dish, and set them in the sun to dry; pound the sugar fine, and strew over them, turning them over to let each part have some; do not put much on at a time, and if any syrup is made, remove them to fresh dishes; when they are sufficiently dry, lay them lightly in a jar, with a little sugar between each layer.

If the peaches are sweet clings, three pounds of sugar to twelve of peaches will be enough, if you dry them a day in the sun before they are stewed.

Sauce of Cherries, or Damsons.

Allow half a pound of brown sugar to every pound of fruit, and to each seven pounds a pint of molasses, and one of strong vinegar; let them cook slowly, so as not to break the skins; take them up in a jar; put in a few cloves, let the syrup boil longer, and pour it over.

13

Frosted Fruit.

Take large ripe cherries, apricots, plums or grapes; if cherries, cut off half of the stem; have in one dish some white of an egg beaten, and in another some powdered loaf-sugar; take the fruit, one at a time, and roll them first in the egg, and then in the sugar; lay them on a sheet of white paper in a sieve, and set it on the top of a stove or near a fire till the icing is hard.

Grapes for Pies.

After the first frost, pick the wild grapes, and put them in a jar, free from stems; fill it with boiling molasses, and tie it up close; set it on a hot hearth, or on the top of a stove, in a pan of water, for several days. These are very useful to make common pies in the winter.

Green Tomatoes for Pies.

Pick the green tomatoes before they are much frosted; scald them and take off the skins; put them in your kettle and let them boil for half an hour; cut them up, and put in a pound of sugar to three pounds of tomatoes, and let them cook for half an hour longer; season them with the juice and peel of a lemon, and put them away in jars.   They make very good pies in the winter, and resemble gooseberries.

Conserve of Roses.

Gather the leaves of the damask rose, while they are fresh; spread a pound of loaf-sugar on your cake-board, and roll in about half a pound of rose leaves, or as many as will work into it, have your kettle cleaned, and stew them in it very gently for about half an hour; put it in tumblers to use when you have a cough.   It is very good for children that are threatened with the croup; you should have some by the side of the bed to use at night.

To keep Damsons for Pies.

To every twelve pounds of damsons take seven pounds of brown sugar; put them together in a stone jar, a layer of fruit and a layer of sugar; tie it up close, and set it in a heated oven; let it stay till it is cold, and continue to set it in, after every baking, for several weeks; or you can cook them on the top of a stove, in a pan of hot water.

Dried Cherries, &c.

Dried cherries should be kept in a jar, with sugar sprinkled among them; they are very useful in sickness; a tea-cupful of cherries, with a quart of boiling water poured on them, and left to draw for half an hour, with sweetening, makes a very agreeable drink when you cannot get lemonade.

When stewed for pies you should allow them plenty of water, and not put in the sugar till they are nearly done.

Boiling water poured on dried apples also makes a good drink in sickness.

Apple Butter,

With Remarks on the Use of Earthen Vessels.

Have your kettle well cleaned, and fill it early in the morning with cider made of sound apples, and just from the press; let it boil half away, which may be done by three o'clock in the afternoon; have pared and cut enough good apples to fill the kettle; put them in a clean tub, and pour the boiling cider over; then scour the kettle and put in the apples and cider, let them boil briskly till the apples sink to the bottom; slacken the fire and let them stew, like preserves, till ten o'clock at night. Some dried quinces stewed in cider and put in are an improvement. Season with orange peel, cinnamon or cloves, just before it is done; if you like it sweeter, you can put in some sugar an hour before it is done. If any thing occur that you cannot finish it in a day, pour it in a tub, and finish it the next day; when it is done put it in stone jars. Any thing acid should not be put in earthen vessels, as the glazing is poisonous. This way of making apple butter requires but little stirring; you must keep a constant watch that it does not burn.

Pears and peaches may be done in the same way, and if they are sweet, will not require sugar.

ANOTHER WAY.

It is important to have a large copper or bell-metal kettle, into which put the cider as soon as it comes from the press; put it over a brisk fire, and boil it half away; then put the cider from the kettle into clean stone jars, (warm the jars to prevent the danger of breaking them;) have your apples pared and cut over night, as many as would fill your kettle twice; have the kettle well cleaned, and in the morning put in half the cider, and fill the kettle nearly full of apples, and put it over a brisk fire; when they begin to boil up, stir them down, which may be done two or three times, before you put in your stick to stir constantly; then put in the rest of the apples and cider, as fast as the kettle will take them, and boil it four hours after the last apples are put in, stirring it all the time; you should have for the purpose a stick made of hickory wood, somewhat like a common hoe, with holes in it.

Candied Preserves, &c.

If your preserves candy, set the jars in hot water for half an hour; if they are in glass jars put them in something else, as glass cracks easily, when exposed to heat. Preserves made with white Havana sugar are not so liable to candy as others. Common preserves are improved, and are more certain to keep well, by being placed on flat dishes and set in a brick-oven after the bread is taken out: they may remain two or more hours without injury. When preserves are about to boil over, you should have a common fan at hand and fan them, which will sometimes answer instead of taking them from the fire.

Cider Marmalade.

Boil two gallons of sweet cider down to one gallon; have ready two gallons of apples, pared and cut; pour the cider out of the kettle, and clean it; then put in the apples, and pour the cider in, and two or three pounds of sugar; if it will not hold all conveniently, add at intervals; let them stew four hours; do not stir till they are nearly done—stirring makes fruit stick to the kettle and burn; if you stir once you must keep on. This is a pleasant sauce for dinner, or eaten with bread and butter at tea, and will keep in a cool place through the winter.

Tomato Figs.

Take six pounds of sugar, to one peck (or sixteen pounds) of ripe tomatoes—the pear-shaped look best; put them over the fire (*without peeling*) in your preserving kettle, their own juice being sufficient without the addition of water; boil them until the sugar penetrates and they are clarified. They are then taken out,

13*

spread on dishes, flattened and dried in the sun, or in a brick-oven after the bread is taken out. A small quantity of the syrup should be occasionally sprinkled over them whilst drying; after which, pack them down in jars, sprinkling each layer with powdered sugar. The syrup is afterwards concentrated and bottled for use. They retain surprisingly their flavor, which is agreeable and somewhat similar to the best figs. Ordinary brown sugar may be used, a large portion of which is retained in syrup.

Molasses Candy or Taffy.

Put a quart of good molasses (not sugar house) in a dutch-oven or iron pot, having previously greased it with butter; let it boil very fast, stirring it all the time for fifteen minutes; then put in a tea-cup of sugar and let it boil fifteen minutes longer, stirring all the time; take a little out on a plate, and when it is brittle, pour it while hot into tin plates rubbed with butter; put it in a cold place and break it up when you want it for use; never put taffy in china or earthen plates, as they would probably be broken in taking it out. Some think it an improvement to add the kernels of black walnuts, nicely picked—put them in just as you take up the taffy and give it one stir; a tea-cup of kernels to a pint of molasses is a good proportion.

Walnut Cheese.

Take a pint of nice kernels and pound them in a mortar with two tea-cups of brown sugar, and a table-spoonful of water; put it in cups or small bowls and it will turn out like other cheese. It is a favorite refreshment with some country children.

CORDIALS, WINES, VINEGAR, PICKLES, &c.

Peach Cordial.

Put a gallon of peach brandy into a wide-mouthed vessel, and five pounds of fine flavored peaches, cut from the stone; boil five pints of water with two pounds of loaf-sugar and a pound of peaches, till it is a clear and rich syrup; pour this boiling hot on the brandy and stir it well; put in two dozen peach kernels, blanched and pounded, and a little mace; let it stand three weeks covered tight—at the end of which time, bottle it for use.   It is a nice seasoning for cake.

Quince Cordial.

Grate the quinces and strain them; to every quart of juice, put a pound of loaf-sugar and a pint of spirits; boil, strain and bottle it.

Cherry Cordial.

Mash and strain the cherries, boil the juice, and to a gallon, put two pounds of sugar, and half a pint of spirits; the sugar should be boiled in it; skim and strain; when cold, bottle it.

Lemon Brandy.

Have a bottle three-quarters full of brandy; when you use lemons for other purposes, pare off the yellow skin very thin, cut it small and drop it in the bottle, till you get it full.   Be careful not to put in any of the tough white part, as that will give it a bitter taste; cork the bottle and keep it to season cakes and puddings.

Rose Brandy.

Fill a large bottle with damask rose leaves, picked while they are fresh; fill the bottle with brandy, or good spirits of any kind; cork it tightly and set it away for use. It will bear filling up several times.

Blackberry Cordial.

Mash and strain the blackberries; put the juice on to boil in a brass or bell-metal kettle; skim it well, and to each gallon of juice put three pounds of sugar and a quart of spirits; bruise some cloves and put in. This is valuable as a medicine for children in summer.

Rose Water.

Gather the damask rose leaves; have a tin pan that will fit under your warming-pan; wring a thin towel out of water, spread it over the pan, and put rose leaves on this about two inches thick; put another wet towel on top of the leaves, and three or four thicknesses of paper on it; put hot embers in the warming-pan, and set it on top of the paper, propped up so as not to fall; when you renew the coals, sprinkle the towel that is at the top of the rose leaves; when all the strength is out of the leaves, they will be in a cake; dry this, and put it in your drawers toscent the clothes; put another set of leaves in, sprinkle the towels, and so till you have used up all your rose leaves. Rose water is a very nice seasoning for cake or pudding; it should be kept corked tightly.

Cologne.

Put into a bottle half an ounce of oil of lavender, one drachm of oil of rosemary, two of essence of lemon, two of essence of bergamot, forty drops of oil of cinna-

WINES. **149**

mon, and a little musk, if you like it; pour on it three pints of best alcohol.

Blackberry Wine.

Gather the fruit when fully ripe, but before the sun has had time to dry the juice; put it in a tub and pour in clear cold water enough to cover it; mash it to a pulp with a wooden masher; strain it through a linen bag or towel; a deal of juice will remain in the pulp, which in order to get you must add some sugar to it, and boil it in your preserving kettle, when you may strain again, and will have little left but seeds; to every gallon of the liquor, add three pounds of good brown sugar; pour it in a keg, (which should stand in a cellar, or cool dry place;) let it stand two or three weeks, with the bung laid loosely on; as the froth works out fill it up, (with some of the liquor kept out for the purpose.) French brandy in the proportion of a quart to five gallons, is an improvement. At the end of three or four weeks, it may be closely bunged and put away in a safe dry closet, where it should remain undisturbed for a year, when it may be racked off, bottled and sealed over.

Gooseberry Wine.

Put three pounds of lump sugar in a gallon of water; boil and skim it; when it is nearly cold, pour in it four quarts of ripe gooseberries, that have been well mashed, and let it stand two days, stirring it frequently; steep half an ounce of isinglass in a pint of brandy for two days, and beat it with the whites of four eggs till they froth, and put it in the wine; stir it up, and strain it through a flannel bag into a cask or jug; fasten it so as to exclude the air; let it stand six months, and bottle it for use; put two or three raisins in each bottle, and cork it up.

Currant Wine.

Pick and mash the currants, either with your hands or a clean block, in a tub; strain them, and to one gallon of juice, put two gallons of water; and to each gallon of the mixture, put three pounds of sugar; stir it until the sugar is dissolved, then put it in a clean cask that has never been used for beer or cider; put it in a cellar or cool place, and let it work out at the bung for several weeks; have a gallon of it saved in a jug to fill up with, as it works out. When it is done working, bung it up.

You may rack it off towards spring, or it will not hurt it to stand a year.

If you want a barrel of wine, you must have eight gallons of currant juice, sixteen of water, and seventy-two pounds of sugar; put in a quart of brandy after it has done working; if you can get a clean brandy barrel to put it in, it is better than a new one.

ANOTHER WAY.

Mash well together equal quantities of currants and water, strain the juice and to every gallon add three pounds of best brown sugar; fill the cask two-thirds full, bung it tight and put clay over; by this means the air is excluded while the process of fermentation is going on; the cask should be iron-bound; rack it off and bottle or put in demijohns the next spring after making.

Elderberry Wine, &c.

To each gallon of berries, put one of water; mash them in a tub, and leave them two days, stirring them frequently; then strain them, and to each gallon of juice put three pounds of brown sugar, and to every five gallons, two ounces of bruised ginger, and one of cloves, which tie up in a bag, and boil in the wine for an hour, and put it in a cask; when it is nearly cold, put in two spoonsful of lively yeast; let it ferment two days, and put in a pint of spirits with the bag of spice, and close it up. This is excellent as a medicine for delicate or elderly persons.

Fill a bottle with elderberries, with a dozen cloves, and fill it up with spirits. It is good to give children that have the summer disease; mix a tea-spoonful of it with sugar and water for a child, or a table-spoonful for a grown person.

Ginger Wine.

Boil nine quarts of water with six pounds of lump sugar, the rinds of three lemons very thinly pared, and two ounces of race ginger pounded; when it has boiled half an hour, skim it, and pour it on the juice of two lemons: when nearly cold, add two-spoonsful of yeast; put a pound of raisins in the cask, with a half a pint of brandy, and half an ounce of shaved isinglass; strain it in the cask, and stop it tight; bottle it in six or seven weeks.

Raspberry Wine.

Pick over the raspberries, and to every quart put a quart of water; bruise them, and let them stand two days; strain off the liquor, and to every gallon put three pounds of lump sugar; stir it till the sugar is dissolved, and put it in a clean barrel, or keg; at the end of two months, bottle it, and put a spoonful of brandy, or a glass of wine in each bottle.

Raspberry Vinegar, and its uses.

Put two pounds of raspberries in a large bowl, and pour on them two quarts of white-wine vinegar; the next day, strain the liquor on two pounds of fresh raspberries; let this stand a day, and strain it into a stone jar; to each pint of the liquor put a pound of loaf-sugar; stir till it is dissolved, and put the jar in a sauce-pan of water, which keep boiling for an hour; skim it, and bottle it when cold. This is used not only as a refreshing drink, mixed with water, but is said to be of use in complaints of the chest. No glazed or metal vessels should be used in making it.

Spruce Beer.

Boil some spruce boughs with some wheat bran, till it tastes sufficiently of the spruce; bruise some alspice, and put in; strain it, and put two quarts of molasses to half a barrel; when it is nearly cold, put in half a pint of yeast; after it has worked sufficiently, bung up the barrel.

To Make Two Gallons of Beer.

Put two pounds of brown sugar in a jug, with a heaped spoonful of ginger, and a pint of strong hop tea; pour in a gallon and a half of warm water, and a tea-cup of yeast; leave out the cork a day—then fasten it up, and set it in a cool place; or if you bottle it, put two or three raisins in each bottle.

Harvest Beer.

To make fifteen gallons of beer, put into a keg three pints of yeast, three pints of molasses, and two gallons of cold water; mix it well, and let it stand a few minutes; then take three quarts of molasses, and three gallons of boiling water, with one ounce of ginger; mix them well, and pour into the keg, and fill it up with cold water.

A decoction of the root of sassafras is good to put in beer.

Porter Beer.

A pleasant drink in summer is to take one bottle of porter, five bottles of water, and a pint of molasses, or a pound of sugar; make a spoonful of ginger into a tea, and mix all well together; have seven clean bottles, with two or three raisins in each; fill them, cork them tight, and lay them on their sides on the cellar floor.

Molasses Beer.

Take five pints of molasses, half a pint of yeast, two spoonsful of pounded ginger, and one of allspice; put these into a clean half-barrel, and pour on it two gallons of boiling water; shake it till a fermentation is produced; then fill it up with warm water, and let it work with the bung out, a day, when it will be fit for use; remove it to a cold place, or bottle it. This is a very good drink for laboring people in warm weather.

To Make Cider.

To make cider that will keep sweet for a length of time, requires particular attention to all the points. All the works and utensils in use must be perfectly clean, so that nothing acid shall come in contact with the pulp or liquor while pressing. The casks should be cleaned in the following manner:

After washing each barrel clean, put in a lump of unslacked lime, and pour in a gallon of boiling water; bung it up, and roll the barrel several times a day,

14

letting it lay with the bung down; in the evening, empty out the lime-water, and wash the barrel clean in several waters; after the water is drained out, burn a brimstone match in it, made of a piece of coarse muslin one inch broad, and four long, dipped in melted brimstone; light one end of the match, and put it in; put the bung on slightly, so as to hold the other end, and allow air sufficient to make it burn; when the rag has burned out, drive in the bung to keep in the sulphuric gas, which, if allowed time, will condense on the sides.

The apples should be kept under cover, and secured from rain. After they have laid to mellow for two or three weeks, select those that are sound; break off the stems and leaves; have the trough perfectly clean, and after they are ground, keep them from the sun and rain for twenty-four hours; then press them, and fill into the casks; the first running is always the best; each cask that is filled should be numbered, so as to know the quality; and after they are all filled, draw off and mix them, the weak with the strong; keep the casks filled up with cider while they are fermenting; when the fermentation is subsiding, there will be a thin white scum rise slowly: when this is all off, lay on the bung lightly; rack it off in a few days in barrels, in which brimstone has been used, and bung it tight; rack it off again in March, and keep the bungs in tight.

To Make Vinegar.

You may always have good vinegar for pickling, and other purposes, by taking a little pains. Get a tight whiskey barrel, if it is clean you need not rinse it, and put into it ten gallons of the best vinegar you can procure, with one quart of whiskey and one quart of molasses; every day for a week, add a gallon of good cider that has not been watered, and shake the barrel each time; let it stand in this state two weeks, shaking the barrel frequently. After this, you may put in a gallon of cider occasionally, with any that has been left at table, or the settlings of decanters or bottles that have had wine in, but do not put in any water. It will make much sooner in the garret or a warm place, but if the barrel is fixed early in the summer, you will have plenty to pickle with in the fall; taste it so as not to add cider too fast. Have a phial with a string attached to it that you can put in at the bung. You should have a barrel of good hard cider before you begin to make vinegar. If you are in want of vinegar, fill a jug from the barrel, and set it in the hot sun, where it will turn sour much quicker. It is a good plan to keep a jug in a closet, where you can empty all the slops of cider and wine; and when you get it full, empty it in the barrel.

After the pickling is done, you can put as much hard cider in the barrel, a gallon at a time, as you have taken out, with a little molasses, and half a pint of whiskey; if you put too much of the latter it will prevent it from getting sour, but a little gives strength to the cider, and the molasses increases the acidity, and helps to color it. If you should have any juice of cherries, currants, or blackberries, put it in, or if you can get cheap sour raisins, they will be an improvement to the flavor of the vinegar; a tea-cup of burnt sugar will give it a good color.

Vinegar made in this way will keep pickles good for several years. If the cider has not sufficient strength it will take longer to make.

To Pickle Mangoes.

Pick your musk-melons at a proper age, before they get too hard; make a slit in the sides and take out the seeds with a tea-spoon; boil a pickle of ground alum salt, that will bear an egg, and let the melons lay in this a week; then make a new pickle, and let them lay in it another week; then wash them, and scald them in weak vinegar, or sour cider, with cabbage leaves around the kettle; put them in a jar, and put the vinegar and leaves in with them; leave them two days, then wipe them carefully, and to two dozen mangoes, have an ounce of mace, one of cloves, some nasturtions, small onions, scraped horse-radish, and mustard seed sufficient to fill them; fill up the inside of each one, and tie them round with strings. Put them in your kettle with strong vinegar, and let them scald a few minutes; then put them in a wide-mouthed jar, and pour the vinegar over; have them covered close, and they will keep good for several years. Large green tomatoes make good mangoes, previously salted and drained, when fill them as other mangoes.

For Pickling Mangoes with Oil and Vinegar.

Cut a square piece out to remove the inside; lay them in salt and water nine or ten days, and afterwards green them as any other pickle. For stuffing, take two ounces of garlic, dried and pulverized, two ounces of horse-radish, prepared as the garlic, two ounces of nutmegs, two ounces of cloves, two ounces of mace, two ounces of whole mustard seed. When the mangoes are large, put a small cucumber, and two beans in each. Wipe each mango perfectly dry before the stuffing is put in; sew each up, and tie twine around it; then put them in a pot, and pour the pot two-thirds full of sharp vinegar; pour sweet oil on the top till covered. The ingredients must be mixed with sweet oil. The spices, &c. mentioned, are sufficient for a dozen mangoes.

Cucumbers.

Gather the cucumbers while they are small, lay them in a jar with salt enough to make a pickle; pour in a little water, and if there is not salt enough to cover them, in a few days put in more. At the end of two weeks put them in a kettle, with cabbage leaves around and through them; fill it up with weak vinegar, and let them scald three hours; put all in a jar for three days, then take out the cucumbers, pour out the vinegar and leaves; put them back in the jar, with some cloves, peppers, horse-radish and mustard; boil some strong vinegar and pour over them.

Small Cucumbers.

Wash small cucumbers from two to four inches long; put a gallon of very strong vinegar in a large jar, with mustard seed, scraped horse-radish, and celery seed, a small portion of each, and a tea-cupful of salt; put the cucumbers in the jar; tie them close. Martina's may be pickled in the same way, or in the old way of pickling cucumbers.

To Pickle Cherries or Peaches.

If peaches, wipe them well with a coarse towel; if cherries, cut the stems half off, but do not stone them; put them in jars, and to every half gallon of vinegar it takes to cover them, put a pound of sugar, and cloves and cinnamon to taste; boil and skim it well, and

14*

when nearly cool pour it over the fruit; for three suc-
cessive days pour off the vinegar, and boil and pour
it on again.

Peaches.

Pick out sound clingstone peaches; lay them in salt
and water for a day, then wipe them on a coarse cloth;
boil up some strong vinegar, with a little ginger, whole
pepper and mustard seed; put the peaches in a jar and
pour this over.

White Walnuts.

Take full grown white walnuts, or butter-nuts, before the shells get so hard that a pin will not run
through easily; put them in a jar; boil a pickle of
ground alum salt that will bear an egg, skim it, and
when it gets cold, pour it on the walnuts; let them lay
in this ten days; then make another pickle as strong as
the first, and leave them in it ten days longer; then
scrape each one carefully, until you get all the rough
skin off, wipe them with a very coarse cloth, and let
them soak in cold water two days; boil them in weak
vinegar, and let them lay in this a week; boil enough
good vinegar to cover them; mix together scraped
horse-radish, mustard seed, cloves, red pepper, onions
and garlic; put a layer of the walnuts in a jar, and
sprinkle the spice over; pour the boiling vinegar over
the top.

English Walnuts.

Gather them when nearly full grown, but not too
hard; pour boiling salt and water on them; let them be
covered with it nine days, changing it every third day;
then take them out on dishes, and put them in the sun
to blacken, turning them over; then put them in a jar
and strew over them pepper, cloves, garlic, mustard

seed and scraped horse-radish; cover them with cold strong vinegar and tie them up.

Black Walnuts.

Gather the walnuts while you can run a pin through them; boil them in an iron pot three hours, to soften the shell; put them in a tub of cold water, hull and wash them, and put them in your jars; pour salt and water over them, and change it every day for a week; at the end of that time scald them in weak vinegar; let them stand in this three days, then pour it off, and for half a bushel of hulled walnuts, have quarter of a pound of cloves, a tea-cup of mustard seed, two spoonsful of black pepper, a pint of scraped horse-radish, two pods of red pepper, some sliced onions and garlic; put these in the jars with the walnuts, and fill them up with strong cold vinegar.

Pickled walnuts will keep for six or seven years, and are as good at the last as the first.

Virginia Yellow Pickles.

To two gallons of vinegar, put one pound of ginger, quarter of a pound of black pepper, two ounces of red pepper, two of cloves, a tea-cup of celery seed, a pint of horse-radish, a pint of mustard seed, a few onions or garlic, and three ounces of turmeric to turn them yellow. The above ingredients should be mixed together in a jar, and set in the sun by the first of July, tied up close, with a block over each jar to keep out the rain. Put whatever you intend to pickle in salt and water for two or three days; then pour boiling salt and water on them; wash them and drop them in the jars of vinegar.

You can pickle any thing in this way but walnuts.

The same pickle, by adding more vinegar to it, will do for two years; if the jars are set by a fire, a much less time will do to take the strength out of the spices; the turmeric should be tied up in a bag.

Tomatoes.

Scald and peel a peck of ripe tomatoes; lay them on dishes, and strew salt thickly over them; let them stand for twenty-four hours, occasionally pouring off the liquor that the salt extracts; then drain them on a sifter, and gently squeeze them, as it is this juice that weakens the vinegar and makes the pickles spoil; take a large jar, put in a layer of tomatoes, then a layer of sliced onions, mustard seed, cloves and white pepper, or whole black pepper; (you may if you like, break two pods of red pepper and put in each jar.) When the jar is full, pour very strong vinegar over, and in a few days they will be ready for use, and will keep all winter. They retain much of the tomato flavor, and should be kept in a cool place.

ANOTHER WAY.

Take small round tomatoes when they are not too ripe; stick them with a needle in several places, to keep the skin from bursting, and let them lay a week in salt and water; then wash them and put them in a jar with some cloves, pepper and small onions; cover them with strong cold vinegar, and tie up the jar.

Pepper Mangoes.

Take fully grown green peppers, cut a slit in the side of each and take out the seeds; make a strong brine and lay them in it for three days; then soak them in clear water a day and night; pack them in a jar, and pour boiling vinegar over them with a piece of alum; let them stay in this three days, when boil the vinegar again, and pour over them; when they are green, stuff them with chopped cabbage, mustard seed, cloves, horse-radish, pepper, and a small onion in each; tie them up, put them in a jar; boil fresh vinegar and pour over.

Observe always to have the kettle you boil vinegar in well cleaned; never put pickles in common earthenware, as the glazing is poisonous.

Onions.

Peel small white onions and pour boiling milk and water over them; when cold, put them in a jar, and make a pickle of strong vinegar, a little mace, ginger, white mustard seed, and horse-radish; boil it and pour over them.

If you want them to be white, do not put in black pepper or cloves.

Mushrooms.

Take the small round mushrooms that are pale pink underneath, with white tops, and peel easily; put them in a jar with a little mace, white mustard seed and salt; cover them with cold vinegar, and tie them close If you put in black pepper or cloves, it will turn them dark.

Nasturtions.

Have some strong vinegar in a jar with a little salt, and as you gather the nasturtions, put them in, and keep the jar tied close.

Cherries.

Take sound morel cherries with the stems on, and put them in a jar; boil spices in strong vinegar, and pour over them hot. Damsons may be done in the same way. A little sugar improves the pickle.

Cabbage.

Take firm heads of purple cabbage, quarter them, sprinkle them with salt, and let them lay three or four days, when shave them fine, drain off the salt and put them in a jar; boil enough vinegar to cover them, with horse-radish, pepper and cloves; when nearly cold pour it on the cabbage, and put in a little cochineal tied up in a bag; it will be fit for use in a week.

ANOTHER WAY.

Cut hard cabbage fine as for slaw; sprinkle salt through it, and let it lay under a moderate pressure for twelve hours; then drain well through a colander; slice a dozen raw onions; have a large jar in readiness, put in a layer of cabbage, strew in some of the onions, a few cloves, a tea-cupful of mustard seed, some whole black pepper; cut six half ripe red pepper pods, and sprinkle in; add a little more salt; boil vinegar and pour on sufficient to cover the mixture.

Cut Cucumbers.

Slice large cucumbers lengthwise—do not pare them—then cut them half an inch thick; if you have small ones, slice them across; put them in a large jar, and sprinkle them well with salt; after standing a day or two, pour off the liquid the salt has extracted; drain them, and wash the jar, and put the cucumbers in alternately, with sliced onions, mustard seed, white pepper, whole black pepper and a few cloves; pour over them strong vinegar, and tie close; keep them in a cool place, but do not allow them to freeze in severe weather, as freezing spoils the flavor of pickles. When pickles do not keep well, pour off the vinegar, and put more on; but if the vinegar is of the best quality, there is little fear of this. Putting alcohol on over paper, will prevent their moulding.

Cucumber Catsup.

Take full grown cucumbers, pare them, and cut out the lines of white pith, which are on three sides; cut them in slices about half an inch thick; to six cucumbers, put one onion, sliced fine; then sprinkle them with salt, placing the fruit in layers, with salt between;—next morning, press the liquor from them; put them in *small jars*, and fill up with strong vinegar, seasoned with pepper, mustard seed, and salt, if necessary. The small jars are recommended—as the cucumbers do not keep well after they have been exposed to the air.

Tomato Catsup.

Take a peck of ripe tomatoes, wash and cut out the stems, but do not peel them; put them over the fire in your bell-metal kettle, cover them, and let them boil till soft enough to mash, when pour them in a colander placed over a pan; drain them and throw away the liquid; then mash and strain the tomatoes, a few at a time, through a hair sifter: this is rather a tedious process; but, as the waste liquor has been previously drained off, the catsup will require but about twenty minutes boiling; throw in the spices before you take it up, fine pepper and salt, mustard, and a few whole cloves, and sliced onions, if you like their flavor; allow a tea-cup of strong vinegar to each bottle of catsup; part of which may be put in with the spices, and the rest in each bottle on top of the catsup, before you cork and seal them.

Walnut Catsup.

Gather the walnuts, as for pickling, and put them in salt and water for ten days; then pound them in a mortar, and to every dozen walnuts put a quart of strong vinegar, and stir it every day for a week; then strain it through a bag, and to every quart of liquor put a tea-spoonful of pounded mace, the same of cloves, and a few pieces of garlic or onion; boil it twenty minutes, and when cold, bottle it. White or black walnuts are as good for catsup as the English walnut, and will keep good for several years.

Green Tomato Catsup.

After the tomatoes have ceased to ripen, slice and put them in a jar, with salt scattered through them; let them stand two days, then drain them in a colander; put them in the jars they are to remain in, strewing sliced onions, cloves, whole pepper, mustard seed, and one or two red pepper pods through them; boil vinegar enough to cover them and pour over; tie them close and put a plate on each jar.

Mushroom Catsup.

Take the largest mushrooms, those that are begining to turn dark, cut off the roots, put them in a stone jar, with some salt; mash them and cover the jar; let them stand two days, stirring them several times a day; then strain and boil the liquor, to every quart of which, put a tea-spoonful of whole pepper and the same of cloves, and mustard seed, and a little ginger; when cold, bottle it, leaving room in each bottle for a tea-cupful of strong vinegar, and a table-spoonful of brandy; cork them up and seal them over.

Tomato Sauce,

Scald and peel a peck of ripe tomatoes; cut them in slices and lay them on a large dish; cover well with salt each layer; the next morning put the tomatoes in a colander or on a sifter, and drain off all the liquid; then mash them with a wooden masher, and to each quart, put a pint of strong vinegar, two table-spoonsful of white mustard seed, a dozen cloves, a dozen grains of black pepper, an onion sliced and chopped, a table-spoonful of salt; if mashed fine you can pour it out of wide-mouthed bottles; put a table-spoonful of spirits in each bottle at the top; cork tight, and seal. If you prefer putting the sauce in small stone jars, put spirits on paper at the top of each.

Spiced Peaches,

Take nine pounds of good ripe peaches, rub them with a coarse towel, and halve them; put four pounds of sugar and a pint of good vinegar in your preserving kettle, with cloves, cinnamon and mace; when the syrup is formed, throw in the peaches, a few at a time, so as to keep them as whole as may be; when clear, take them out and put in more; boil the syrup till quite rich, and then pour it over the peaches. Cherries may be done in the same way.

Mushroom Sauce,

Gather large mushrooms, that have not turned dark, peel them and cut off the stems; put them in a pan and strew salt over each layer; when all are in, mash them well; then put them in a jar, put a plate on the top,

15

and set it in a pot of cold water; let it heat gradually, and boil for fifteen or twenty minutes; to each quart of the pulp put three tea-cupsful of strong vinegar, two tea-spoonsful of powdered mace, or one of cloves, two of white mustard seed, one of black pepper; put it in jars or wide-mouthed bottles, with a spoonful of alcohol at the top of each, and secure it from the air. This is by some preferred to the catsup.

TO CURE BACON, BEEF, PORK, SAUSAGE, &c.

To Cure Bacon.

To one thousand weight of pork, put one bushel of fine salt, one pound and a half of saltpetre rolled fine and mixed with the salt; rub this on the meat and pack it away in a tight hogshead; let it lay for six weeks, then hang it up and smoke it with hickory wood, every day for two weeks, and afterwards two or three times a week for a month; then take it down and rub it all over with hickory ashes, which is an effectual remedy against the fly or skipper. When the weather is unusually warm at the time of salting your pork, more care is requisite to preserve it from taint. When it is cut up, if it seems warm, lay it on boards, or on the bare ground, till it is sufficiently cool for salting; examine the meat tubs or casks frequently, and if there is an appearance of mould, strew salt over; if the weather has been very warm after packing, and on examining, you should find evidence of its spoiling, lose no time in unpacking the meat; for a hogshead of hams and shoulders that are in this state, have six pounds of brown sugar, three pounds of salæratus, mixed with half a bushel of salt; rub each piece with this, and as you pack it in the hogshead, (which should be well washed and cleaned,) sprinkle a little coarse salt over each layer of pork, and also on the bottom of the hogshead. I have known this plan to save a large quantity of pork, that would have been unfit for use, if it had not been discovered and attended to in time. Some persons use crushed charcoal to purify their meat. Shoulders are more easily affected than hams, and if the weather is warm the ribs should be cut out of the shoulders. Jowls also require particular care; black pepper, about a pound to a hogshead, sprinkled on the meat before it is hung up to smoke, is valuable as a preventive where flies are troublesome; have a large pepper-box kept for the purpose, and dust every part that is exposed; pepper is also good to put on beef before it is hung up to dry; wash it off before cooking, and it does not injure the flavor.

To Pickle Pork.

Take out all the ribs, and cut it in pieces of about three pounds each; pack it in a tight barrel, and salt it well with coarse salt; boil a very strong pickle made of coarse salt, and when it is cold pour it over the meat, and put a weight on the top; if you wish pork to keep, do not put saltpetre in, as it injures the flavor.

To Cure Hams and Shoulders.

To cure five hundred weight of hams and shoulders, take fifteen quarts of common salt, one pound and a half of saltpetre rolled fine, half a pound of red pepper pods chopped fine, and four quarts of molasses; mix them all together and rub the meat well; pack it down; cover it close, and let it remain six weeks; then hang it up and smoke it with green hickory wood for three weeks. If there is a damp spell of weather, it is best to make a fire in your meat-house occasionally through the summer, to keep the meat from moulding.

To Make a Pickle for Chines.

Rub the chines with fine salt, and pack them in a tight barrel; make a pickle of coarse salt, strong enough to bear an egg; boil and skim it, and when nearly cold pour it on; let there be enough to cover them, and put a weight on the top. Chines are good smoked.

It is best to make a separate pickle for the heads; wash and scrape them, cut off the ears and noses, and take out the eyes. The jowls may be packed and smoked with the bacon.

Sausage Meat, &c.

Separate the tender parts of the meat from the rough and bony pieces, and chop each sort separately; to twenty-two pounds of meat have half a pound of salt, three heaped table-spoonsful of sage, three of pepper, and two of thyme. If you have a box large enough to hold this quantity, sprinkle it over the meat before it is chopped, and it will be thoroughly mixed by the time it is done. It is best to have a small piece fried to taste, and if it is not seasoned right, it can be altered; you should have some pieces of fat, chopped in with the meat.

The sage and thyme should be carefully dried, but not heated too much, neither should it be hung up too near the fire, as it would spoil the flavor; rub it through a wire sifter, and if that should not make it fine enough, pound it in a mortar or grind it in your pepper mill. The pepper should be ground and ready some days before it is needed, as the pork season in the country is (while it lasts) one of the busiest in the year; every thing should be prepared before hand that you possibly can. It is a good plan to have plenty of bread and pies baked, and a quantity of apples stewed, vegetables washed and ready to cook, so that every member of the family, that is able, may devote herself to the work of putting away the meat which is of so much importance for the coming year; while some are cutting up the fat to render into lard, others may be employed in assorting the sausage meat, and cutting it into small pieces for the chopping machine, by trimming off every part that can be spared. You can have one hundred pounds of sausage from twelve hundred weight of pork, and since the introduction of sausage choppers, a great deal more sausage is made, than formerly, by the old method. Clean a few of the maws, and soak them in salt and water, and fill them with sausage meat; sew them close; let them lay in pickle for two weeks; then hang them up, and when your meat is smoked, let them have a few days smoke. In this way sausage will keep all summer, and is very nice when boiled slowly for several hours, and eaten cold. The best fat to chop in with sausage is taken from the chines or back bones. To keep sausage for present use, put it in small stone pans, and pour melted lard over the top; for later in the season, make muslin bags that will hold about three pounds, with a loop sewed on to hang them up by; fill them with meat, tie them tight, and hang them in a cool airy place; they will keep in this

15*

way till August; when you want to fry them, rip part of the seam, cut out as many slices as you want, tie up the bag and hang it up again. If you have a large quantity, a sausage chopper is a great convenience.

Liver Sausage.

Take four livers, with the lights and hearts; have two heads cleaned, and boil them with any scraps, or skinny pieces you have; skim the pot; take out the livers when they are done, and let the heads boil longer; when they are done, pick out the bones, and chop all together; season with sage, thyme, sweet marjoram, salt and pepper; put it in pans, and fry it as sausage.

Bologna Sausage.

Chop ten pounds of beef, with two pounds and a half of the fat of fresh pork; pound one ounce of mace, and one of cloves, and mix in; let it stand a day, then stuff it in large skins; let them lay in brine ten days, then hang them up to smoke a few days; they can be put in the same brine with beef or tongues.

Hogs' Head Cheese.

Take off the ears and noses of four heads, and pick out the eyes, and lay them in salt and water all night; then wash and put them on to boil; take out the bones carefully, chop and season them well, and pack it in bowls; they will turn out whole, and may be eaten cold with vinegar, or fried as sausage.

Pigs' Feet.

Pigs' feet should be well cleaned by dipping them in scalding water, and scraping off the hairs; leave them in weak salt and water two days, changing it each day; if you wish to boil them for souse, they are now ready; but if the weather is cold they will keep in this a month. They should be kept in a cold place, and if they are frozen there is no danger of their spoiling; but if there comes on a thaw, change the salt and water; soak them in fresh water all night before you boil them. In this way they are good to eat with pepper and vinegar while hot, or may be dipped in batter and fried after they are cold.

To make Souse.

Boil the feet till the bones come out easily, and pick out all the large bones; pack them in a stone pan with pepper and salt, and cover it with vinegar; they may be eaten cold, or dipped in flour and fried. Another way is to pick out all the bones, season them with salt, pepper and sage, and warm them up as you want to use them.

Pigs' feet, after being boiled, are very nice stewed as terrapins; make the gravy with butter and water; they are nourishing food for delicate persons.

Vessels for salting meat should be cleaned well after the meat is hung up, and set on boards in the cellar; if they do not smell sweet, they should be washed and soaked before meat is packed in them again. You should see that the hoops are sound, and have covers made to fit them. If taken care of in this way, they will last a number of years.

Scrapple.

Take eight pounds of scraps of pork, that will not do for sausage; boil it in four gallons of water; when tender, chop it fine, strain the liquor and pour it back into the pot; put in the meat; season it with sage, summer savory, salt and pepper to taste; stir in a quart of corn meal; after simmering a few minutes, thicken it with buckwheat flour very thick; it requires very little cooking after it is thickened, but must be stirred constantly.

Dried Beef.

An experienced housekeeper has furnished the following method for curing and drying beef, which will keep good for two years, without being injured by must or fly, and is much admired. Have the rounds divided, leaving a piece of the sinew to hang up by; lay the pieces in a tub of cold water for an hour; then rub each piece of beef that will weigh fifteen or twenty pounds, with a handful of brown sugar and a table-spoonful of saltpetre, pulverized, and a pint of fine salt; sprinkle fine salt in the bottom of a clean tight barrel, and lay the pieces in, strewing a little coarse salt between each piece; let it lay two days; then make the brine in a clean tub, with cold water and ground alum salt—stir it well; it must be strong enough to bear an egg half up; put in half a pound of best brown sugar and a table-spoonful of saltpetre to each gallon of the salt and water; pour it over the beef; put a clean large stone on the top of the meat to keep it under the pickle, (which is very important;) put a cover on the barrel; examine it occasionally to see that the pickle does not leak,—and if it should need more, add of the same strength; let it stand six weeks, when hang it up in the smoke-house, and after it has drained, smoke it moderately for ten days; it should then hang in a dry place; before cooking, let it soak for twenty-four hours: a piece that weighs fifteen or twenty pounds should boil two hours—one half the size, one hour, and a small piece should soak six or twelve hours, according to size. Beef cured in this way will make a nice relish, when thinly sliced and eaten cold, for breakfast or tea, or put between slices of bread and butter for lunch; it will keep for several weeks,—and persons of delicate stomachs can sometimes relish a thin slice, eaten cold, when they cannot retain hot or rich food.

This receipt will answer for all parts of the beef, to be boiled for the dinner table through the summer.

To Cure Beef.

Make a pickle of six quarts of salt, six gallons of water, half a pound of saltpetre, and three of sugar, or half a gallon of molasses; pack the beef in a barrel, with fine and coarse salt mixed; when the pickle is cold, pour it over, and put a weight on the top; let it stay two weeks, when you can hang it up and smoke it, to boil through the summer; or boil the pickle over again, and leave it in till you want to use it: this is for two hundred pounds.

A New Method of Curing Beef.

Take six gallons of water, nine pounds of salt, (fine and coarse mixed,) three pounds of sugar, one quart of molasses, three ounces of saltpetre, and one ounce of pearl-ash or salæratus; boil and skim it well, and let it stand till entirely cold, when pour it on beef that has been sprinkled with salt for several days. You can boil of this beef from the brine all winter, or hang it up, and smoke it with your bacon.

To Cure a Dozen Tongues.

Soak the tongues an hour in a tub of cold water to extract the blood, and cut off most of the root; mix together a quarter of a pound of saltpetre, finely powdered, one pound of brown sugar, and a pint of salt; rub the tongues with this, and put them in a tight barrel; then make a pickle that will bear an egg, which pour over them; turn them every three days, and let them stay in the pickle two weeks; then smoke them two days, and hang them up in a dry place; boil and skim the pickle that the tongues have been in, and it will do for a round of beef.

Pickle for Two Rounds of Beef.

Cut the rounds in a suitable shape for drying; mix together two pints of salt, one of molasses, or a pound of sugar, and half a pound of saltpetre; rub them with this, and pack them in a tight vessel; make a pickle that will bear an egg, and pour it over; put a weight on the top, and let it lay for ten days, when take it out, and smoke it two days; hang it up in a dry place; it will be fit to slice and broil in a week; or cut it very thin, and stew or fry it with butter and cream. Legs of mutton may be salted as rounds of beef, and will resemble venison, when dried and chipped.

In preparing pickle for any kind of meat, observe that one gallon of water will hold, in solution, a quart of salt and two ounces of saltpetre.

To Corn Beef, Pork or Mutton.

Rub the meat well with salt, and pack it in a tub. If the weather is warm, it will require a good deal of salt, but no saltpetre.

To Restore Meat that has been kept too long.

When meat has been kept too long in summer, it may be improved by putting it in sour milk for several hours, or washing it in vinegar is good, some hours before it is cooked; you must wash it well in cold water several times; if it lays all night in sour milk, or salt and vinegar, it should be put in soak early in the morning in cold water. In very hot weather, when you have fresh meat, fowls, or fish left at dinner, sprinkle them with strong vinegar, salt and pepper; warm this up the next day, either as a fry or stew; the vinegar will evaporate, and not injure the taste. Cold rock fish is good, seasoned with salt, pepper and vinegar, to use as a relish for breakfast or tea.

To Keep Meat Fresh.

Where persons live a distance from market, and have no fresh meat but what they kill, it is important to know how to keep it fresh. In winter, if it is hung up in an out-house, it will keep very well for six weeks, or more; when it has once frozen, it is safe till a thaw comes on, when rub it with salt. In the summer, if you have an ice-house, you can keep it without trouble. If rubbed with salt, and pinned in a cloth, it will keep in the cellar two days; or by lowering it down your well, attached to a rope, and changing the cloth every other day, it will keep good a week in hot weather.

To Put up Herring and Shad.

Those that put up their own fish should be careful to have the barrels tight and well cleaned; if the pickle leaks from them, they are liable to spoil. Scale the fish and wash them, as it will save much time; when you prepare them for cooking, take out the gills, but leave on the heads of herrings.

The heads should be taken off the shad, and split them down the back; put a layer of fish, then a layer of ground alum salt,—and after they are packed, put on a weight to keep them down. If herring are well cured, they will be good at the end of two years.

To Put up Herring,
According to the Harford Mode.

First put the herring into the brine left from curing bacon; or, if you have none of that description, make a brine that will bear an egg, and let them remain in it thirty or forty hours; then, if for pickled herring, change them into new brine, which must also bear an egg, and head them up to keep. If for red herring, hang them up, and smoke them thoroughly. A little saltpetre, added to the brine, is an improvement. It is better to take out the roe.

BUTTER, CHEESE, COFFEE, TEA, &c.

Butter.

It is of the first importance that every thing connected with milk and butter should be kept clean; if the milk acquires an unpleasant taste, it communicates it to the butter. Tin pans are best to keep milk in, and they should be painted on the outside to keep them from rusting when they are put in water.

In summer, milk should be kept as cool as possible; before it is strained, the pans and strainer should be rinsed with cold water, and the milk not covered until it is cold; as soon as the cream rises sufficiently, it should be skimmed, and put in a large tin bucket with

a lid that fits down tight, and stirred every day. Butter will be spoiled by neglecting to stir the cream; a
yellow scum will form on it, which gives it an unpleasant taste. And if you leave a pan of milk till the
cream is covered with spots of mould, you had better
throw it away than put it in, as it will spoil the taste
of a whole churning.

If you have no way of keeping your cream cool in
hot weather, it ought to be churned twice a week; the
earlier in the morning the better. Always put cold
water in your churn the night before you use it, and
change it in the morning just before you put in the
cream. When the butter is gathering, take off the lid
of the churn to let the heated air escape, and move it
gently; have your butter-ladle and pan scalded and
cooled; take out the butter and work it till all the milk
is out; scrape some lumps of salt, and work in; cover
it up, and set away in a cool place till the next morning,
when work it again.

If you have neither an ice, or spring-house, a box by
the side of the pump, with a cover over it, is very
convenient to put cream and butter down the well;
put them in tin kettles with covers to fit tight, and
fasten them to strong tarred ropes twenty feet long.
The air of a well will keep butter sweet for several
weeks in the hottest weather. It is best to have one
kettle or basket to put the butter in that is used at the
table; it should be deep enough to hold five or six
plates, each covered with a saucer. It can be kept in
this way as firm and sweet as in an ice-house. You
can have a separate kettle to put a large lump of butter
in for seasoning vegetables. If you print butter for
home use, it is not necessary to weigh it; make it out
in little lumps that will weigh about half a pound; scald

16

the print and ladle, and put them in cold water; as you print each lump, lay it on a dish.

In winter it is more difficult to have good butter, as much depends on the food of the cows; the milk should be kept in a cellar, where it will not freeze; if you have a safe to keep it in, it need not be covered. Cream takes much longer to rise in winter; after it has stood two days, to put it on the top of a moderately heated stove will assist it; when it is hot, set it away to skim the next day, when the cream will be thick and rich, and churns easier.

If the weather is very cold, and the cream has been chilled, have a large pot of water over the fire, set in the bucket when it is near boiling heat, and keep stirring till it is milk-warm; have the churn scalded and put it in; by churning steadily, it will come as quick as in summer; one good working answers very well for butter in winter; always scald the churn before you put in the cream in cold weather.

To put up Butter for Winter.

Work it well, and salt it rather more than for table use, and pack it in stone pans or jars, with a thin cloth on the top, and salt on it an inch thick; keep it in a cool place, and if it is sweet when made, it will keep good till spring. It should be tied up with paper to exclude the air.

To Cure Butter that will keep for a Length of Time.

Reduce separately to a fine powder two pounds of the best fine salt, one pound of loaf-sugar and half a pound of saltpetre. Sift these ingredients one above another, on a large sized sheet of paper, then mix them well together; keep this mixture covered up close in a nice jar, and placed in a dry closet.

When your butter is worked and salted in the usual way, and ready to put in the jars, use one ounce of this composition to every pound of butter; work it well into the mass.

Butter cured in this way, (it is said) will keep good for several years. I have never kept it longer than from the fall until late in the spring, it was then very sweet and good.

It will not do to use for a month, because earlier, the salts will not be sufficiently blended with it. It should be kept in wooden vessels, or nice stone jars. Earthenware jars are not suitable for butter, as during the decomposition of the salts, they corrode the glazing; and the butter becomes rancid and unhealthy.

A friend of mine, and a lady of much experience, remarked on reading the above—"This is an admirable receipt, and by attention to its directions, butter may be packed away with success even in the summer months. Thus in cities during warm weather butter is often cheap, a house-keeper may then purchase her winter supply.

"Select that which is sweetest and most firm; begin by putting a layer of the prints in the bottom of a stone pot, press the butter down close, so that no cavities for the admission of air may remain, then strew more of the mixture over it; proceed in this manner until the vessel is filled, when put on the top a small muslin bag filled with salt, and tie the jar up close. It is very important to keep the butter in a cool place."

A great deal depends on the butter being well worked. Persons that have large dairies should always have a machine to work it. A large churning may be more effectually cleared of the butter-milk in a few minutes, than in the old way in an hour. By doing it quickly, it does not get soft and oily in hot weather.

A Pickle for Butter.

To three gallons of water, add four and a half pounds of good brown sugar, one and a half ounces of salt-petre, one ounce of salæratus; put them into an iron pot, and let them come to a boil; take off the scum; when cold it is ready for use; the butter should be salted in the usual way, and well worked; then made into rolls of two or three pounds each; have little bags of coarse muslin, tie each roll in a bag and put them in a large stone jar or clean firkin; when the pickle is entirely cold, pour it over, and put a plate on the top, with a weight on it to keep the butter under; tie it up close and keep it in a cold place; when a roll is wanted, take it out of the bag, and slice it off for table use. It should be put on little plates, and each covered with a saucer, to exclude the air. If the butter is good when put up in the fall, it will keep till you can get grass butter, in the spring. The jars for this purpose should not have been previously used for pickles.

Cheese.

Persons living in the country sometimes have more milk than they can use, of which cheese may be made. Put four gallons of new milk in a clean tub that is kept for the purpose; skim your night's milk, and put two gallons of it over the fire; when it is near boiling, put it in the tub with the new milk, and the rest of the night's milk; it should be rather more than milk warm, if it is too warm the cheese will have a strong taste. The day before you make cheese, put a piece of rennet three inches square in a tea-cup of water, and stir it in the milk; cover the tub and let it stand in a warm place; when the curd begins to form, cut it in squares with a long wooden knife, and spread a thin towel over it. When the whey comes through the cloth, you can dip it off with a saucer, then put a thin towel in the cheese vat, put in the curd, spread the cloth over the top, put on the lid, and press it moderately about half an hour; then put it back in the tub and salt it to your taste; mix it well, and if you want it very rich put in a quarter of a pound of butter; it is always better to skim the night's milk and put in butter, as the cream is apt to press out.

Have a clean cloth in the vat, put in the curd, close it over and put on the cover; if you have no cheese press, a heavy stone will answer the purpose; press it very gently at first, to keep the richness from running out. The next morning draw it out by the cloth, wash and wipe the vat, put in a clean cloth, and turn in the cheese upside down; do this morning and evening for two days; when take out the cheese, and put it on a clean board; set it where the mice and flies will not get at it; rub it every morning with a little butter, and turn it three times a day; dust it over with cayenne pepper if you cannot keep it from the flies, and if it should crack, plaster on a piece of white paper with butter; it is fit for use in two weeks.

Cheese made in this way has a rich, mild taste, and most persons are fond of it. If you get eight gallons of milk a day, you may make cheese twice a week, and still have butter for the family. You should keep four thin cloths on purpose for cheese.

16*

Pennsylvania Cream Cheese.

The cheese called by this name is not in reality made of cream. Take three gallons of milk, warm from the cow, and strain it into a tub; have a piece of rennet two inches square, soaked in half a pint of water for several hours; drain off the water, and stir it in; when it is sufficiently turned, cut the curd; spread a thin linen cloth over the top, and as the whey rises, dip it off with a saucer; put the curd as whole as possible into a cheese-hoop about the size of a dinner plate, first spreading a wet cloth inside, then fold the cloth smoothly over the top; put a weight on the top heavy enough to make the whey drain out gradually. In six or seven hours it will be ready to take out of the press, when rub it over with fine salt; set it in a dry dark place; change it from one plate to another twice a day, and it will be fit for use in less than a week.

To Prepare Rennet for making Whey or Cheese.

When the rennet is taken from the calf, wash it, lay it on a plate well covered with salt; put more on in two days, keep it in a cold place; in three or four days it will do to stretch on sticks; hang it up in a dry cool place, with as much salt as will stick to it; when quite dry, put it in a paper bag and hang it up; a piece two inches square soaked in two table-spoonsful of water will make a cold custard; the same piece salted and dried will do several times.

Cottage Cheese, or Smearcase.

The best plan of making this dish, is to set the tin-pan of clabber on a hot stove, or in a pot of water that is boiling over the fire. When the whey has risen sufficiently, pour it through a colander, and put the curd or cheese away in a cold place, and just before going to table, season it with salt and pepper to your taste, and pour some sweet cream over it.

Roasting Coffee.

Pick out the stones and black grains from the coffee, and if it is green, let it dry in an oven, or on a stove; then roast it till it is a light-brown: be careful that it does not burn, as a few burnt grains will spoil the flavor of the whole.

White coffee need not be dried before roasting, and will do in less time. Two pounds is a good quantity to roast for a small family. The whites of one or two eggs, well beaten, and stirred in the coffee when half cold, and well mixed through it, are sufficient to clear two pounds, and is the most economical way of using eggs. It will answer either for summer or winter. Some persons save egg shells for clearing coffee.

Many persons use coffee roasters,—but some old experienced housekeepers think that the fine flavor flies off more than when done in a dutch-oven, and constantly stirred.

If you are careful, it can be done very well in the dripping-pan of a stove. Let the coffee get quite cold, and put it away either in a canister or tight box, and keep it in a dry place. Coffee may be roasted in a dripping-pan in a brick oven. After the bread is taken out, there will be heat sufficient; put about two pounds in a pan; stir it a few times—it will roast gradually, and if not sufficiently brown, finish in a stove or before the fire. If you have a large family, by using several pans, six pounds of coffee can thus be roasted, and but little time spent on it.

Boiling Coffee.

A large tea-cupful of unground coffee will be sufficient for six persons, unless they take it very strong, (which is injurious to health;) grind it, and put it in the tin pot, with half a tea-cup of cold water, and the white of half an egg; shake it till it is mixed; then pour boiling water on it, and let it stand close to the fire, and just come to a boil; stir it, and do not let it boil over; let it keep at boiling heat five or ten minutes; then take it from the fire, and put in half a tea-cup of water to settle it; let it stand five minutes, and pour it off;—if you wish it particularly nice, strain it through a thin linen cloth, kept for the purpose; keep it by the fire till it goes to table. If you boil coffee too long, the aromatic flavor flies off.

Tea, &c.

Always be sure that the kettle is boiling when you make tea, or the flavor will not be so good; scald the pot, and allow a tea-spoonful for each person. Let green tea draw by the fire from two to five minutes. Black tea should draw ten minutes, and is much more suitable for delicate persons than green. Persons with weak nerves should never drink strong tea and coffee. I have known instances of persons being afflicted with violent attacks of nervous head-ache, that were cured by giving up the use of tea and coffee altogether; and their general health was also improved by it. Before pouring out tea, it should be stirred with a spoon that the strength of each cup may be alike.

Milk is the best drink for children; but if that cannot be had, sweetened water, with a little milk, will do.

A New Mode of Preparing Chocolate.

Have a pound of chocolate pulverized, and put in a jar, with the same quantity of rice flour, and an ounce of arrow root; put on coals a quart of milk; when it boils, stir in a heaped table-spoonful of the above preparation, (dissolved in a tea-cup of water;) keep stirring it until it boils again, when pour it out; drink it with sugar and cream to your taste.

This is called by some Rac-a-haut chocolate, and is very nice for delicate persons, as well as those in health.

LARD, TALLOW, SOAP AND CANDLES.

Rendering Lard.

THE leaf lard should be rendered by itself, as it does not take so long as that with the skin on. Cut it up fine and put it in a clean pot with half a pint of water; stir it frequently and let it boil fast at first; when the cracklings are light-brown and float on the top, it is nearly done, and should cook slowly; when done, strain it into your vessels with a thin cloth put over a colander. If you put lard in stone or earthen jars, it should be cooled first, as there is danger of their cracking; white oak firkins with iron hoops, and covers to fit tight, are good to keep lard, and if taken care of will last for twenty years.

The fat that has the skin on should be cut very fine, taking the skin off first. It takes longer to boil than leaf lard, and there is more danger of burning; put a pint of water in the pot.

The skins should be boiled alone, and will do for soap-fat after the lard is out of them.

Soak the inside fat all night in salt and water; wash it in the morning, and put it to boil without any water in the pot. It is not so nice as other lard, and should be strained by itself. It does very well for frying. Lard keeps well in large tin vessels with tight covers and is not apt to mould.

Rendering Tallow.

Cut the tallow fine, and put it to boil in a large pot with a quart of water; stir it frequently and keep it boiling moderately for six hours; when the cracklings begin to turn brown, it should boil very slowly till done.

Put a little water in the bottom of your dutch-ovens or tin pans, and strain it in with a cloth over the colander, or the settlings will run through and hurt the looks· of your candles.

Soap.

It requires some care and experience to have good soap; but when you once get beforehand, it is easy to keep up the supply if the ashes are good. The leystand should be made of cedar or pine boards, in the shape of a mill-hopper, and have holes bored in the bottom for the ley to run through; have four posts planted in the ground to support it; let it be high enough for a small tub to set under.

If you cannot have it under a shed, there should be a tight cover of boards to protect it from the rain. Put some sticks in the bottom of the ley-stand, and some straw, and pack in a bushel of ashes, then half a peck of lime, and when it is half full of ashes, put in two buckets of water, and another when you get near the top; pack it well, and put on some more water; then cover it over; pour on hot water three times a day for several days. When you are ready to make soap, have a large pot of water, which must be kept boiling, and put it on as fast as it will bear; save the strongest ley by itself; (if the ley will float an egg, it will answer;) have your soap-fat laying in strong ley through the winter; put a gallon of this in a large pot, and put to it a gallon of the strongest ley; let it boil an hour, stirring it often, then put in two gallons more of strong ley; when this has boiled, put in weak ley till the pot is full; let it boil an hour or two slowly, and be careful that it does not go over; cool some on a plate, and if thick, it is done, but if not, boil it longer. Put it away in a tight barrel, and prepare to make more soap; if you have two large pots both of them can be kept going at the same time. Several barrels of soap can be made from one ley stand. A large oil cask is good to keep soap in. If a barrel leaks, set it under a spout in a rain, or fill it with water. It is of the greatest importance to keep the soap-fat in strong ley. Have an oil barrel in the cellar, half full of strong ley, and put in cracklings, bacon skins, pot skimmings, beef bones, or any scraps; when eaten by ley it will take but little boiling. It is much the easiest and safest way, where there are children, to make the soap without boiling. Put four gallons of soap-fat that has been eaten with ley, in a barrel with eight gallons of strong ley, stir it two or three times a day, for a week or two, then fill it up with weaker ley; you may have several barrels making at a time, so as always to have some for use; it takes some time to make it in this way. But if you are careful, and once get ahead, you need not boil the soap unless you prefer it so; if your ley is not strong, dissolve potash in hot water and add to strengthen it.

Hard Soap.

Have fifteen pounds of clean fat to twenty gallons of clear strong ley; let it boil until thick, when put in half a peck of coarse salt; if it does not curdle in two hours, put in more salt till it does, then pour it out in a tub to cool till the next day, when put on your pot with some weak ley, cut the soap out of the tub and boil it in this an hour; then put it in the tub, let it get cold, cut it in squares and put it on a board to dry. Unless you have plenty of ashes and soap-fat, it is much cheaper to buy hard soap than to make it. If you have but a barrel full of ashes you can make a barrel of soap; bore a hole in the bottom of a barrel, put a few sticks across, when half full of ashes put in a quart of lime and some water; keep the hole plugged up till you are ready to make the soap.

You can have a barrel of ashes put in the cellar in winter to use for washing and scrubbing; keep a tub under it to hold the ley as it drops.

Potash Soap.

Persons living in cities frequently have grease that would do to make soap, but are at a loss for ley, in consequence of burning coal instead of wood. Twelve pounds of pure grease of any kind, put with ten pounds of potash in an oil barrel, and filled with water, makes good thick soap, and is much cheaper than buying hard soap. It should be stirred frequently, and if the ingredients are put together in warm weather, and the barrel stands where it can be exposed to the heat of the sun, without danger of getting rain in it, it will be fit for use in a few weeks without the aid of fire; if you wish to make soap immediately put three pounds of potash, four of grease, and about ten gallons of water in a large iron pot; boil it over the fire, and it will make good thick soap in a few hours; it need only boil long enough to dissolve the potash, which is sometimes in very hard lumps. If you use the crumbled potash, you must put rather more of it, as it is not so strong, and a little lump of quick lime will make it turn quicker.

ANOTHER RECEIPT.

Two days before you wish to commence your soap, pour about two gallons of boiling water on ten or twelve pounds of potash, to dissolve it; then put it in an iron pot or kettle, with ten gallons of rain water; hang it over the fire, and when it has dissolved, pour twelve pounds of grease, which has been purified by boiling in water, (or weak ley,) into a well hooped barrel, (an oil barrel from which one head has been taken, and the bung well fastened, is best;) then pour the water in which the potash was dissolved over the grease in the barrel, and stir it for half an hour; afterwards fill up the barrel with cold soft water, and stir it every day for two weeks. If at the end of that time, the fat swims on the top, beat a pound or two more of potash fine, throw it in the barrel, stir it well, and the soap will be finished.

Labor-saving Soap.

Take two pounds sal soda, two pounds yellow bar soap, ten quarts of water. Cut the soap in thin slices, and boil all together two hours, and strain it through a cloth, let it cool and it is fit for use. Put the clothes in soak the night before you wash, and to every pail of water in which you boil them, add one pound of the soap. They will need no rubbing, merely rinse

17

them out, and they will be perfectly clean and white. This soap can be made for two cents per pound.

Ley and Soda Preparation for Washing Clothes.

To sixteen gallons of water, put one gallon of lime water; twelve ounces of soft soap, or if hard soap it must be first melted, and four ounces of soda; put them together in your wash kettle, and when nearly boiling, put in the clothes, being careful to have them as much of a kind as possible; they should be wet first with common water; boil one hour, then wash, scald and blue as usual. The limestone should remain in the water at least four days before it is used, and be about of the strength of limewater for drinking, and the same stone will do for several times if good. The ley will do for boiling a second set of clothes by adding a little more, and afterwards for towels and coarse things. Prints and flannels must not be boiled.

Volatile Soap,
And Directions for Washing Clothes.

Cut up three pounds of country hard soap into three pints of strong ley; simmer it over the fire until the soap is dissolved, and add to it three ounces of pearl-ash: pour it into a stone jar, and stir in half a pint of spirits of turpentine, and a gill of spirits of hartshorn; cover the jar tight, and tie a cloth over it.

To use the soap, have a tub half full of water as hot as you can bear your hands in; assort the clothes, and, beginning with the cleanest of them, rub a small quantity of the soap on the soiled parts of each article, and immerse them in the water one by one, until it will cover no more: let them soak for fifteen or twenty minutes, then stir them well for a few minutes, and boil them for half an hour in eight or ten gallons of water, to which a table-spoonful of the soap has been added; rinse them, using blue water where it is required as usual, and they are ready for drying. After the white clothes are finished, the same waters will answer for the colored ones, adding hot water and more soap. By the use of this soap, most of the rubbing can be dispensed with, and it is not injurious to the texture of the clothes. It has been proved that the clothes washed in this way are more durable than with the common soaps, and the rubbing required in connection with them.

It is particualrly recommended for washing flannels, and calicoes. The above quantity is sufficient for a family of four or five persons for a month, varying slightly as the clothes are more or less soiled. Its cheapness recommends it to all housekeepers.

Candles.

Weigh the tallow, then you can judge how many candles you can make; six and eight candles to the pound do very well for working and reading by; ten to the pound does to use in the kitchen or to carry about the house. Put the wicks on the rods the day before you expect to make candles, and dip them in a little melted tallow, you can then straighten them out. Have a large pot nearly half full of hot water; melt the tallow in another pot and fill it up, and keep more tallow at the fire to fill in as it is used out; put coals under the pot to keep it at a proper heat. Have poles set on stools about a foot apart, to support the rods; dip the rods in the pot, alternately, until they are as large as you wish them. Wax makes candles burn longer, but turns them yellow. The best way is, to put in two pounds of wax, when you first begin to dip, and it will be used up before they are dipped the last time; when they are done, cut off the ends and put them in boxes. Most good managers in the country make enough candles at a time to last a year. If you have not enough tallow to dip candles, you can mould some; mutton tallow is very good for this purpose.

MISCELLANEOUS RECEIPTS.

Clear Starching.

WASH your muslins nicely; rub hard soap on them, and pour boiling water on; let them lay in this half an hour, or if they are very yellow, boil them in water that has a little blue, in a bell-metal kettle; let them dry in the sun; boil your starch half an hour, as it will be clearer, and the things will take less clapping; rub the starch over the muslin until it is well covered, then clap it a few times; afterwards stretch out the muslin and hold it to the fire until it smokes, then stretch, clap, and shake it until the piece is dry enough to iron. When you begin to starch, have a pile of plates near, and as fast as the things are ready to iron, fold them up, and put them between the plates to keep moist. It is a good plan to have a board about three feet long and a foot wide, with a piece of blanket tacked on round the edges, to iron your collars and handkerchiefs on.

There is an art in doing up muslins, which will take but little time when once it is acquired. The same directions answer for clear starching crape, (which must first be bleached as flannels are done,) and add some drop lake to the blue coloring. In cold weather, to rub your hands over with a little clean tallow prevents them from chapping, and will not alter the appearance of the muslin.

To make Corn Starch.

Gather the corn when it is a proper age for table use; have a large tin grater, and grate the corn into a clean vessel, into which drop the cobs as you grate them until the vessel is about half full; rub the cobs and squeeze them dry as possible, and put them into another vessel of clean water; rub and squeeze them again; the third rinsing will take all the starch out; let it settle, and then pour all the starch together and strain it through a coarse cloth, and then through a flannel, and let it settle until the next morning, when you will find a thick yellow substance under the water, covering the pure white article in the bottom of the vessel; remove the yellow substance and pour clean water on the starch and stir it up; as soon as it settles thoroughly again, pour off the water and put the starch on dishes, and set it in the sun to dry. When you want to use it, moisten it with cold water and pour boiling water on, till it is the right consistency for use. It requires no boiling.

Potato Starch.

Pare the potatoes and scrape or grate them in a pan of water; when this is done stir them well, and let them stand a few minutes to settle; pour off the water and

17*

the pulp from the top; pour water on the starch that
has settled, and stir it up; let it settle again, when it
will be nice and white, and may be put on plates to
dry in the sun; after which it may be put away in a
box or paper bags. It may be used immediately. Stir
it in boiling water as other starch, but boil it much
less. It is said that potato starch will injure muslins
when left to lay by for some time; it is used in some
preparations of confectionary, and answers the same
purpose as Poland starch.

To make Common Starch.

Mix a pint of wheat flour with cold water, till it is
the consistence of batter; stir it into a gallon of boiling
water; let it boil a few minutes, when strain it and mix
in the blue—when it is ready to thin for white clothes.
Some put a small piece of tallow in the starch as it
boils—it makes it clearer.

Washing Calicoes, &c.

Calicoes may be kept from fading by washing them
in the suds after white clothes; if it requires more soap,
stir it in the water, as putting it on the garment will
fade it; have the water moderately warm, and put in a
handful of salt; when all the dirt is out, rinse them in
clean water; starch, and hang them to dry on the wrong
side, where they will get the air but not the sun. Alum
is good to set colors. If you want to wash a calico
dress, which you know will fade, make a corn mush,
and as it boils, pour off half, which use as soap in
washing the dress, and with the other half, (which
should be boiled well,) starch it, and hang it out immediately. In washing bed quilts, to prevent fading,

spread them on the clean grass wrong side up; this prevents the colors running into each other.

For chintz or lawn dresses have very nice starch, and clap it into them, after they are hung on the line; they iron much better this way, and look almost like new; sometimes to wash the cuffs and lower part carefully, and press it all over, will do without washing the whole dress. For ironing the skirt have a narrow ironing board, covered with a piece of blanket, to slip inside the dress.

Table Cloths, &c.

When two or three spots get on a table cloth, dip a towel in clean water and rub them off, and dry the cloth before it is put away; this saves washing, and if done carefully it will look like a clean cloth. If table cloths are stained with fruit, pour boiling water on the spots before soap is put on; when it is so deep that this will not take it out, apply lemon juice and salt; dry it in the sun, and put it on several times. You should always have cup-plates, as the marks of a coffee-cup spoils the appearance of a cloth, and the stain is hard to get out. When table cloths and towels get yellow, soak them in sour milk several days. Unbleached table cloths are very good to save washing in winter, and can be laid by in summer; care should be taken to hang them to dry in the shade, as that will keep them from bleaching. New table cloths do not require any starch, but those that are partly worn look better for a little; every thing washes easier that has starch in. Nice table cloths, and all fine things, after being sprinkled and folded, should be tightly rolled up in towels, and ironed till perfectly dry, they will then retain their gloss. Large table cloths should be brushed clean from crumbs, and folded without shaking, as that tumbles them; those in daily use should be put under a press—a heavy book is suitable, or a board may be made for the purpose; they will keep in credit much longer than when laid in a drawer. It is well to put a common muslin cloth under a damask one on the table, as it improves the appearance.

Flannels.

Have the water in which you wash flannel as hot as you can bear your hands in, and rub the soap in the water, or it will shrink the flannel. The water it is rinsed in should also be hot.

When flannels have become yellow and fulled up, I have often smoked them with brimstone, and they will be as white as new, and the fulled places will open. The best plan is to have a box or chest, with strings put across to hang the flannels on, and a drawer to pull out where you can set in a pan with coals and brimstone. Have the flannels nicely washed, and put them in wet, close it up till you think it wants more brimstone, when you can pull out the drawer and renew it.

After they are bleached, they should hang up in the air to let the smell of the brimstone escape. If you have but a few things to do, you can put strings across the top of an old barrel, (with both the heads out,) cover it with a thick cloth, and lift it up to put in a pan of brimstone and coals. Always wash scarlet flannel with hard soap.

Mending Clothes.

All clothes should be looked over before they are put away, and if any require mending it must not be neglected; a broken stitch that can be mended in a few minutes, if left till it has been worn again, will require much more time. If young housekeepers suffer their mending to get behind-hand, it will discourage them. After mending a shirt, it should be pressed before it is put away. If stocking heels are run while they are new, and the thin places darned in time, it saves much work.

Washing Windows,

A little soda dissolved in the water is valuable for washing windows; do not let it run on the sash, or it will stain the paint; rinse them in clear water, and wipe dry with a clean soft towel. When they are but little soiled, clear water will answer, but if smoked or coated with any thing, soda should be always used. Some persons rub their windows with soft buckskin or newspaper, when they are dry and clean, to give them a polish.

To Make White or Colored Washes, Dyeing, &c.

Take half a bushel of unslaked lime, slack with boiling water, covering it during the process to keep in the steam. Strain the liquid through a fine sieve or strainer, and add to it a peck of clean salt, previously dissolved in warm water, three pounds of ground rice boiled to a thin paste; stir in, boiling hot, one pound of Spanish whiting, one of clean glue, dissolved by soaking it well, and simmering over a slow fire in a small kettle within a larger one containing water; add five gallons of boiling water to the whole mixture; stir it well, and if you are not ready to use it, cover it close. It should be put on quite hot; for this purpose, it can be kept in a kettle on a portable furnace. Coloring matter may be added to make any shade desired. Spanish brown stirred in will make a pink color, more or less deep according to the quantity; a delicate tinge of this is very pretty for inside walls. Indigo mixed with the Spanish brown makes a delicate purple, or alone with the mixture, a pale blue. Lamp-black, in moderate quantity, makes a slate color, suitable for the outside of buildings.

Lamp-black and Spanish brown together, produce a reddish stone color; yellow ochre, a yellow-wash, but chrome goes further and makes a brighter color. It is well to try on a shingle, or piece of paper, or board, and let it dry to ascertain the color. If you wash over old paper, make a sizing of wheat flour like thin starch; put it on, and when dry, put on the coloring; for a white-washed wall, make a sizing of whiting and glue water. This precaution should always be taken before using chrome yellow or green, as the previous use of lime injures the color of the chrome. When walls have been badly smoked, add to your white-wash sufficient indigo to make it a clear white.

To Mix White-wash.

Pour a kettle of boiling water on a peck of unslaked lime; put in two pounds of whiting, and half a pint of salt; when all are mixed together, put in half an ounce of Prussian blue, finely powdered; add water to make it a proper thickness to put on a wall.

White-wash for Buildings or Fences.

Put in a barrel, one bushel of best unslaked lime; pour on it two buckets of boiling water, and when it is mixed put in six pounds of fine whiting; fill up the barrel with water; stir it well, and keep it covered from the rain; let it stand several days before you use it, when stir it up; thin it with milk as you use it, and put half a pint of salt to each bucket full.   This makes a durable wash for a rough-cast or frame house, or for fences; the salt prevents it from peeling off.

Chrome Yellow-wash.

Mix four pounds of whiting with as much water as will go over the room; dissolve a tea-cupful of glue, and put in; then wash the walls with this to prevent the lime from affecting the chrome; if they come in contact, the walls will be striped, and will not look at all well.   Mix a wash of whiting, water and glue, and color it with two pounds of chrome yellow.   After walls have been yellow, and you want to have them white, they must be washed over with whiting and glue, and then white-washed in the usual way.

Yellow Ochre-wash.

Dissolve a pound of glue in hot water, and stir into it three pounds of yellow ochre, and one of whiting; mix it well, and thin it with water or skim milk.   It is a suitable wash for a common room or kitchen.

Lamp-black mixed with molasses, and put in white-wash, makes a good color for a kitchen.

To Dye Orange Color.

For five pounds of woolen yarn, have one pound of annotta; dissolve it in boiling water, and put it in a pot of soft water with half a pound of pearl-ash; boil them ten minutes, stirring it well; wet the yarn in soap-suds; put it in, and let it boil twenty minutes; then hang it in the sun, and when dry, if it is not deep enough, dip it in again; and after it is thoroughly dry, wash it in soap and water.

Green-wash.

Take four pounds of blue vitriol, pound it fine, and mix with it three pounds of best whiting, and half a pound of potash; pour on them six quarts of boiling water, and mix in half a pound of glue dissolved in water. Wash the walls with whiting before it is put on.

Chrome Yellow for Dyeing Carpet Rags.

Dissolve the chrome in warm water in an earthen vessel; dip the rags in vinegar and water, then in the chrome dye, and hang in the sun to dry. This color will stand for years in a rag carpet, and is very little trouble. Six cents worth of chrome will dye several pounds.

To Dye a Dark Drab.

For ten pounds of cotton or wool, have half a bushel of maple bark, the same of sumach berries, and a peck of walnut hulls or bark; put a layer of this in an iron pot, and a layer of the wool, till all is in; cover it with water, and boil it slowly for three hours, keeping the pot filled with water; then hang it out, and when dry, wash one skein, and if it is not dark enough, strain the dye, and put in a tea-cup of copperas; put in the yarn, and let it scald a few minutes; take it out, dry it, and wash it well with soft soap and water.

To Dye Cotton or Woollen Black.

To each pound of yarn, have one ounce of copperas, nine of logwood, a handful of salt, and a quart of good vinegar, which boil with copperas ten minutes in a brass kettle; shave the logwood, and boil it in an iron pot; when the color is extracted, strain it into the vinegar; put in the yarn, and let it simmer twenty minutes, stirring it; then hang it in the air, and if it is not black enough, boil it over. You should have a clear day to do all coloring in.

Cedar Dye.

Boil the boughs of cedar in two or three gallons of water, for several hours, in an iron vessel; strain it off, add half a tea-spoonful of copperas, put it on the fire, and put in the articles you wish to dye; let them boil a few minutes, then hang them up to dry. This will dye sage color, and can be used for cotton, woollen or silk, and has the advantage of retaining its color.

The cedar boughs should be used in the fall of the year, when the berries are on them. Pear bark is an improvement and makes the color darker.

To Dye Olive.

Make a strong sage tea, and add copperas and alum till it is dark; strain it; dip the cloth or silk in weak soap-suds, and then in the dye, and air it, till it is the color you wish.

Maple bark and copperas make a good dark color for common purposes.

To Dye Yellow.

Boil peach leaves when they are turning yellow in the fall, with a little alum.

Onion skins boiled with alum make a good yellow.

To Dye Brown.

Take young walnuts, with some of the leaves and bark; wash your wool in soap-suds; put a layer of it in a barrel, and a layer of the walnuts; fill it up with water, and put a weight on the top; at the end of a

18

week wring it out, and let it lay in the hot sun two hours; put it back in the dye, and at the end of another week, sun it again; keep it in until sufficiently dark, when wash it in soap-suds. This makes a pretty brown that will not fade, and is stronger than when dyed with copperas.

To Dye Red.

To four pounds of yarn, take one pound of fine alum, and boil it in as much water as will cover the yarn; put in the yarn, and let it boil gently half an hour; then take it out and dry it; make a dye of two pounds of madder, and two ounces of crude tartar pulverized, and boil it; then put in the yarn, and let it boil half an hour; take it out and air it, and if it is not dark enough, put it in again, and boil it longer.

Brazil Wood Dye.

Tie two pounds of red or Brazil wood in a thin bag, and boil it for several hours in a brass or copper kettle in water; take out the Brazil wood and add a pound of alum, then put the rags in, and let them boil some time; hang them in the sun, and dry without washing them. This will dye woolen *red*, and cotton *pink*. Washing in soap suds will change it to purple.

Lead Color.

Take four ounces of red wood, two of logwood, half an ounce of pounded nut-galls, and quarter of a pound of green copperas; boil them in ten gallons of water, and strain it; wash the wool or cloth in soap-suds, put it in, and let it remain till it is as dark as you wish it; dry it in the sun, and wash it in soap-suds.

Sugar paper, boiled in vinegar, makes a good lead color for stockings.

To Dye Scarlet.

Take one pound of blood root, and one pound of madder, boil them in six gallons of ley, then stir them three or four times in twenty-four hours, till there are signs of fermentation. This dyes ten pounds of cotton or linen.

To Dye Yarn Green.

Take one ounce of best Spanish indigo, finely powdered, and half a pound of oil of vitriol; put them in a bottle, and let them stand in the sun a week; shake it often, but do not cork it tight, lest it should burst the bottle; take four pounds of black-oak bark, and the same of hickory, shave them fine, and soak them till wet through; then boil them in ten gallons of water till all the color is extracted; when take out the chips, put in a pound of alum; shake the bottle of indigo and vitriol, and pour it in; let them boil together a few minutes, and put in the yarn; turn it over several times, and let it boil half an hour; then spread it out in the sun for about an hour, and wash it well in strong soapsuds through two waters, to keep it from becoming tender. This will color ten pounds of yarn. You may have a fine blue color by omitting the bark. It will not answer for any thing but wool or silk, as the vitriol will destroy linen or cotton.

To Dye Cotton Blue.

Boil a pound of chipped logwood in water enough to cover the cotton; take out half a gallon, and dissolve in it an ounce of verdigris, and one of alum; boil the yarn in the logwood water an hour, stirring it, and keeping it loose; then take it out, and mix in the verdigris; put back the yarn, and let it boil four hours;

stir all the time, and take it out every hour to give it
air; dry it in the sun, and the next day boil it in soap-
suds. This will dye six pounds of cotton a deep blue.
After it is done, you may put in as much more, and it
will dye a pale blue.

To Keep Apples in Winter,

Pick them carefully, so as not to bruise them; put
them in an out-house, exposed to the north, either in
boxes, or barrels, or lying in heaps; after they have
been several weeks in this situation, pick them over
and put them in barrels which should be headed; if the
weather is not severe, let them remain in this cold
situation as long as it will be safe, without their being
frozen, then remove them to the cellar. Do not shut
the windows till the severe weather comes on. Some
persons pack them in dry chaff, or sand, and put them
in barrels and boxes in a cool garret.

Directions for Making Matresses,

If you have an old curled hair matress, you can
make two, that will be equally useful as those that are
composed of curled hair, by using cotton and hackled
corn husks, in alternate layers with the hair.

Some persons use a quantity of green corn, and
save all the husks, and strip them with a fork, or
hackle, and spread them on a garret floor to dry; they
are nicer in this state than prepared from the dry husk;
but if you have not sufficient, take the dry husks from
corn that has been stripped off the top and blade in the
field, and have it hackled as flax; for one matress,
have as much as will fill two flour barrels tightly
packed; sixteen pounds of refuse cotton, (such as is
sometimes sold very low at the factories,) and half the

hair of an old matress, (which should be well picked;) measure the bedstead you wish it for, and allow to each breadth of the ticking, a quarter of a yard in length over; for a small matress less should be allowed, and the same in width, (as it takes up in making;) cut the side strips as deep as you wish the matress, fit the corners, cut out a place for the foot posts, or fit each end square alike; after the bottom and sides are sewed together, run a tuck all round to save binding, sew the tick in a quilting frame, and stay it to the end pieces as a quilt; put a table under to support the weight, (which can be shifted as it is sewed;) first put a layer of hair, then cotton, then husks alternately, till it is done; be careful to let the hair be next the ticking; put some all round the sides and edges. When all is in, put on the top, and baste it down with strong thread; then with a chalk line strike across, to form squares to sew it by. Have a long needle prepared and polished smoothly, threaded with twine, or several strans of strong shoe thread; this should be well waxed, and long enough to go through and back again; have tufts, or two pieces of strong cloth prepared, to secure the stitches on both sides; one person should be under the frame, to pull the needle through and put it back; it should be tied tightly as possible; when you have done stitching, the matress should be sewed all round, taken out of the frame and the raw edges bound. They can be made of cotton and husks, without hair, or cotton alone. Those that have sheep can use the coarse wool, (and such as is not profitable for manufacturing,) with the husks, it is more elastic than cotton. Many persons are deprived of one of the greatest comforts in summer, and sleep on feathers, when a little care in pre-

18*

paring the materials, and putting them together would furnish your chambers with the most healthy and pleasant beds; a large cotton sheet should be kept on a matress, or a case made of unbleached muslin, this covering should be occasionally washed and starched. If you cannot get husks, straw will answer, or hay.

To Make a Rag Carpet.

Ten pounds of purple warp, ten of green, four of yellow, seven of red, will make a pretty stripe, mingled and arranged according to your fancy; the above quantity of warp, with fifty-eight pounds of rags will make forty-two yards, yard wide. In most cities warp can be purchased ready colored. A very good proportion is a pound and a quarter of rags, and three-quarters of a pound of warp to the yard. Save all the scraps in cutting out work; have a bag for the purpose hanging in a convenient place, and when you have leisure cut them. Old muslin garments that are not worth giving away, may be torn in strips and colored. In cutting out clothes for boys, from men's garments, there will always be scraps and strips. By purchasing a little red flannel to mix in, the appearance is improved. A carpet wears cleaner to be about one-third cotton, and two-thirds woollen rags to mix the colors. Do not sew a strip that is longer than three yards, and the cotton should be much shorter, as the warp is usually of that material, there is more danger from fire.

To Keep Furs and Woollens.

Crack the grains of black pepper, and sprinkle in among your furs and woollen clothes; after they have been shaken and aired, fold them smooth and put them in linen bags or sheets; keep them in a large trunk or dark closet, and look at them once through the summer to see that they are safe. Tobacco and camphor are also good to pack them in, but the smell continues with them a long time, and is disagreeable to some persons. They should be well shaken and aired before they are worn.

To Keep Curtains.

Take the curtains down in the spring, shake them carefully and brush the dust from them; let them air a day, but not so that the sun will fade them; then fold them neatly, and pin them up in sheets.

Moreen or worsted curtains require the same care as woollen cloths.

To Keep Blankets in Summer.

If you have any blankets that are soiled and require washing in the spring, have it nicely done; when they are perfectly dry, put them on a bedstead in a spare chamber, keeping out one to use on each bed through the summer; spread a large sheet over; tuck under all round, and secure the corners with pins; this will keep them from dust and moths, and makes a good bed to use in hot weather.

Carpets, &c.

When you take up carpets in the spring to put down matting, have them well shaken, and if there are any spots on them, they should be washed off with a stiff brush and dried; if there is oil or grease spilt on them, mix up whiting or nice clay with water; spread it on both sides of the spot, and baste thick paper over it. When dry, fold it up the size of a bedstead, and pin a coarse sheet round it. In this way they will be secure from moths, and the addition of a few quilted comforts on the top, makes a very pleasant bed in summer. The small moth-fly appears early in the summer, and should always be destroyed when seen, as the moth is produced from the eggs which they deposit in woollens; by being careful to kill them when they first come, a house may be kept nearly clear of them. Select the softest brooms for sweeping carpets, as stiff ones wear them out.

House Linen.

Have a book in which to set down all the bed and table linen, towels and napkins; every article of which should be marked and numbered, and counted at least once a month.

To Clean Paint.

Rub some whiting very fine on a plate; have ready some clean warm water, and a piece of flannel, which dip in the water and squeeze very dry; then take as much whiting as will stick to the flannel, and rub the paint to remove dust or grease, then wash it well with clean water and wipe it dry with a soft cloth.

Bran boiled in water, and left to settle, is very good to clean paint; use a soft cloth or flannel; it will take off fly specks and impart a gloss to the paint; wipe it quite dry. Unless soap is used with great care, it will injure paint.

Varnished paint requires nothing but clean warm water and to be wiped dry.

To Clean Bedsteads.

In the summer, bedsteads should be brushed and searched every week; if they are infested with bugs, boil the sacking in ley and water, or put it in an oven, on some boards, after the bread is taken out, to kill the eggs; fill a large bottle with red pepper pods of the strongest kind, and fill it up with vinegar; put this in each crack of the bedsteads every morning, until they entirely disappear; never omit to search the bedsteads longer than a week. It is a good way to fill up all the cracks of the bedsteads with resin soap. After they are cleaned, move the bed from the wall and fill up every crack in the plastering with calcined plaster and water, or putty.

Sometimes bed-bugs are brought in the cleanest houses before the family are aware of it. When persons return from travelling, the trunks should always be examined before they are taken into the chambers, or put away; a little care at the proper time will prevent much trouble. Some persons scald their bedsteads with boiling vinegar; the acid is said to dissolve the shell of the egg. If poison is used, great care is necessary.

It is said that lard is good to use on bedsteads that are infested with bugs; the grease prevents their increase. All the cracks should be filled after the bedstead has been well searched.

To Clean Floors.

Scour all the spots with soap and sand, then go all over with the long scrubbing brush, a few boards at a time; rinse it well and wipe it dry. A floor that has been well cleaned, and dried without being walked on, will keep clean much longer than one that has been half done; too much soap or ley makes a floor look yellow.

Bare floors are very pleasant in summer, and when they get a few spots, they can be taken out with dry white sand, and a shoe-sole, and will not need scrubing more than two or three times in a summer.

Cleaning Cellars.—Rats, Roaches.

In the spring, cellars should be swept, and all refuse vegetables taken out; if left till warm weather, they will become putrid, and endanger the health of your family. The sprouts should be rubbed from the potatoes; all the barrels should be moved and swept under. Have boards laid on the floor for meat and fish barrels, and after they are emptied, have them washed and drained ready for use. Empty flour barrels should be swept out and the heads and hoops saved. Have lime sprinkled over the cellar floor twice during the summer, or oftener if it should be necessary. If the windows are kept shut in warm weather, the air will be unwholesome. Do not trust to servants, examine and see that it is done thoroughly.

The apartments where cold meat and milk are kept should be cobwebbed and swept once a week, and the safe washed out at least that often. If the cellar is paved with brick, keep a part of it washed clean, to set cold meat and milk on; cover them with tin pans and put a weight on the top if rats are troublesome. If there are rat holes have them stopped with pieces of brick, and broken glass bottles; never use ratsbane without the greatest caution, as it is a dangerous remedy. No food or milk should be in the cellar at the time, and keep it locked up all the while it is there. I have heard of lives being lost by it. Have water set about in pans for the rats to drink, and after three days, clear it all away and have the cellar cleaned and aired before putting any thing in it. Several persons have been in great danger from burning the arsenic; when it is used it should be put deep in the ground and covered up.

Mice are kept under by a good cat, and traps. If roaches are troublesome, set bowls or deep dishes, with molasses and a plate on the top, with room for them to get in, and set it close to a wall. I have seen hundreds caught in this way in one night, and it is much safer than setting any thing poisonous about the kitchen or pantry. They should be burnt in the morning, and the dishes set again at night. If you find a closet infested with ants, remove every thing that will attract them, scald and clean it well, and they will soon leave it. It is said that strips of cotton or linen dipped in spirits of turpentine, and placed about the closets, will drive them away.

Mats should be placed at all the outside doors, and at the top and bottom of the cellar stairs.

Putting Straw under Carpets.

It is thought that carpets wear better when straw is spread over the floor before they are put down, and it will prevent the dust from rising so much. Care should be taken to have them well tacked down, as it is dangerous on account of fire. Where straw is used, they may be kept down a much longer time without being shaken.

Picking Geese, &c.

When you pick geese and ducks, have a tub of boiling water; dip each one in, turning it over to let every part be well scalded, and as each one is scalded, wrap it up in a cloth, and when they are nearly cold, pick them. In this way the pen feathers are loosened, and they can be picked much cleaner. Wetting the feathers does not hurt them if they are well dried. They should be put in bags, and frequently sunned. Baking them in the oven after the bread comes out, cures them more thoroughly than any other way.   Turkey and chicken feathers are not so good for beds as goose and duck; they may be picked in the same way.

Marble, &c.

Marble mantles should be washed but seldom; wipe off spots with a damp cloth, and rub them dry. Hearths should be washed with soap and water.   When there is a spot of grease, mix clay or whiting with soft soap, and put on.   Soap-stone hearths may be scoured with soap and fine sand, and washed off.

To Restore Colors taken out by Acid, &c.

Hartshorn rubbed on a silk or woollen garment will restore the color without injuring it.   Spirits of turpentine is good to take grease or drops of paint out of cloth; apply it till the paint can be scraped off.   Rub French chalk or magnesia on silk or ribbon that has been greased and hold near the fire; this will absorb the grease so that it may be brushed off.

To make New Feather Beds.

In making new feather beds, put half a pound of cayenne, and half a pound of black pepper in each bed; this will prevent the moths from getting into new feathers that have not been well cured.   It is best to air your beds frequently, and shake them up, even if they are not slept in.   It is the oil in the feathers that makes them smell bad, and when in constant use the heat of the body dries it up gradually; when beds or pillows have acquired this unpleasant smell, open them and put a few pounded cloves in each.

When new beds are covered with cases, the moth will sometimes eat through without its being discovered. Covers also prevent the air from sweetening the feathers, and when new they should never be covered unless in use. When beds are slept on, it is best to have a thick cotton sheet, or if it is cold weather, a blanket between the under sheet and the bed, and have them washed and aired occasionally.

To Clean Silver,

Wash the silver in soda water, rub it with whiting, and polish it with a piece of dry buckskin. Embossed silver requires a stiff brush. Another way is to let the silver lay in chalk and water for an hour, then take it out, and wipe it dry on flannel; polish it with a piece of buckskin.

Britannia Ware,

First wash it clean in soap-suds, then rub it with a woollen cloth and whiting, and polish off with dry buckskin.

Brass,

First rub the brasses with turpentine, vinegar or whiskey, then with rotten-stone and a woollen cloth, and polish off with a piece of soft leather.

For brasses that have been long out of use, chalk and vinegar may be used.

To Clean Stoves or Grates,

Have the stove slightly warm, and if there is rust on it rub it off with a dry brush; mix some black lead or British lustre with boiling water, rub it on a small part of the stove at a time, and polish it with a stiff brush. If the stove needs but little cleaning, wet the spots with water, dust a little lead on the brush and rub it quickly. The black lead should be washed off several times a

19

year, and then renewed. Sheet iron stoves should be rubbed with a woollen cloth, as a brush is apt to streak. The lead may be mixed with the white of an egg in cold water. Alum water is good to mix lustre; it prevents the stove from rusting.

To polish the hearth of a Franklin stove, rub it over with a piece of grindstone, or use coarse sand with the sole of a shoe; when it begins to look bright, polish it with pumice stone.

Cement to Mend Cracks in Stoves.

Take two parts of ashes, three of clay, and one of sand; mix them well together with water, and put it on when the stove is cold. It is also good to stop a leak in a roof.

Fire-proof Cement.

Slack a peck of lime in boiling water; put into it three pounds of salt, three of brown sugar, and one of alum; mix them well together, and color it with lamp-black or ochre. This has been recommended to put on the roof of a building that is exposed to fire.

To Take Spots out of Mahogany.

Put a piece of paper on the spot, and hold a warm iron over it, then rub it with a waxed cloth. If furniture is hurt with flies, it should be well washed with a cloth, and rubbed with a cork and a waxed cloth.

Varnished furniture should be first rubbed with sweet oil, and then with a waxed cloth.

To Take Grease out of Floors.

Mix clay or fullers' earth with ley, and put a thick coat on the grease spot; scrape it off every few days, and put on more. To put soft soap on the place, and rub it over with a hot iron, will take out the grease.

Wash for Hearths.

Mix red ochre in milk, and put it on the hearths with a brush.

Blacking for Boots and Shoes.

Take one ounce of vitriolic acid, one wine-glass of olive oil, two ounces of ivory black, an ounce of gum arabic, a quart of vinegar, and a tea-cup of molasses; put the vitriol and oil together, then add the ivory black and other ingredients; when all are well mixed, bottle it.

To Make Boots and Shoes Water-proof.

Take one pint of linseed oil, one ounce of Burgundy pitch, two of beeswax, and two of spirits of turpentine; melt them carefully over a slow fire. With this you may rub new or old shoes in the sun, or at a short distance from the fire, and they will last longer, never shrink, and keep out water.

To Make Blacking for Morocco Shoes.

Pound some black sealing wax, and put in a bottle with half a pint of alcohol; shake it frequently, and when it is dissolved, you may rub it on morocco shoes when they are scaled or defaced, and they will look almost like new; dry it on in the sun.

To Grease Eggs for Winter.

In the spring when eggs are plenty and cheap, it is very well to put up several hundred, to use in the winter, when it is very difficult to get them, even in the country.

Grease each egg with sweet lard, and as you do so, lay them in a keg or jar, or old tin vessels that are out of use; put them in a dry closet and keep them covered over; if they are put in the cellar, they are liable to mould, which spoils them entirely. Do not put in any cracked ones, or they will injure the rest.

In this way they have been known to keep a year, and were nearly as good for puddings, or batter cakes, as fresh eggs. They do not do to boil, or make pound or sponge cake, as they lose part of their lightening property.

To Keep Eggs in Lime Water.

Pour two gallons of hot water on a pint of lime and half a pint of salt; put the eggs in a jar or keg, and when it is cold, pour it over them, and put them in a cellar to keep ; be sure that there are no cracked ones. Eggs may be kept a month or longer, spread out separately on dishes, so as one will not lay on another. They will keep best in a dark closet.

To Clean Soiled Eggs.

When eggs are discolored from laying on the ground, wash them first in strong vinegar, and then in cold water, and wipe them dry on a soft towel.

Chloride of Lime.

A few spoonsful of chloride of lime dissolved in some water in a bowl or saucer, is very useful to purify the apartment of an invalid, or in any case where there is an unpleasant smell, of any kind. It is a cheap article, and should always be kept convenient where there is sickness in the house.

To Take Lime out of Cloth.

Lime spots on woollen clothes may be effectually removed, by putting a little strong vinegar on the part, which completely neutralizes the lime, and does not usually effect the color; but it will be safest to wash it over with a cloth dipped in water, and rub it till nearly dry.

Hartshorn and alcohol mixed together are very useful in taking spots out of cloth or merino, applied with something that will not leave lint.

To Take Wax or Spermaceti out of Cloth.

Hold a red hot flat-iron within an inch or two of the cloth, and this will make the wax or spermaceti evaporate entirely; then rub the place with a towel (that is free from lint) or clean brown paper.

To Remove a Stopper from a Decanter.

Wet a cloth with hot water and wrap it round the neck of the bottle; this will cause the glass to expand, and the neck will be enlarged so as to allow of the stopper to be withdrawn without any trouble.

Precautions against Fire.

Perhaps it may not be improper to remark that houses have been saved from being destroyed by fire at night, by there having been buckets of water left in the kitchen.

Never go to bed without seeing that there is a supply in readiness. Housekeepers should also arrange their family affairs so as to have as little going about with lights by servants as possible. Chimneys should be swept at proper intervals, and if you burn them, let it be on a rainy morning and never at night.

19*

To Take Ink and Stains out of Linen.

Dip the spotted part in pure melted tallow, then wash out the tallow and the ink will come out with it. If you get a stain of fruit of any kind on linen, boil a little new milk, and dip the parts in and out for a few minutes; this must be done before any water is used, or it will not be likely to succeed. Oxalic acid, or salt and lemon juice are good, and care should be taken to rinse the articles well after the application.

Herbs, Gardens and Yards.

If you have a garden, be careful to raise herbs, both for cooking and to use in sickness. Parsley, thyme, sage and sweet marjoram occupy very little room in a garden, and cannot very well be dispensed with for kitchen use; and every family should have a bunch of wormwood; it is a fine tonic, either made while fresh, cut fine, with cold water, or after it has been dried, made with boiling water. Tansey is also a useful herb. Hoarhound is excellent for coughs, and is particularly useful in consumptive complaints, either as a syrup or made into candy. Balm is a cooling drink in a fever. Catnip tea is useful when you have a cold, and wish to produce a perspiration, and is good for infants that have the colic. Garlic is good for colds, and for children that have the croup; you should have some taken up in the fall to use through the winter. The root of elecampane gathered in the fall, scraped, sliced, and strung with a needle and thread to dry, will keep its strength for several years, and is useful for a cough with hoarhound. Rue is a valuable herb; a tea made of it and sweetened is good for worms.

It is not expected that persons living in a town

should have room in their garden for herbs, but they are generally to be purchased at market, and should always be kept in the house, as sometimes in the winter they are much needed when it is difficult to find them.

Herbs should be spread out on a cloth to dry; turn them every day; when dry, put them in thick paper bags, and close up the top, so as to exclude the air. They can be kept hanging up, or laid on the shelf of a closet, where they will not be affected by damp.

Such herbs as sage, thyme and sweet marjoram, when thoroughly dry, should be pounded, sifted, and corked in bottles. Parsley should be cut fine with a pair of scissors, dried, and put in bottles; it is nearly as good this way as when fresh; keep it in a dark closet.

Where you have a garden, do not throw away the soap-suds that are left from washing, as they are very good to water herbs and flowers.

It is very important to have early vegetables. A garden that is spaded, or ploughed in the winter, is ready to plant much earlier. There are many things that will bear the spring frosts without injury, and if planted early will be ready to grow when the fine weather comes. Tomatoes should be sowed in boxes or a hot-bed to be ready to transplant.

The scrapings of a cellar are good to put in the garden to enrich it. Ashes sprinkled on a yard, or grass plat, will keep down the coarse grass, and produce white clover.

The grass should be cut out of a brick pavement with a knife, and boiling ley poured on to kill the roots.

Seeds should be saved as they ripen, from the finest plants; they should be kept in a box with a tight lid to keep them from mice.

Greasers for Bake-irons.

Take pieces of fat from the back bone, or chine of pork; cut them in pieces of half a pound each; leave the skin on; salt them. They will do to grease the bake-iron where you have buckwheat cakes every morning in winter, and should be kept in a cool place; after remaining in salt several weeks, they may be hung up in an airy place. This is nicer than suet.

Cement for the Tops of Bottles or Jars.

Take equal parts of rosin and brick-dust pounded fine; a lump of beeswax; stew them together, and keep in an old tin, melting it when you want to seal your bottles or jars.

Cement for Mending Cast-iron.

To mend a crack or sand hole in an iron pot, beat up the white of an egg, and mix equal weight of salt and sifted ashes; work it very smooth and fill up the crack, let it harden before it is used. If it is a large sand hole you wish to mend, put in a rivet and secure it with the cement, if it gets loose it is easily fastened by the same process.

Weather Proof Cement.

Take of fine sand one part, two of clay, three of ashes; mix with linseed oil to the consistency required. Put it on with a towel or brush. It is said to become as hard as marble.

To Cleanse Vials, &c.

Put ashes and water in each one, and boil them in water, letting them heat gradually. Pie plates may be cleansed in the same way. Iron pots that have been used for boiling milk, may be cleaned by boiling ashes and water in them.

Mending China with Milk.

China can be mended if not too badly broken, by boiling it in skim milk, it should be entirely clear of cream, or the oily particles will prevent its adhesion. Tie the pieces with tape or fine cord, put them into a kettle of cold milk, and let them boil two hours, then take it off the fire, and when cold take the china out, and set it away; let it stand for several months. China pitchers, tea-pot lids, cup-plates and dishes, have been used for years after being mended in this way.

Mending China with White Lead.

Take the bottom of an old paint keg, and carefully with a small knife, put it on the edge of glass or china, close the parts together, and place away; if badly broken, mend the small parts first, and set away; then when dry, putty the edges you wish to join carefully, and set on the top shelf of a closet, where it will be undisturbed for a year.

Linseed Oil for Furniture.

For polishing mahogany or walnut furniture, (that has never been varnished) linseed oil has been recommended. It possesses a tendency to harden and become solid, on long exposure to the air. It is this peculiar quality that renders it useful in its application to furniture. Rub the furniture you wish to polish (having previously washed all the wax from it with soap and water) all over with the oil; a small piece of sponge is suitable for the purpose, let it remain a few minutes so as to sink in the wood; then rub it in with a soft cloth, and again with a clean cloth. Do this every other day and your table will soon be fit to use for breakfast or tea without fear of spoiling the polish; when you wash it off it should be done with plain warm water, as soap will injure it. It is best not to use a table till it has had several rubbings wiht the oil, and then apply it once a week. The pores being filled with the application it becomes hard. Always give a table that is in use a rub with a dry cloth every morning.

For Filtering Water.

Put a thick layer of pounded charcoal, (say six inches,) at the bottom of a large earthen flower-pot; over this, lay a bed of fine sand, which has been washed, (to prevent its giving a taste to the water;) pour the water in the filterer and put a large stone pitcher under to receive it.

ON A LARGER SCALE.

Prepare a tight barrel by charring it on the inside, (by having some hickory or oak shavings burnt in it,) then put in half a peck of quick lime, and fill it with water. After the lime water has stood in the barrel for two weeks, it will be ready for use.

This preparation of the barrel is necessary to remove the acid from the wood, which would communicate an unpleasant taste to the water.

Fit a partition in the barrel, (perforated with many holes,) about three inches from the bottom of the barrel, and having put in a tube, to go down from the top through the partition nearly to the bottom, put on the perforated partition some broken charcoal, then finer charcoal a foot thick, then about a foot of clean washed sand.

To use this filter pour the water through the tube, (which should be open at the top like a funnel;) the water runs to the bottom, and filters upward, leaving all the impurities at the bottom.

The pure water is drawn off from the top of the barrel by means of a spile or faucet.

To Keep Water Cool in Summer, when you have not Ice.

Where you live at a distance from water, and wish to keep it cool, put a large stone vessel in the coldest place you can find; fill it with water, cover it with a towel and wrap a wet cloth around it; this will keep it cool for some hours, which is a comfort in warm weather.

To Purify Water.

To put a small lump of lime into your water-cask is useful. Agitating and exposing it to the air, will help to keep it fresh.

Strain muddy water through a sieve, in which a cloth or sponge, (or a layer of fine sand or charcoal,) has been placed.

Hard water may be softened and rendered suitable for washing, by adding to every twelve gallons of water, about a quarter of a pound of sal soda.

Gum Arabic Paste.

Pulverize in a mortar an ounce of gum arabic, pour on boiling water and stir it till dissolved; do not put too much water. If you wish to keep this paste any length of time, put it in a wide-mouthed phial, and pour alcohol over it; keep it corked, and as you use it, you may thin it with water if required; put it on with a feather or brush.

Preserving Kettles.

Bell-metal, copper and brass kettles require very nice cleaning immediately before they are used, or it will endanger your health. Vinegar with salt or ashes should be used; save the vinegar that is left in the pickle jars for this purpose.

To Clean Knives and Forks.

In some families the knives are a great care to the housekeeper, but by proper management it is rendered easy. After using them, they should be wiped with a cloth, dipped in warm water, then wiped dry, (the handles should never be put in hot water,) then polish them with Bristol or Bath brick, which, with the rubbing cloths, should be kept in a small box, with a strip of leather nailed on one edge, on which to polish them after they are rubbed with the brick.

Knives that are not in daily use should be wrapped in raw cotton and then in paper, and if kept in a dry place will not be liable to rust.

To Clean Teeth,
With Remarks on Fixing the Habit, &c.

Pulverized charcoal mixed with honey, is very good to cleanse teeth, and make them white. A little Peruvian bark put in a phial with lime water is excellent to use occasionally by those that have offensive teeth; and tincture of myrrh mixed with a little water, may be used with advantage, to harden the gums. A little Peruvian bark put in the teeth just before going to bed, and washed out in the morning, is an excellent preservative of teeth. It is very important for parents to insist on children cleaning their teeth, at least, it is well for them to begin before they lose their first set, as it makes them last longer, and fixes the habit, which is of great importance.

To Clean Kid Gloves.

Take a piece of flannel; moisten it with a little milk; rub it on a cake of mild soap, and apply it to the soiled spots on the gloves; as soon as the dirt is removed, rub the spot with a dry piece of flannel, and dry them on the hands. Care must be taken that the gloves are not made too wet, or they will have a wrinkled appearance. Dark gloves that are worn in winter, should be exposed to the sun for about a quarter of an hour in the spring, before putting them away, or they will be liable to spot.

To Clean Papered Walls.

Cut the crust off of stale bread very thick, and rub the walls carefully from top to bottom, in a straight line, using a fresh piece of bread as soon as it looks much soiled.

To Take Old Putty from Window Glass.

Warm an iron, and rub it on the glass opposite the putty; this melts the oil, and you may easily remove the putty.

Cutting Glass for Mending Windows.

If you want to cut glass for mending windows, and have no diamond, dip a piece of cotton twine into turpentine, and stretch it tightly across the glass where you wish to break it; then set the string on fire, and after it is burned, break the glass while it is warm.

20

SIMPLE REMEDIES.

THE following remedies are for diseases which occur in almost every family, and have been proved to be useful in a number of instances. As most old house-keepers have their favorite recipes, it is for the young and inexperienced these are particularly intended, and may be used with safety, when a physician is not at hand.

Remarks upon a Deeply Seated Cough.

It is very important to begin in time with a cold. Consumption is sometimes prevented by very simple remedies. To put Burgundy pitch plasters on the breast and back of the neck, often has a good effect; they should be re-spread frequently, and when one part is irritated, change them to another place. Put one on your side if you have a pain there.

Flannel should be put on next the skin by all means, which, with the above simple remedies, will cure a cold, if begun with in time.

I have frequently known new flannel put on those that usually wore it, greatly to benefit a delicate person. The increased irritation of the new flannel acts on the pores of the skin and promotes circulation. Hair soles worn in the shoe, or socks made of flannel, or soft buckskin worn under the stockings, are very good to keep the feet warm and dry. Persons predisposed to consumption should have nourishing food, and not eat too much at a time; they should avoid strong tea or coffee, and drink milk. Eggs, oysters, fresh fish and fowls, are very good for them. Fruit of all kinds is useful.

They should take exercise in the air, particularly riding on horse-back, or take a short walk, but not so as to be fatigued; to work moderately in a garden, when the ground is not too damp, is good exercise for a delicate person; the smell of fresh earth, and of flowers, is beneficial to both body and mind. After taking exercise, a glass of lemonade is very refreshing, and promotes appetite.

If there should be perspiration at night, change the sheets and pillow-cases frequently, and the under garments; air the chamber and bed-clothes every day; if the weather is too damp to raise the windows, shake up the bed, and leave it unmade half of the day, and put it out in the sun occasionally.

By all means avoid strong medicine, or any thing that has a tendency to weaken the body.

Sometimes blisters are used with very good effect; also, rubbing the breast and back with camphor or spirits, or with a piece of dry flannel.

Taking anodyne drops, particularly laudanum, should be avoided, if possible; they may still the cough during the night, but it will come on with increased violence in the morning; they weaken the stomach, increase the fever, and sometimes cause delirium.

Every thing that tends to excite or irritate the mind, should be kept from them. It is very important to talk cheerfully to sick persons, particularly if confined to their chamber, which can be done without lightness or trifling.

If they see gloomy faces around them, it has a very disheartening effect; and, if the mind sinks, such is its intimate connection with the body, that it is hard to raise it.

I have known persons by judicious management to

live for many years, after it was thought they were in a deep decline, by avoiding weakening medicines, taking exercise on horse-back and on foot, and never indulging in a full meal.

Sometimes such persons have very good appetites, and it is a satisfaction to their friends to see them eat heartily; but they should eat something frequently, rather than over-load the stomach too much.

When they come in hungry from a ride, to beat up an egg with a tea-spoonful of wine, and a little sugar and nutmeg put in a tumbler with some milk, and taken with a cracker or biscuit, or a piece of thin toast broken up in it, has a very strenghtening effect.

Persons are seldom benefitted by a strict diet, but it is sometimes enforced till they lose their appetite and cannot eat.

If the weather is so that exercise cannot be taken out of doors, some method should be devised for taking it in the house. Rubbing furniture and playing battle-door, are good exercise for a female, but should not be taken too much at a time.

Men that are confined to the house are sometimes very much at a loss what to do; if such would purchase a few tools, and appropriate a spare room as a work-shop, it would promote their health. I have known men that were but little acquainted with the use of tools, do many useful and ornamental pieces of work, that were greatly valued by their friends; and the exertion kept their spirits from sinking, when the weather was too inclement to take exercise in the open air.

For a Cough.

Take a wine glass of the juice of the green hoar-hound, or if that cannot be obtained, a strong decoction from the dry herb will answer; mix it in half a pint of new milk, sweetened either with sugar or honey; take this half an hour before breakfast. It has been known to cure obstinate coughs, and persons that have taken it for four weeks or more, have gained strength and flesh, and the pain in the breast was relieved. Flannel should be worn.

Elecampane and Hoarhound Syrup,

Put a pint of hoarhound in a quart of water, and let it draw by the fire; put a tea-cupful of dried elecampane root in a pint of water, cover it close, and let it boil till all the strength is out; strain it and the hoarhound together, and put them to boil with a pound of sugar; when it is a rich syrup, pour it in a pitcher to cool, and bottle it. Take a table-spoonful at a time when the cough is troublesome. Sometimes flaxseed is a useful addition to this syrup.

Brown Mixture for a Cough.

Take of paregoric, liquorice and gum arabic, each an ounce, from fifty to one hundred drops of antimonial wine and two gills of hot water; mix them well together, and when cold, bottle, and cork it tight; take two tea-spoonsful at a time; if it should nauseate, give a smaller quantity. If this produce profuse perspiration avoid going in the air unless well wrapped up. This has been useful in the latter stages of the whooping cough.

Ginger Tea,
With Remarks on its Use, &c.

Strong ginger tea, sweetened and taken hot on going to bed, is very good. Where persons have been exposed to the air, and think they have taken fresh cold, keep

20*

the feet warm by taking a hot brick to bed, and do not increase the cold the next day. If it is not deeply seated, taking this a few nights will give relief. A piece of ginger root, kept about the person to chew, is good for a tickling in the throat, which many persons are subject to, when sitting in close heated apartments, in lecture rooms, or places of worship.

Lemon Mixture for a Cough.

Put two fresh eggs in a jar; cover them with the juice of six large lemons; let it stand until the hard shell of the eggs is eaten off; then beat it together; strain it, and add half a pound of rock candy, one gill of brandy and two table-spoonsful of sweet oil.

Mixture of Lemon Juice and Honey.

Take half a pint of honey and squeeze the juice of four lemons on it; mix well together, and add a small portion of sugar; take a tea-spoonful every time the cough is troublesome.

Hoarhound Candy.

Put two pounds of sugar in a pint of hoarhound tea, as strong as can be made, which may be done by drawing two sets of hoarhound in the same water, till the strength is out of each; when it is cold, mix in the sugar and the white of an egg; when it begins to boil, take off the scum as it rises, boil it slowly till it becomes thick, so that when you drop it on a plate, it will be hard and crisp, and pour it out in plates that have been greased with a little sweet butter; when cold, you can break it up for use, and tie it up in a jar. This is quite as useful as the candy you buy, and is much cheaper; it is very convenient for persons that have a cough, to have a little box of this about them to take when there is a tickling in the throat.

Mustard Bath for the Feet—Soap Stones, &c.

It gives relief to a bad cold in the early stages, to soak the feet in warm water, in which you have put half a tea-cup of salt and two table-spoonsful of pulverized mustard, and to drink ginger tea. You may keep your feet in the bath for half an hour, and then retire with a warm soap stone wrapped in a cloth and placed near them. A soap stone, the size of a brick will, when thoroughly heated, keep warm till morning, and is invaluable for an elderly person or one that suffers with cold feet.

Liverwort Syrup.

Make a quart of strong liverwort tea by extracting two sets of herbs in the same water; tie a tea-cup of flaxseed in a bag and put with it; keep it covered while drawing; when the strength is all out, strain it on a pound of sugar, and let it boil slowly till it is thick—keeping it covered to prevent the strength from going off; when cold, bottle it, and set the bottle in a cool place while using it. Take a table-spoonful at a time about six times a day. This has been used for a cough with great benefit.

For Sore Throat.

Make a gargle of cayenne pepper, honey and spirits; or sage tea, with alum and honey; or figs boiled, mashed and strained, and use it once in two hours. If it is very bad, steam the mouth with a funnel held over hot vinegar, and put on a hot poultice of hops, boiled in weak ley and thickened with corn-meal; there should be a little lard spread over; renew it every time it gets cold. Another very good poultice, is hot mush strewed with powdered camphor; put it on as hot as can be borne, and change it when cold. A purgative should be given, either of senna and salts, castor oil, or rhubarb and soap pills. An emetic is of great importance, and has caused the throat to break when persons have been very ill.

Sore throats have been cured when quinsy was apprehended, by using powdered camphor and lard on flannel. It is a good way, when persons are subject to it, to keep an ounce of camphor mixed with lard, in a wide-mouthed bottle, or jar, and corked tight. The cayenne pepper and honey gargle should also be kept ready mixed, and used when the first symptoms appear; or in a violent attack, a plaster of snuff and lard may be applied with benefit, keeping it on only a few minutes at a time. Sometimes a bag of hot ashes sprinkled with vinegar, and applied hot as can be borne, has cured a sore throat in one night. Persons that have been afflicted for years with repeated attacks of sore throat and quinsy, have been cured by bathing the throat, neck and ears with cold water every morning. The constant use of the shower bath is very important. Keep the feet warm.

Molasses Posset for a Cold.

Take a pint of the best molasses, a tea-spoonful of powdered ginger, a quarter of a pound of fresh butter, and let them simmer together for half an hour; then stir in the juice of two lemons, or if you have not these, two table-spoonsful of strong vinegar; cover over the sauce-pan, and let it stand by the fire five minutes longer. Some of this may be taken warm or cold.

For Whooping Cough,

Dissolve a scruple of salts of tartar in a gill of water; put in half a scruple of pulverized cochineal, sweeten it with loaf sugar; give an infant a tea-spoonful of this mixture four times a day, and a child four years old or upwards, a table-spoonful. In some cases the relief is instantaneous.

ANOTHER REMEDY.

Half a pint of honey, half a pint of vinegar, two table-spoonsful of sweet oil, stewed together a few minutes; when cold put it in a bottle, and put in a tea-spoonful of laudanum; shake it well, and give a table-spoonful when the cough is troublesome, and a dose just before going to bed. For an infant of six months, a small tea-spoonful is a dose, and for a child of four years, two tea-spoonsful. Where there is not much fever, a little port or claret wine, mixed with sugar and water, and taken with toast broken in it, is beneficial. Children should be taken out riding if possible, and should be well wrapped up.

For the Croup,

Put the child in warm water, and keep up the temperature by putting in more hot water; keep it in fifteen or twenty minutes, then wipe it dry and put it in a warm bed, or wrap a blanket round it and hold it on the lap; give it an emetic, and put powdered garlic and lard to the throat and soles of the feet; keep up the perspiration, by giving a few drops of antimonial wine every half hour. The next morning give it a dose of rhubarb tea or castor oil, and keep it from the air for several days. This treatment has been very beneficial when a physician was not at hand; and if nothing had been done till his arrival, perhaps the child would have been too far gone to recover.

In cases of croup, to wet a piece of flannel with alcohol, and apply it to the throat as hot as it can be borne, has often a salutary effect, applied frequently. It is also good to use for a bad cold, &c.

Molasses stewed with a lump of butter, and a table-spoonful of vinegar, taken just before you go to bed, and to grease the nose, forehead and breast with mutton tallow, will sometimes cure a child without any thing else. To pound garlic in a rag and squeeze out the juice, mix it with molasses, and give a tea-spoon-ful at a time, has given relief when a child was very ill. Sliced onions, or garlic stewed with sugar and water, or molasses, is very good to take for a cold. Where children are subject to the croup, you should always have a pot of water over the fire, and light-wood near, to heat it as quick as possible. Children that are subject to these attacks should have their feet kept warm and dry, and always wear flannel next to the skin.

It is the duty of parents to make use of the most simple remedies, which may always be in readiness, and, if applied in time, may prevent the necessity of giving strong medicines, which injure the constitutions of young children. The least symptom of the disease should be attended to. Lobelia is a certain remedy for croup. If the case is light, a few drops of the tinc-ture, increasing the dose according to the age of the child, given at short intervals, will cause it to vomit and prevent danger; but if the attack is a severe one, you should give the "third preparation of lobelia;" for a child of ten years, ten drops, and so on in proportion; mix it with sugar and water. Every mother should keep lobelia at hand, as it has been known to give certain relief in many cases.

A child of twelve months, may take of the tincture ten drops every fifteen or twenty minutes, till it acts as an emetic, or relieves by perspiration; one of two or three years may take twenty or thirty drops. The third preparation is of much greater strength than the tincture.

Infants' Colic, &c.

Tea made of catnip, and sweetened, given to an infant when it appears to be in pain, is often useful. Sweet marjoram tea also relieves pain, and has a soothing effect on the nerves.

To put the feet in warm water, and put a warm piece of flannel to the stomach, is important; but if neither of these relieve the child, put it in warm water for about ten minutes, and cover it from the air carefully; wipe it dry, and keep it warm afterwards.

A little weak ginger tea is good for the colic; as also tea made of dried damask rose leaves; a teaspoonful of leaves will make a tea-cupful of tea.

Uneasiness is frequently caused by their stomachs being overloaded with food, and care should be taken in this respect.

Having lately met with some remarks in the "Baltimore American," with which I am much pleased, I take the liberty of inserting them. "Narcotics and anodynes cannot be given with too much caution; the sensitive and nervous system of an infant should never be acted upon by these powerful drugs unless in extreme cases, and of these, few mothers should presume to judge. Two drops of laudanum, says the London Medical Gazette, have been known to kill an infant; and a single drop, it is said, stole the life of a new born babe.

"The most experienced medical men never administer medicines of this class to the very young, without exercising the utmost caution, and making the most accurate calculations.

"In the present day, the more general diffusion of correct facts in physiology and pathology has caused a large class of young mothers to reject the old system of giving narcotic drugs to infants. In carrying out this salutary reformation like all other reformers, they have a strong opposition to contend with; old fashioned nurses do much harm in opposing all nursery reformations, consequently young mothers will have a hard task to execute.

"Too many have not the steady courage to hold on to the end in mild, but firm opposition to all erroneous, but well meant interference. But there are others whose pure and unswerving love for their tender offspring keeps them firm to their duty; to these the next generation will owe much. They are the little band of true-hearted reformers, whose good example will be like leaven, spreading until its influence is felt throughout the wide circle of maternal responsibility."

Summer Diseases.

The food of children in summer, should be light and nourishing; if of milk, be careful that it is sweet. If you cannot get it fresh as often as you want it, boiling will keep it sweet. Sour milk and improper food sometimes bring on the summer disease, which is easier prevented than cured.

A little rhubarb tea or tincture, with a small quantity of prepared chalk, will sometimes check it in its early stages, but the most effectual medicine that I have tried is called by some apothecaries, "red mixture," of which I will give a recipe.

Chicken water, slightly salted, is very good; make but a little at a time, and have it fresh.

Rice gruel, sweetened with loaf-sugar, and a little nutmeg, is nourishing. To make a drink of slippery-elm, shave the bark fine and put it in water; strain it, mix it with milk, and sweeten it. Elderberry and blackberry cordials are also good in cases where there is no fever.

The stomach and back should be bathed with spirits; and a little bag of pounded spices, wet with spirits, applied to the stomach, may be used with safety, when not within reach of a physician.

A bark jacket has been used with success in many instances; cut it out of fine muslin, to be double, spread it open, and cover one side with about two ounces of the best Lima bark, and twelve pounded cloves; put on the other side, sew it up, and quilt it across; put on shoulder straps and strings of soft ribbon; sprinkle it with spirits twice a day.

The child should have the benefit of the morning and evening air. If it is not convenient to ride it out, walking will answer, in the arms of a careful nurse, carried on a pillow, with an umbrella to protect its eyes from the light.

When a child is taken sick in a city, removing it to the country often has a beneficial effect. Milk thickened with arrow root is good diet for children. Flour dried in an oven for several hours, and used to thicken milk or water, is also good, sweetened with loaf-sugar, and is nutritious. They should eat but a small portion of any thing at a time.

21

To cut slices of lean fresh beef or mutton, put it in a bowl, and pour a pint of boiling water on it, and let it set close to the fire for an hour, is very good to give children occasionally, with but little salt; the stomach will sometimes retain this when other things are rejected. As thirst is an attendant on this disease, much salt should be avoided in all their food. Every thing about a sick child should be kept clean, and its clothes well aired before changing them. If it is too ill to carry out of doors, have it changed from one room to another, and the apartment it left well aired.

Children who are afflicted with this disease, sometimes crave fruit. Ripe peaches, fresh from the tree, or ripe apples, baked or roasted before the fire, may be occasionally administered in small quantities with perfect safety.

To make toast-water, the bread should be toasted on both sides very dry, and boiling water poured on it.

I hope these hints will be useful to persons that cannot procure a physician, which is often the case in the country.

Mustard Whey.

Boil a pint of milk, and the same of water, with an ounce and a half of bruised mustard seed, until the curd separates—when strain the whey. This is a most desirable way of administering mustard; it warms and invigorates the system, promotes the different secretions, and in the low state of nervous fevers, will often supply the place of wine. It is also of use in chronic rheumatism, palsy and dropsy.

Red Mixture.

Take sixteen grains of powdered rhubarb, thirty of soda, fifty of prepared chalk, and two drops of the oil of spearmint, mixed in a vial with two ounces of water; keep it corked up and shake it before giving a dose. A child of ten months old should take a tea-spoonful every three or four hours. If there is much pain, two drops of laudanum may be added to every other dose. A table-spoonful is a dose for a grown person.

Erysipelas.

The decoction of sarsaparilla has proved useful in cases of erysipelas. Take two ounces of sarsaparilla, one of sassafras, one of burdock root, and one of liquorice; boil them slowly in three pints of water, keeping it covered close, until reduced to one-half. Take two table-spoonsful four times a day.

While taking medicine for the erysipelas, meat and all strong food should be avoided, and every thing that has a tendency to inflame the blood. Dusting the parts affected, with rye or buckwheat flour, sometimes has a cooling effect, and bathing with camphor or spirits will allay the irritation.

Nettle rash is very much like erysipelas, and the same treatment is good for both. Slippery-elm bark, chipped, and let to stand in cold water till it becomes thick, is a very cooling drink. It may be filled up the second time. Barley water is also a suitable drink.

Erysipelas is frequently brought on by violent exercise, and the perspiration being checked too suddenly. Persons that have once had it, should avoid extremes of heat and cold, and pay strict attention to diet—not eating any thing that disagrees with them. All acids, particulary pickles, are improper.

The stomach should be cleansed by emetics. Small and frequent doses of senna and salts, if taken just at going to bed, will not occasion much sickness, and tend greatly to relieve the system of this unpleasant disease. Where the case is slight, the rhubarb pills sometimes give relief. The pores of those that are subject to it are generally open, and flannel should be worn all the year, to prevent too sudden a check of perspiration.

Magnesia, Charcoal and Salts,

Form a valuable compound for family use: one ounce of each mixed together, and put in a wide-mouthed bottle; it is useful for head-ache, or diseases of the skin. Cases of erysipelas have been cured by its continued use. Take a tea-spoonful of the mixture, in a little water two or three times a day, or on going to bed at night. Persons of sedentary occupations, that are in the habit of taking pills, will find it to their relief to use this simple remedy. It has been found beneficial in cases of tetter and ring-worm in the head, using at the same time, as a wash on the part affected, borax dissolved in strong vinegar.

In cases of erysipelas, the "charcoal mixture" has been used with great benefit; it is excellent for purifying the blood. Take it in small doses for two or three weeks, then discontinue it, and take it again at intervals. If this medicine should be found unpleasant, take a tea-spoonful of jelly, or something of that kind after it. It will answer quite as well to keep the magnesia, charcoal and salts in separate bottles, and mix them just as you take the dose, taking about an even tea-spoonful of each.

For Dropsy.

Put a quarter of a pound of cream of tartar, and a pound of new nails, in a stone jug, with half a gallon of water; let it stand three or four days, occasionally shaking it; take a table-spoonful three times a day, on an empty stomach, and half an hour after each dose, take two spoonsful of mustard seed or scraped horse-radish. If the swelling abates, you may take the medicine less frequently, or omit every other day, but do not leave it off until you are entirely cured. After it has stood some time, it becomes stronger, when you may put in more water. This has been highly recommended for the dropsy.

ANOTHER REMEDY.

Take a quart of gin, put into it one handful of the white buds of the common pine; shake it frequently, and take half a wine-glassful at a time, twice a day, about an hour before a meal, and occasionally eat a little brown mustard seed; this should be persevered in, and has been known to afford great relief, in two obstinate cases.

For Rheumatism.

Persons are liable to have the rheumatism from taking cold in the winter. Where the pain is most violent, put on plasters of Burgundy pitch, spread on leather. Persons that are subject to it, should always keep pitch in the house to use, as it will give relief; a silk handkerchief tied round the joint, keeps it warm and relieves stiffness. If the pain is in the back part of the head, put a blister on the neck, by all means. When persons have a bad spell of rheumatism, they should always take medicine, and avoid eating meat for a few days. Equal parts of rhubarb and castile soap, made into pills, with a little water, is a valuable medicine for rheumatism, and suits aged persons; the pills should be taken at night on going

21*

to bed. They are easily made, and should always be at hand: it is valuable as a cathartic in almost every case where mild medicine is necessary. The use of the shower bath is also beneficial. Flannel should always be worn next the skin, and the feet kept dry. Bathing with camphor sometimes relieves the pain, but there is a danger of driving it to a more vital part. Salt and water is useful to bathe for the rheumatism, when it is of long standing.

Deafness, Remarks, &c.

A remarkable case of deafness was cured by the following remedy: (An aged person, whose hearing had been very good, gradually became so deaf as not to be able to hear common conversation; after suffering some months, the patient thought of trying the following remedy:) of honey, brandy and sweet oil, each a tea-spoonful, warm and mix well together; sew a soft linen rag to the eye of a strong darning needle; dip this mop in the mixture while warm, and put it in the ear; hold it in till cold, when renew and move it gently about; by so doing, wax that had accumulated, hardened, and stopped the cavity, was discharged, and the hearing of the patient restored. Wool should be worn in the ears, and an occasional use of the mixture; also flannel round the head at night. A young person was relieved by the persevering use of the following remedies: Put a small blister of Spanish flies behind the ears, very high up on the hard part, so as to be clear of the leaders, (or it will occasion pain;) when drawn, dress them in the usual way, and as soon as healed renew them; repeat this several times, keeping wool in the ears dipped in sweet oil, and at night put in small pieces of fat bacon that has been boiled, and tie a handkerchief around to keep them warm. When the blisters are healed, the hair should be cut short, to enable the patient to bathe the head in cold water, which should be poured from a pitcher; begin with it a little warm and gradually get it colder; this should be persevered in, even in cold weather; wipe the head and tie it up till dry. I have been induced to make these remedies public, by seeing several interesting young persons suffering from deafness, with a hope that they may be of use.

Remedy for Sick Head-ache.

A table-spoonful of table salt, dissolved in a pint of water, as warm as you can drink it; take at two doses, and drink freely of luke-warm water, until it causes vomiting; put a hot brick to the feet, and avoid the air, which will check the perspiration.

The Oil of Butter.
A Remedy for Dysentery, &c.

Put half a pound of fresh butter in a quart of boiling water, to extract the salt; let it melt and boil up. If there should be any curds on the top, take them off, then skim off the clear butter, and keep it covered by the fire; give from one to two table-spoonsful at a time, three or four times a day.

This is useful in cases of dysentery, and is also soothing to the stomach, after violent vomiting for a long time. Sometimes a plaster of mustard put on the stomach stops vomiting.

For Dysentery and Diarrhœa.

The following prescription from an eminent physician has proved valuable: Take of calcined magnesia two drachms, of aromatic spirits of ammonia two and a half drachms, of water half a pint; mix well together, and as a dose for a grown person, give a table-spoonful every half hour until relieved.

Some country nurses recommend dittany tea, or spice-wood berries boiled in new milk. A large poultice on the stomach and bowels, made of new milk, thickened with light bread, has given relief— keeping it warm.

Be careful to keep the patient's feet warm, and to bathe the back and stomach with spirits. Where the dittany and spice-wood cannot be obtained, other aromatics, as cinnamon and cloves, are good substitutes.

Remedies for the Dysentery and Cholera Morbus.

Take the roots of the low running blackberry or dewberry; make a strong tea; sweeten it, and drink it occasionally. Take a large apple; cut out the core, and wrap in wet paper; cover it up in hot ashes, and when cooked, take off the paper and eat it cold.

Take one pint of good hard cider, that is entirely sound, put a table-spoonful of hot ashes into it, and stir it as soon as it settles; take a table-spoonful once every hour for a grown person, until relief is obtained.

Remedy for the Ear-ache.

Mix a few drops of French brandy with sweet oil and a drop of laudanum, and pour it in the ear a little warm.

Another valuable remedy is to take a few wood lice, and stew them in a little lard, (which should be very pure,) for three or four minutes; then strain it and pour some in the ear before it gets cool.

This gives almost immediate relief. The heart of a roasted onion put warm in the ear, and tie around the head a silk handkerchief, has given relief.

A Wash for Sore Ears.

Make a tea of the black or candle-alder, wet a soft rag with it, and lay it on; it should be applied three times a day, and occasionally wash it with castile soap and water. The patient should take a mild purgative. If the ears are very much inflamed, there should be a bread and milk poultice put on occasionally. Elder ointment is also beneficial.

Weak Eyes.

Make a strong decoction of chamomile flowers, by boiling them in new milk; with this bathe the eyes several times a day—continue it for several weeks; to bathe the eyes in cold water before going to rest, is also good. Pure rye whiskey is very good to bathe weak eyes. Persons that are afflicted with sore eyes, have often been benefitted by putting a small blister behind the ears, very high up on the hard part, so as to avoid the leaders. Infants should not be exposed to the light too soon; it sometimes weakens the sight and seriously injures the eyes. The pith of sassafras put in water, is good to bathe inflamed eyes; a decoction of young hyson tea is also used with benefit. Persons afflicted with weak eyes should avoid a strong light, and should not strain their eyes with reading or sewing at night. I have known small doses of "charcoal mixture," relieve the eyes when there was slight inflammation. Attention to diet is necessary. Fold a linen handkerchief, dip it in cold water, and bind it over the eyes at night on retiring, and you will experience relief. Pain in the eyeballs is also relieved, by gently rubbing the finger and thumb over the lids towards the nose. This was published some years since, and I have known it give relief and strengthen the eyes.

For Worms.

Equal parts of salt and sugar, taken while fasting, are good for worms; a tea-spoonful is sufficient for a child two years old; to take half a cup of chamomile, rue or wormwood tea, with a little sugar, two hours before breakfast, is also good. Give a dose of senna after they have been taking this three days. It is very important to bruise garlic and rue, to apply to the stomach; put it in a bag, and wet it with spirits every day. The garlic and rue is said to keep the worms out of the stomach. Wormseed oil, a few drops at a time, has given relief, but should be used cautiously. Old cheese grated and given to a child, has been known to afford relief: it is also beneficial when a child is seized with sudden illness from having eaten too many cherries.

For Tooth-ache.

Reduce two drachms of alum to a very fine powder, and mix with it seven drachms of nitrous spirits of ether; apply it to the tooth. Alum burnt on a hot shovel, and powdered, is sometimes good; also half a drop of the oil of cinnamon, on a piece of cotton or lint, where the tooth is hollow. Cayenne pepper on cotton, and moistened with spirits of camphor, has been known to afford relief. A poultice of hops applied to the cheek, or a piece of raw cotton with red pepper dusted on it, or a mustard plaster, will relieve a swelling which proceeds from tooth-ache.

Cure for Cholera Morbus,

Put a table-spoonful of hot ashes in half a pint of good hard cider, and give the patient three table-spoonsful of it at a time. This has given relief in half an hour.

Another cure is to take a soft cork and burn it thoroughly; when it ceases to blaze, powder the coal very fine on a plate. Mix a table-spoonful of this powder with a little milk or water, or any thing agreeable to the palate; repeat the dose till the disorder ceases, which it generally does after two or three doses. This has given relief to a person in the greatest agony with the bilious colic.

For Colic.

Drink strong ginger tea, while hot, and put hot bricks to the stomach and feet; if this does not give relief, take a dose of rhubarb or castor oil. Persons subject to the colic should keep a piece of ginger about them to chew after eating; wear flannel next the skin, and be careful to keep the feet dry: they should avoid strong coffee and tea, and eat nothing that disagrees with them. Dry toast without butter, and crackers, are good for persons that have the colic. For violent cases, take two table-spoonsful of brandy, and half a tea-spoonful of black pepper.

For Bilious Colic and Indigestion,

Pour three quarts of boiling water on a quart of hickory ashes and a tea-cup of soot; let it stand a day, then filter it, and if the complaint is bad, take a wine-glassful before and after each meal. This has been very beneficial to persons with the above complaint.

Warner's Cordial for Gout in the Stomach.

Take one ounce of rhubarb, two drachms of senna, two of fennel seed, two of coriander seed, one of saffron, and one of liquorice; stone and cut half a pound of good raisins, and put all in a quart of good spirits; let it stand in a warm place for ten days, shaking it every day; then strain it off and add a pint more spirits to the same ingredients; when all the strength is extracted, strain it and mix the first and last together. Take from two to four spoonsful of this cordial in as much boiling water as will make it as hot as you can take it; if the pain is not removed in half an hour, repeat the dose, and if your stomach will not retain it, add ten drops of laudanum.

Dr. Warner remarks, "after twenty years' experience of this medicine in myself and others, it is impossible for me to speak of it in terms higher than it deserves. When the vital parts are affected, persons subject to the gout should never sleep without it in their chamber."

Cure for Tetter.

Take one tea-spoonful of powdered Spanish flies, put them in half a pint of French brandy; wash the part affected occasionally. This has been highly recommended to me, as a remedy for tetter on the hands, but I have never seen it tried.

For Cramp in the Stomach.

Dissolve a tea-spoonful of table salt, in a tea-cup of warm water; if this does not stop the vomiting and cramp, repeat the dose; this is very useful in stopping the operation of an emetic, when it has continued too long. Flannel cloths dipped in hot spirits, and sprinkled with cayenne pepper, and applied to the stomach, sometimes relieves the pain; a mustard plaster is also of use.

For Cramp.

A foot-board to the bedstead is of great service, when you are taken with the cramp in the night, and by placing the foot against it, will sometimes give relief. Another remedy is to tie a string round the limb, between the body and the pain, about as tight as a physician does to draw blood; wear a bandage filled with pounded brimstone round the limb, to prevent a return of it. Sometimes to hold a roll of brimstone in each hand will relieve the cramp, and persons subject to it should keep some by the bed-side to use in the night.

For Scalds and Burns.

When persons are badly scalded or burned, to put raw cotton on immediately, and wet it with spirits, is very good; other remedies are, linseed oil and lime water; starch and cream; scraped potatoes, molasses, and eggs beaten up and put on immediately. Almost any thing will relieve the pain, that excludes the air. Be careful not to break the skin, as it will be longer in healing.

If a foot is scalded, pour cold water over it and cut the stocking. You should be careful to use linen rags about a burn, as cotton rags cause irritation.

After the place begins to heal up, a salve may be applied, made of equal parts of Burgundy pitch, beeswax, sheep's tallow, and sweet oil, melted together over the fire; renew it twice a day, washing the place each time with milk and water, and a little castile

22

soap. A wash of weak sugar of lead water, is also good for burns. A poultice of powdered elm bark mixed with water, and put on frequently, wetting the sore with thick cream, is also soothing; be careful that the limb does not contract, as there is great danger if the sinews are affected. If there should be fever, a mild cathartic should be given. "Comstock's Pain Extractor" sometimes gives great relief; you may also apply immediately, with benefit, a tea-spoonful of air-slacked lime and a table-spoonful of lard; sift the lime and rub them well together. For a burn by vitriol or any caustic substance, apply whites of eggs mixed with powdered chalk, putting it on with a feather. Linen rags dipped in cold water and changed every few minutes, I have known applied day and night to give relief to a bad burn on the foot; but avoid putting the foot in water, although it gives present relief, it is dangerous.

For Ague.

Take half an ounce of coarsely powdered race ginger, infused in three gills of boiling water; when cool, strain and sweeten it; and for a dose give a heaped tea-spoonful of Peruvian bark, in a wine-glassful of the ginger tea, every two hours during the absence of the fever. To one ounce of best Peruvian bark, add two ounces of cloves powdered, and a half an ounce of cream of tartar; mix them well, and give two tea-spoonsful at a time every two hours: when clear of fever, begin at four in the morning, and give it until twelve at noon. Wormwood seed, a heaped tea-spoonful in a cup of water, as a dose, is also good. A third recipe is to take two ounces of best Lima bark, twelve heaped tea-spoonsful of magnesia, to be well mixed together, and divided into twelve doses.

Take four doses on each well day, at intervals of four hours each; this has cured a number who had suffered with ague a long time.

Chilblains.

Put as much alum in hot water as will make it very strong; put the feet in when it is as hot as can be borne, and keep them in till it is cold; warm it over, and soak them every evening till they are entirely cured; by beginning in time, it need only be applied two or three times.

When blisters are formed, take one ounce of camphor, one of sheep's tallow, and one of sweet oil; stew them together gently till it becomes an ointment, and rub the feet with it.

Take an ounce of glue, and melt it in a pint of hot water over the fire; stir it until the glue is dissolved; pour it out and dip the part that is affected in this dilution until the uneasiness or burning is allayed, which is mostly in a few minutes.

Lock-jaw.

If lock-jaw is apprehended from a scratch or wound, bathe the injured part frequently with weak ley, or warm pearl-ash water; make a poultice by boiling bitter herbs in weak ley, and thicken it with corn-meal; put a little grease in just as you put it on. Bacon skin and the rind of fresh pork bound tightly on, are said to be good.

Falls.

If a child receives a fall, examine every part, and rub your hand on its back to tell if any part is injured. There are instances of persons being cripples for life, from receiving a hurt, that was not known of at the

time.   To rub with camphor and sweet oil, and bathe
the child in warm water, is soothing.

For the Bite of a Spider.

Moisten a slice of wheat bread with sugar of lead, or
pearl-ash water; bind it on, and keep wetting it as it
becomes dry.   If the place swells very much, take a
table-spoonful of sweet oil every hour, till it is relieved.   To drink water with salæratus dissolved in it
has been useful.

For the Sting of a Bee.

Rub the place with hartshorn or salæratus water,
immediately after it is stung, to prevent it from swelling; bruised peach leaves bound on, are also good,
and laudanum, where it is very painful.   If it swells
very much, apply a poultice of onions and cream, or
ley and bitter herbs.

For Bruises.

The oil of St. Johnswort applied on lint, is an
excellent remedy for bruises, and if used immediately
will prevent the blood from settling on the place;
when children get their fingers or toes mashed, this is
very good, and soon gives relief; salt butter is also
very good.   The leaves of the Jamestown weed,
mashed with cream, are good for a stone-bruise.

For Felons.

Make a poultice of quick lime slacked in soft soap,
and bind it on the finger; renew it every half hour.
The leaves of Jamestown weed, bruised with cream
or lard, are also good.   Also, roast coarse salt in a
piece of wet brown paper, or a cabbage leaf, about

twenty minutes; when cool, pound it and mix it with resin soap; bind it on the felon; it is said to be a certain cure. The white of egg, with unslacked lime, has been known to give immediate relief.

For a Sprained Limb.

Strong vinegar and salt, put on brown paper, will soon cure a slight sprain, if applied frequently. If very painful, a bath should be made of bitter herbs, bran and vinegar, put on as hot as you can bear it. Great care should be taken not to use the limb too soon after it has been sprained. Some sprains of several months' standing have been greatly relieved by taking several electric shocks a day. St. Johnswort oil is good to rub on a sprained limb.

For a Sprained Ancle.

Of chalk, soft soap, salt, and brandy, take a spoonful each, and add the white of an egg; beat the mixture, and spread it on raw cotton, and apply it at once, when it will generally afford relief; and after repeatedly changing, it may be left off in twenty-four hours. The ancle is often weak when recovering, and benefit is derived from pouring cold water on it from a pitcher held high above you. Tallow and salt, mixed and spread on a piece of muslin, are good for a sprain.

Cuts or Wounds, &c.

When cuts bleed very much, tie a handkerchief tight above the wound, or place a finger on it until you can get a physician: in the country, persons should be supplied with a surgical needle and adhesive plaster, and have lint scraped and linen rags in a convenient place. Balsam apple put in a bottle when

22*

fresh, and whiskey poured on it, is an excellent application for fresh cuts or bruises. For the stick of a needle or pin, try to make it bleed, and hold the finger in strong vinegar and salt, as hot as you can bear it, this will prevent a gathering. A mashed finger should be held in hot water a few minutes. No. 6 is a most valuable remedy for cuts or wounds; bind a linen rag over the cut, and pour on the No. 6.

For Tetter, Warts, &c.

Dig up the pocoon root that grows in the woods, wash and slice it, and put it in a bottle with strong vinegar; bathe the parts with it several times a day. Celandine root is also good, used in the same way, and either of them will remove warts and ringworms.

Poisons, Accidents, &c.

These are valuable remedies, and should hold a place in the memory of every one, if possible.

Mix a spoonful of powdered mustard in a tumbler of warm water, and drink it immediately; it acts as an emetic, and has proved effectual where an ounce of poison had been taken into the stomach. Where the skin is poisoned, use a wash of smartweed steeped in water, or mix soot and cream, and apply it frequently; bruised Jamestown weed and cream is also good. If you have been exposed to poisonous plants, wash your face and hands immediately in salt and vinegar, or salt and water. When "corrosive sublimate," has been swallowed, the whites of two eggs taken immediately will neutralize the poison, and change the effect to that of a dose of calomel.

Persons struck by lightning should be laid on the ground, and pour water over them till life is restored.

When "oil of vitriol" or "aqua fortis" have been swallowed in large quantities, sweet oil should be taken, (as much as can be retained on the stomach.) For "oxalic acid," give magnesia or chalk and water.

For "tartar emetic," give Peruvian bark and water, (or a strong decoction of green tea, if you have not the bark.) For "saltpetre," give an emetic of mustard seed with water, and afterwards elm bark mucilage, and small doses of laudanum. This is also good in cases where arsenic has been swallowed.

When a child has swallowed a cent, pin or needle, give it the white of egg immediately; this forms a coating round the metal, and prevents injury in most cases; then give moderate doses of medicine, such as castor oil or salts.

When a fish bone has been swallowed, take the white of an egg, which will help to carry it down the throat; also eat a hard crust of bread.

Insects taken into the stomach, may generally be destroyed by taking a small quantity of vinegar and salt. When insects get into the ears, use a little salad oil, or melted lard.

Tar Ointment for the "Milk Crust."

Take a quarter of a pound of lard, and the same of sheep's tallow, three table-spoonsful of tar, an even spoonful of sulphur, an ounce of white turpentine, a lump of beeswax the size of a hickory-nut, the same quantity of powdered resin and scraped chalk, a tea-cupful of the inside bark of elder, a little celandine, southern wood, and English mallows; bruise the herbs, and put them on to boil, with the lard and tallow, and a little water to keep it from burning; when all the strength is out, strain them, and put the grease back in the pot, with the tar, and add the other ingredients a little at a time, and stir till all is melted; then strain it in a jar, and keep it covered for use.

Tar ointment is good for ring-worms in the head, which some children have, and has cured children where the head and face was covered with what is called the "milk crust."

Before it is applied, the place should be washed with milk and water, and a gentle purgative should be administered occasionally. Rhubarb tea is good for this purpose.

If it is wanted in the winter, when you cannot get all the herbs green, dried ones will do; and when made, it will keep good several years.

If there is much hair on the head of a child, it should be cut off before this is put on.

It is very dangerous to give infants that are affected with the milk crust, calomel, or any strong medicine. They should be carried out in the air occasionally, and not kept all the time in a warm nursery; sometimes a change of food is attended with a good result.

There have been instances of infants dying very suddenly, where powerful medicines had been administered.

Hop Ointment.

Take a table-spoonful of the yellow dust of hops, and put it in three spoonsful of melted lard, and mix it well; put it away in a cup for use. This has proved beneficial in cases of swelling of the breast; when cold has been taken, it will sometimes backen gatherings; bathe the place with a warm hand several times a day, and keep flannel over it. Young mothers should keep this ready, as it is much better than preparations of camphor, which are injurious.

Precipitate Ointment, &c.

Take one ounce of Venice turpentine, half an ounce of powdered precipitate, half a pound of lard, and two table-spoonsful of cold water; mix the turpentine and precipitate together with a knife; then add the lard and water, a little at a time, till it is well mixed; then put it in little boxes. This is useful to dry up a breaking out on the face or hands; care should be taken while using it, not to take cold.

Camphor dissolved in alcohol, or any white spirits, is very good to use on pimples on the face.

Blister Ointment.

Sometimes after a blister has been drawn with cabbage leaves, it becomes very sore and inflamed; a salve may be made of the leaves of evergreen, (a plant which grows in gardens with a thick leaf;) pound the leaves, and stew them in cream or sweet lard; spread it on a fine linen rag, and apply it to the blister after it has been washed with milk and water.

Another salve for blisters is to bruise the leaves of the English mallows with a little southern wood; stew them in sweet lard until they are crisp, and strain it; apply it three times a day. This is good to heal a burn.

Lily Ointment.

Gather the flowers of the sweet white lily, while they are fresh, and stew them in sweet lard. This is good for a swelling or sore.

Elder Ointment for Burns, &c.

After peeling off the outside bark of the elder, scrape off the green bark that is under, and stew it in lard till it is crisp; then strain it in a jar, and put it away to heal a blister or burn, or an old sore.

St. Johnswort Ointment, and its Uses.

Gather the yellow flowers of St. Johnswort while in full bloom; put them in a wide-mouthed bottle, and fill it with equal quantities of lard and sweet oil; tie a skin over it, and hang it in the sun for a month; then strain it, put it back in the bottle, and cork it up. This is one of the most effectual remedies for bruises, or for a mashed foot or hand. It should always be kept where there is a family of children.

Ointment for Mortification.

Take the berries, leaves and bark of the black alder, and bruise them well in a mortar; stew them in lard for an hour, stirring all the time; then strain it, and add a small piece of beeswax.

A poultice can be made for mortification, of the berries, leaves and bark of black alder, boiled in sweet cream, and thickened with wheat bread.

Another good poultice may be made of the inmost bark of sassafras root, pounded and boiled in weak ley, and thickened with corn meal. The patient should drink tea made of the roots of sassafras and burdock.

Bread and Milk, and Flaxseed Poultices.

Boil half a pint of sweet milk, and thicken it with crumbs of bread; let it boil till soft. This is the mildest poultice that can be made.

A tea-cup of flaxseed boiled till soft, requires no addition to make a good poultice.

Hop Poultice, and its Uses.

Boil a handful of hops in a pint of water till very soft; when thicken it with corn meal. This is very good for a sore throat, tooth-ache, or swelled face.

Onion Poultice.

Slice the onions and boil them in water till very soft; then mash and boil them with milk and some crumbs of bread. This will draw a bile or gathering to a head very soon.

Lily Root Poultice.

Pound the roots of the sweet white lily, and put them on to boil in rich milk; when soft, thicken it with crumbs of bread. This is a most valuable poultice for a gathering, and has given relief in many instances where the suffering was great.

Cream Poultice.

Put to boil a tea-cup of cream; mix two spoonsful of flour in milk, and stir in when it boils.

Ley Poultice.

Tie a spoonful of ashes in a rag, and boil it in a pint of water for fifteen minutes, with some catnip or life-everlasting; when the herbs are soft, take out the ashes, and thicken it with corn meal; spread some grease over as you apply it.

Adhesive Plaster.

Take three pounds of resin, one-quarter of a pound of beeswax, one-quarter of a pound of mutton tallow, melt together in an iron pan; then pour out about one-third into a bucket of water, turn up the edges until you can take hold with the hands and pull it as you would shoemakers' wax: grease papers ana put the plaster on them for use; you may then pour out the rest and treat it in the same way.

A Valuable Salve for Burns and other Sores.

Take of high mallows, heal-all, night shade, and elder bark, a large handful, and about half the quantity of Jamestown weed; boil them for several hours; strain off the liquid, and add to it one pound of beeswax, one pound of mutton tallow, one pound of resin, half a pound of lard; boil them slowly for about two hours, and let it cool on the liquid. This salve will do to apply immediately to a burn or scald, or after other remedies have been used; it is also good to heal old sores or gatherings.

Deshler's Salve for Gatherings or Sores.

Take half a pound of sheep's suet, the same of resin and beeswax, a quarter of a pound of thick turpentine, and half a pint of linseed oil; pound the resin, and cut the beeswax and suet; put them over the fire with the other ingredients, and keep stirring till they are mixed, but do not let them boil; put it in a jar, and tie it up. It is good for burns, biles, gathered breasts, &c.

Salve for Corns, or Bunions.

Take a pint of sweet oil, half a pound of red lead, two ounces of Venice turpentine, two of beeswax, and one of white turpentine; boil the oil and red lead in brass or bell-metal till they turn brown, stirring it constantly; have the wax and white turpentine sliced, and put them in by degrees; take it off the fire, and stir till all is melted; then add the Venice turpentine, and continue to stir till it is cold; when dip your hands in cold water, and make it out in rolls about two inches long; wrap each roll up in paper, and keep them in a box. After soaking and scraping the corn, bind it on, spread on a soft rag. To warm a small piece of common adhesive plaster and apply it, gives almost immediate relief.

Sassafras Poultice,

Take the bark of the root and mash, or pound it; boil it in a little water, and take out the bark, and thicken it with crumbs of bread, and milk.

Balsam Apple in Spirits,

Cut a ripe balsam apple in small pieces, and fill a bottle with it; pour Holland gin on it.

This retains its strength for years, and is useful to take a few drops at a time for the colic; it is also valuable to apply with sugar to a cut or wound.

Cure for Biles,

Use equal quantities of resin soap, brown sugar, and powdered resin, worked well together, with a few drops of molasses. A poultice of onions, sassafras, or bread and milk may be used with advantage. For musquito bites, apply spirits of hartshorn and camphor.

For Scurvy of the Gums.

Take a quarter of an ounce of bark, and a piece of new lime the size of a hazle-nut; put them in a bottle with half a pint of water; wash the mouth with this three times a day.

For an Infant's Sore Mouth.

Make a strong sage tea; put in a little bark and borax or alum, with honey to sweeten it; cork it up in

23

a vial, and wash the child's gums with it three times a day, using a fresh rag every time.

For Affection of the Kidneys.

Boil some onions soft, mash, and apply them where the pain is seated. This has given great relief.

For a Gathering on a Finger.

Mix together equal parts of castile soap and chalk; wet it with camphor, and bind it on, or dip the finger in honey and camphorated spirits, as hot as you can bear. A little burnt alum put on lint is good; also a bread and milk poultice, with pounded sassafras root stewed in it, and renewed frequently. Honey and camphor mixed is useful for gatherings that have been of long standing.

Take of the following ingredients a tea-spoonful each: black pepper powdered finely, ginger, spirits of camphor, laudanum, and honey; beat them well with the yelk of an egg, and thicken with rye flour, or if you cannot obtain rye, corn and wheat flour mixed will answer; this will form a soft poultice, and should be applied in sufficient quantity to keep moist, and changed once a day. I have known this to cure several gatherings that threatened to be severe.

Huxham's Bark Tincture.

Take two ounces of bark, three drachms of Virginia snake root, one ounce of orange peel, and one quart of good spirits; set it in a warm place, and shake it daily for two weeks; then pour it off, and add a pint more spirits to the ingredients.

This is very useful to take, when recovering from the ague or billious fever, or in the fall of the year;

when these are apprehended, take two tea-spoonsful a day, before breakfast and dinner.

Wine Bitters for Debility, &c.

Take two ounces of chamomile flowers, two of centaury flowers, one of iron filings, and an ounce and a half of Jesuit's bark; put these in two quarts of good wine, and set it in the sun three days, shaking it frequently. Half a wine-glass of this taken twice a day, with water, is useful in cases of debility, where there is no fever.

Chamomile, and wormwood teas, are both excellent tonics, as is also wild cherry tree bark, made in strong tea, and taken cold.

Spice Wood Berries.

Boil in a pint of new milk, a table-spoonful of bruised spice wood berries. This has a very healing effect in cases of dysentery, and summer disease in children.

Spiced Rhubarb.

Take two ounces of rhubarb, half an ounce of cloves, the same of cinnamon, and quarter of an ounce of mace; stew them in a pint and a half of water till one half is evaporated; then strain it and add half a pint of good spirits. Two tea-spoonsful is a dose for a child a year old, with the summer disease, and two table-spoonsful for a grown person.

For Chapped Lips.

Put a tea-cupful of rich cream over some coals to stew with three table-spoonsful of powdered loaf-sugar. This has a healing effect.

Another remedy, equally good, is to a tea-cupful of honey, add half the quantity of mutton tallow, and stew together till well mixed; pour it out in a cup, and keep stirring till cold.

For chapped hands, mix together equal quantities of rich cream and strong vinegar, and rub it over every time you wash your hands.

Bathing.

Almost every family, even if their circumstances be moderate, can have a shower bath; they may save the expense, by improved health and strength; one bucket full of cold water is sufficient. You should wear on the head an oil-cloth cap. For a person in strong health, the bath may be taken on first rising in the morning; but for one disposed to be delicate, two or three hours after breakfast is the most proper time. To produce warmth, rub the person with a crash towel, or horse hair glove. You should be careful to take some exercise after the bath, or you will be more liable to take cold. Never take a bath soon after a meal, as that is injurious. Persons subject to colds, sore throat, rheumatism, sick head-ache, nervous disease, or general debility, have been greatly benefitted by the daily use of the shower bath. Children that are oppressed with heat are much refreshed, and will rest well after a bath; the water should be moderated for them. Infants should be bathed every morning in a tub of water about milk warm, and may be very early accustomed to its use; they will become fond of it, and are less liable to take cold from exposure to the air. They generally take a refreshing nap after coming out of the bath. They should not be allowed to remain in more than five or ten minutes; should be well wiped with a soft towel, and then rubbed with flannel and dressed; their clothes being warmed to prevent a chill.

Elderberry Jam for Colds, &c.

A quart of nicely picked elderberries, to a pound of loaf-sugar and a tea-cup of water; let them boil slowly for an hour. If you prefer it without the seeds, strain the berries after boiling them for a few minutes, before you add the sugar. This is useful and agreeable for colds, taken through the day, or at night, when the cough is troublesome. It is said also to purify the blood, and is taken to prevent erysipelas.

Black Currant Jelly, a Remedy for Sore Throat.

Take ripe black currants, mash and strain them, and to every pint of the juice, add a pound of loaf-sugar; boil it until it becomes a jelly. It is valuable for sore throats.

Quince seeds dried, and boiling water poured on them, make a useful gargle for sore throat.

Lavender Compound.

Pick the lavender blossoms, and put them in a bottle, with a few blades of mace, and some cloves; fill up the bottle with good spirits, and let it stand corked up, till all the strength is extracted; when strain it off, and color it with a little cochineal.

FOOD FOR THE SICK.

Remarks on Preparing Food for the Sick.

FEW young persons understand cooking for the sick. It is very important to know how to prepare their food in an inviting manner; every thing should be perfectly clean and nice. Avoid giving an invalid any thing out of a cup that has been used before; even if it is medicine, it will not be so hard to take out of a clean cup. It is well to have a stand or small table by the bedside, that you can set any thing on. A small silver strainer that will just fit over a tumbler or tea-cup, is very useful to strain lemonade, panada or herb tea.

If you want any thing to use through the night, you should prepare it, if possible, beforehand; as a person that is sick, can sometimes fall asleep without knowing it, if the room is *kept perfectly still.*

Boiled Custard.

Beat an egg with a heaped tea-spoonful of sugar; stir it into a tea-cupful of boiling milk, and stir till it is thick; pour it in a bowl on a slice of toast cut up, and grate a little nutmeg over.

Panada.

Put some crackers, crusts of dry bread or dried rusk, in a sauce-pan with cold water, and a few raisins; after it has boiled half an hour, put in sugar, nutmeg, and half a glass of wine, if the patient has no fever.

If you have dried rusk, it is a quicker way to put the rusk in a bowl with some sugar, and pour boiling water on it out of the tea-kettle. If the patient can take nothing but liquids, this makes a good drink when strained.

Egg Panada.

Boil a handful of good raisins in a quart of water; toast a slice of bread and cut it up; beat two eggs with a spoonful of sugar, and mix it with the bread; when the raisins are done, pour them on the toast and eggs, stirring all the time; season to your taste with wine, nutmeg and butter.

Oat-meal Gruel.

Mix two spoonsful of oat-meal, with as much water as will mix it easily, and stir it in a pint of boiling water in a sauce-pan until perfectly smooth; let it boil a few minutes; season it with sugar and nutmeg, and pour it out on a slice of bread toasted and cut up, or some dried rusk. If the patient should like them, you can put in a few raisins, stoned and cut up. This will keep good a day, and if nicely warmed over, is as good as when fresh.

Corn Gruel.

Mix two spoonsful of sifted corn-meal in some water; have a clean skillet with a pint of boiling water in it; stir it in, and when done, season it with salt to your taste, or sugar, if you prefer it.

Arrow-root.

Moisten two tea-spoonsful of powdered arrow-root with water, and rub it smooth with a spoon; then pour on half a pint of boiling water; season it with lemon juice, or wine and nutmeg. In cooking arrow-root for children, it is a very good way to make it very thick, and thin it afterwards with milk.

Sago.

Wash the sago, (allowing two table-spoonsful to a quart of water,) and soak it an hour; boil it slowly till it thickens; sweeten it with loaf-sugar, and season it with wine or lemon juice.

Tapioca Jelly.

Wash the tapioca well, and let it soak for several hours in cold water; put it in a sauce-pan with the same water, and let it boil slowly till it is clear and thick; then season it with wine and loaf-sugar. The pearl tapioca will require less time to soak, and no washing. Allow three table-spoonsful of tapioca to a quart of water.

Milk Porridge.

Put half a pint of milk, and the same of water, in a sauce-pan to boil; mix two spoonsful of wheat flour in milk till very smooth, and stir in when it boils; keep stirring it five minutes, when pour it in a bowl and season with salt.

Barley Water.

Boil two table-spoonsful of barley in a quart of water; it is a cooling drink in fevers. If the weather is cold, you can make a larger quantity. Some boil whole raisins with barley; take it with or without seasoning.

To Poach Eggs.

Put a pint of water in a clean skillet, with a little butter and salt; when it boils, break two eggs in a plate, and put them in; in about a minute, take them up on a plate, in which there is a slice of bread toasted and buttered. This is a very delicate way of cooking eggs.

Barley Panada.

Boil a small tea-cup of barley in water till it is soft, with a tea-cup of raisins; put in nutmeg and sugar, and break in it toast or dried rusk.

Calf's Foot Blancmange.

Put a set of nicely cleaned feet in four quarts of water, and let it boil more than half away; strain through a colander, and when it is cold, scrape off all the fat, and take out that which settles at the bottom; put it in a sauce-pan, with a quart of new milk, sugar to your taste, lemon peel and juice, and cinnamon or mace; let it boil ten minutes and strain it; wet your moulds, and when it is nearly cold, put it in them; when it is cold and stiff, it can be turned out on a plate, and eaten with or without cream. This is very nice for a sick person, and is easily made.

Cream Toast.

Cut a slice of stale bread, and wet it with cream; toast it slowly and butter it; this is very nice for an invalid, and an agreeable change.

Milk Toast, &c.

Boil a tea-cup of milk, and put in a spoonful of butter; toast a slice of bread and moisten it with water, then pour on the boiling milk. This is very good for sick persons, and can be eaten without much exertion. In making water-toast, the butter should be melted in boiling water, and put on while hot.

To Stew Dried Beef.

Chip some beef very thin, pour hot water on it, and let it stand a minute or two, then drain it off, and stew it in a skillet with a little cream and butter. If it is preferred dry, it may be fried in butter alone.

To Stew Ham, &c.

Cut a slice of ham into small pieces, and pour boiling water on it; let it soak a few minutes to extract the salt, and stew it in a little water; just before it is done, put in some cream and parsley.

If you broil ham that is uncooked, it should always be soaked in water a few minutes.

To Stew Chickens or Birds.

When sick persons are tired of broiled chickens, or birds, it is well to stew them for a change; the wing, with part of the breast of a chicken, will make a meal; stew it in a little water, and put in parsley, cream, pepper and salt, just as it is done.

Chicken Water.

If you have a small chicken, it will take half of it to make a pint of chicken water. Cut it up and put it to boil in a covered skillet with a quart of water; when it has boiled down to a pint, take it up, and put in a little salt and slice of toasted bread. This is valuable in cases of dysentery and cholera morbus, particularly when made of old fowls.

Beef Feet

Soak the feet and have them nicely cleaned; boil them slowly, and take off the scum as it rises; when they are soft and tender, take them up, and separate the bones from the glutinous part, which is very nice for a sick person, and conveys nutriment in a form that will hardly disagree with the most delicate stomach, and has been taken when nearly all other food was rejected; a few drops of vinegar, and a little salt, renders it more palatable.

Beef Tea, &c.

Take a piece of juicy beef, without any fat, cut it in small pieces, bruise it till tender, put it in a wide-mouthed bottle, and cork it tight; put this in a pot of cold water, set it over the fire, and let it boil an hour or more.

When a person can take but a small quantity of nourishment, this is very good. Mutton may be done in the same way.

Mutton and Veal Broth.

Boil a piece of mutton till it comes to pieces; then strain the broth, and let it get cold, so that the fat will rise, which must be taken off; then warm it, and put in a little salt. Veal broth may be made in the same way, and is more delicate for sick persons.

Wine Whey.

Boil a pint of milk, and put to it a glass of white wine; set it over the fire till it just boils again, then set it off till the curd has settled, when strain it, and sweeten to your taste.

Rennet Whey.

Warm a pint of milk, but do not let it get too hot, or it will spoil the taste of the whey. Wash the salt from a piece of rennet the size of a dollar, and put it in the milk; when it turns, take out the rennet; wash and put it in a cup of water, and it will do to use again to make whey. If you have rennet in a bottle of wine, two tea-spoonsful of it will make a quart of whey; but if the person has fever, it is best to make it without wine.

Mulled Jelly.

Take a table-spoonful of currant or grape jelly, and beat with it the white of an egg, and a little loaf-sugar; pour on it half a pint of boiling water, and break in a slice of dry toast, or two crackers.

Mulled Wine.

Beat together an egg, a glass of wine, and a spoon-ful of sugar; pour on it half a pint of hot water; stir all the time to keep it from curdling, and when you pour it in a tumbler, grate a little nutmeg over it.

Toast Water.

Cut slices of bread very thin, and toast dry, but do not let it burn; put it in a pitcher, and pour boiling water on it. Toast water will allay thirst better than almost any thing else. If it is wanted to drink through the night, it should always be made early in the evening.

Apple Water, &c.

Roast two apples, mash them and pour a pint of water on them; or slice raw apples, and pour boiling water on them.

Tamarinds, currant or grape jelly, cranberries, or dried fruit of any kind, make a good drink.

Coffee.

Sick persons should have their coffee made separate from the family, as standing in the tin pot spoils the flavor. Put two tea-spoonsful of ground coffee in a small mug, and pour boiling water on it; let it set by the fire to settle, and pour it off in a cup, with sugar and cream. Care should be taken that there are no burnt grains.

Chocolate.

To make a cup of chocolate, grate a large tea-spoonful in a mug, and pour a tea-cup of boiling water on it; let it stand covered by the fire a few minutes, when you can put in sugar and cream.

Black Tea.

Black tea is much more suitable than green for sick persons, as it does not affect the nerves. Put a tea-spoonful in a pot that will hold about two cups, and pour boiling water on it. Let it set by the fire to draw five or ten minutes.

Rye Mush.

This is a nourishing and light diet for the sick, and is by some preferred to mush made of Indian meal. Four large spoonsful of rye flour mixed smooth in a little water, and stirred in a pint of boiling water; let it boil twenty minutes, stirring frequently. Nervous persons who sleep badly, rest much better after a supper of corn, or rye mush, than if they take tea or coffee.

24

DOMESTICS.

Hints on the Management of Domestics, &c.

SOME families are always changing their domestics, and weary their friends with complaints of those they have, and inquiries for others.

Deliberate before you make a change; if servants are honest, speak the truth, and have an obliging disposition, it is better to bear with a few defects, than to discharge them; these are qualifications for the foundation of a good servant; and some of the most valuable I have had, were such as could hardly be put up with at first. By being patient, and speaking to them in a kind manner, they become attached and fearful of doing any thing to offend.

When they break any thing, or an accident occurs, accustom them to inform you of it immediately. Few mistresses, of well regulated minds, will be offended when openly told of accidents; but if they are left to be found out, you always feel more disposed to blame and reprove them. By speaking to them in a mild and forgiving manner, careless servants will become more careful.

A considerate mistress may, without loss of dignity, make them feel that she regards it as her duty to be their friend, and that she feels herself under an obligation to advise them in difficulties and promote their comfort.

We should reflect that theirs is a life of servitude, and if they over-exert themselves, or are too much exposed in early life, it will bring on disease that will shorten their days, or render old age a burden.

Some young persons are too indolent to wait on themselves, and ring for the servants on the most trifling occasions; when if they were accustomed to perform these little offices, their health would be much better, and we should not hear of so many complaints, the result of want of exercise. All female servants should have time to attend to their clothing; many have to work so hard through the day that their only leisure is at night, and then they hurry over their things in a careless manner.

Where your circumstances permit, a good man-servant is a valuable acquisition; and they are sometimes more easily governed than females.

If mistresses were better informed, they would not complain so much of the ignorance and awkwardness of their domestics. Always give them their orders in time. If a new dish is to be cooked, superintend its preparation yourself.

If you are capable of directing, a cook will soon learn to do without your constant attention.

If they are slow in their movements, insist on their beginning early to prepare a meal, so that there will be time sufficient for every thing to be done properly.

If you expect company, have every thing prepared, that can be done with safety, the day previous. In summer there are but few things that can be done without risk of spoiling: a ham or tongue may be washed ready to boil; castors and salt-stands put in order, and pastry or dessert prepared, that will not spoil by being kept a day.

In winter, many things can be kept for days in a state of preparation for cooking; and it greatly assists the work of the family, to have every thing done beforehand.

Do with as few domestics as possible; assist with the work yourself, rather than keep one too many. Those that take orphan children to bring up, are often rewarded for their trouble; as sometimes a girl of fifteen will be more useful than one much older: and where a family is small it does very well; but in large families, a little girl is so often called from her work, that it has a tendency to unsettle and make her careless.

Never allow your children to call on or interrupt servants when at their work or meals, to do any thing which a child could do for itself; children that treat domestics with respect, will generally find them willing to render any assistance in their power. I have known a few house-keepers, who have kept the same servants for years; who have assisted in rearing the children, until they almost viewed them as their own; and these were not faultless. If they had been discharged for trifles, they might have wandered, from one family to another, without being attached to any, until they became so indifferent, as not to be worthy of employ; but by the kindness and patience of their employer, they became so grateful and attached, as to be a treasure to her family. When they become weary of such constant servitude, would it not be better, instead of discharging, to give them time for rest and recreation in visiting their friends? I have known them to return, renewed in health and spirits.

Encourage them to lay by as much of their wages as they can possibly spare, in such institutions as are thought the most safe, that they may have something to look to in case of sickness, or any event which would require its use.

Promote their reading in such books as are suited to their capacities; they sometimes have a little leisure, that could be well filled up in this way. I have found it to increase the happiness of those under my care, to encourage a fondness for reading, and improving their minds; it tends to keep them from unprofitable company, and too much visiting, to which so many are addicted.

Young girls should make and mend their own clothes, and keep them in good order, and they should be taught to knit. The material of which stockings are composed costs but little, and they wear much better than those that are bought. Knitting fills up leisure moments, and promotes industrious habits; and when age comes on, they will have a resource, although it appears so simple, yet if it is not learned while young, it is hard to acquire when old.

When servants are guilty of faults that cannot be looked over, instead of publicly reproving them, take an opportunity when alone, and talk coolly; tell them of your sorrow at being obliged to notice their conduct, encourage them to pursue a different course, and that you will forgive them if they will strive to do better. I have known them much improved by this mode of treatment.

By inspecting every department, not only will waste be prevented, but dishonesty. In cities many persons find it necessary to lock up nearly every thing; and it is a lamentable state of things that so few are to be trusted.

Sometimes treating servants with confidence will have a good effect; but let them be aware that you have a knowledge of every thing that is going on.

Some young persons are completely at the mercy of their domestics. I have known great uneasiness to be experienced, and much loss; but by showing a little

24*

moral courage, and discharging those that are irre-claimable, an ascendancy was gained. Never suffer them to treat you with disrespect or impertinence. If it is known that they will be discharged for these faults, they will be on their guard.

If you have taken a boy or girl, to bring up as a domestic, endeavour to teach them, at least to spell and read; they are sometimes very fond of their books, and if you once get them to reading, it will become to them a favorite evening amusement; I have known them take up their books on every occasion of leisure. I have seen boys that worked hard through the day, spend all the evening with their books, slate, and occasionally a little writing. Sometimes, I have in the evening felt fatigued and listless, and would much rather read, and amuse myself, than go out to teach two or three in the kitchen; but in attending to this, (which I consider a duty,) have felt a sweet reward—indeed, their grateful thanks expressed by words, have encouraged me to keep on. I have thought a little instruction in this way, arouses their faculties, and tends to make them more industrious. When I have been prevented from teaching them for some time, by indisposition, or other causes, I have observed they were not so cheerful in the performance of their work. If they are reading any thing they do not fully understand, take a little time to explain it to them. It will be, my young friends, like sowing the good seed, and you, as well as they, will receive the reward.

I wish to encourage you in the most affectionate manner to attend to *this* duty; you will find it will strengthen you in the performance of others. " The more we exert our faculties, the more we can accomplish. He that does nothing, renders himself incapable of doing any thing. While we are executing one work, we are preparing ourselves to undertake another."

REMARKS.

Remarks on Carving, &c.

I do not think it necessary to say much on the subject of carving, as those who are accustomed to sit at a well ordered table, and who observe the manner of the host and hostess, can soon acquire the art, both of carving and helping with ease. And when placed at the head of their own table, the knowledge thus gained will be found a great assistance.

The proper time for children to acquire good habits at meals, is not when there is company; it should be an every day lesson. As when parents are engaged with their friends or guests, they have no time to devote to the manners of their children, and to reprove them at table is very unpleasant, as well as mortifying.

Young children will soon acquire the manner of sitting quietly till they are helped, if they are made to understand that they will not be permitted to eat with their parents and friends, unless they behave with propriety.

I have thought it a great assistance to the good order of a large family, for every member to be punctual in their attendance at meals, and all to sit down together, with a short pause before the carving and helping commences. In those moments of quiet, the heart is sometimes awakened to a feeling of gratitude to the Almighty dispenser of our blessings.

At the table, different members of the family meet; and where affection and kindness, those aids to true politeness, preside, it is truly a delightful treat to be the guest of such a family.

Every symptom of selfishness should be discouraged, for if suffered to take root in a child, it lays the foundation of much that is disagreeable to themselves and others.

Inculcate this excellent rule, "of doing unto others, what you wish others to do unto you," and always preferring others to yourself.

It is the custom in some well regulated families, to permit the younger members, (as they arrive at a suitable age,) to take turns in presiding, not only at breakfast and tea, but at the dinner table. I have known quite young girls that had been taught in this way, carve a fowl or joint of meat with ease and grace. In helping, they should be taught not to overload the plate, as it takes away the appetite of some persons to be helped too largely.

The gravy should be stirred so that all may be helped alike, and a small quantity put on the meat or fowl, to which it belongs, and not on vegetables unless it is particularly desired.

If there should be a rare dish on the table, it is best to hand it round and let every one help himself, after it has been nicely cut up. Ham is much nicer to be cut in very thin slices. So is salt beef and tongue.

Young housekeepers in selecting their dishes for dinner, (if they have not an experienced cook,) should avoid those that are difficult to prepare. Never try a new dish when you expect company. Your guests will be more gratified with a neat and moderate table, with a few plain and well cooked dishes, accompanied with the smiling countenance of the hostess, than with a great variety of ill cooked and badly arranged viands.

Economy the Source of Charity,

If your circumstances will not admit of giving away much, you can, by economy, give a little, and a blessing will attend it. There are few of the very poor, that know how to repair old clothing to advantage; a garment will be of much more service, that is well mended before it is given to them.

It has been remarked, that the poor are ungrateful, and forget the favors conferred upon them.

I have seldom found them deficient in this respect; and when they are, if we would reflect, that if some of us received no more than we deserve, we should be but poorly off.

We know in our own families, how acceptable is a nice present of something that a sick member can eat; and it is sometimes the means of restoring the appetite, when any thing cooked in the house is rejected. The feeling of love with which it is presented, is as a cordial to a sick person.

How much more acceptable will something nourishing be to one oppressed with poverty, as well as sickness.

When the rich are diseased, the physician often finds it necessary to enjoin strict abstinence; but very different is it with the poor, who frequently suffer for want of nourishment.

When the mother of a poor family is ill, how greatly are her sufferings augmented by the knowledge that her children are deprived of her services; and how acceptable to such a family would be a loaf of bread, or a large bowl of soup, which could be made of materials that would hardly be missed.

Dried beans or peas, and onions, are a cheap and valuable addition to soup; also cold vegetables. The liquor that fresh meat is boiled in, should be carefully saved for that purpose, if there are those near you that need it.

It may seem at first troublesome to a young house-keeper, to take the necessary care to save for the poor. It is certainly much easier to let the cook have her own way, and waste or not, as she pleases; but for your encouragement my young friends, permit me to say, you will be sweetly rewarded for your attention to them.

One eminent for his charities, near the close of life, made this remark: "What I spent I lost, but what I gave away remains with me."

To Encourage Children in Acts of Kindness to the Aged and Afflicted.

Young children may early be taught to administer to the wants of the aged and infirm.

Some mothers are in the practice of giving a small sum of money to their children, as a reward for some little service or piece of work that they have done. The money thus obtained, to be laid out for a sick or old poor person. This method has an excellent effect on the minds of children; it incites them to industry, teaches self-denial, and the feelings of love and charity which are thus early instilled into their tender minds, make a lasting impression.

If they spent their little fund in trifles for their own use, they would acquire a habit of selfishness; which, when once formed, it is most difficult to eradicate.

I have remarked the pleasure with which children will relate the incidents of a visit, which they have been permitted to make to a poor family; and it is a refreshment to persons advanced in life, to see a young family thus trained.

As soon as little girls can sew, they should be encouraged to make garments for the poor, or repair their own old ones as a present to a child of their own size, or make patchwork out of old dresses for a bed covering for poor people. Their being permitted to do these things, should be as a reward for good behavior in attention to their lessons or other duties.

When they are old enough to make a loaf of bread, a pie, or a little plain cake, allow them to do it, and take as a present to, or make broth or panada for a sick person. This teaches them to prepare these things while young, and may be useful to them in after life.

How cheering it must be to the aged or afflicted, to see smiling young faces enter their dwellings, bearing their little offerings of food or clothing, the work of their own hands.

Be encouraged my dear young mothers; if you thus train your children to works of charity, you will be doubly blessed.

Early Rising Promotes Punctuality.

It is an old and true saying, "that if you waste an hour in the morning, it is seldom recovered all that day." This dispirits you, and the next day there is still something left undone.

A late riser is rarely punctual in her engagements, and more of the happiness of married life depends on forming a habit of strict punctuality, than young persons are generally aware of.

If you are distressed at having acquired habits of late rising, and want of punctuality, remember by perseverance, they can be overcome. Fix an hour for rising, and let nothing but illness prevent your being up at that time. While forming this useful habit, you should retire to rest early.

Many things can be better attended to at an early, than a late hour in the morning.

Where families rise before the sun, the day seems much longer; all the active employments of the early riser are accomplished before her later neighbors have finished their breakfast.

The duties of the bath and toilet being performed, her chamber well aired and arranged—and her parlor in order, she is ready for the more quiet employments of reading and sewing.

In a well regulated household, servants perform their duties with life and energy. Determine on an hour for your meals, and if all the members of the family adhere to it, scrupulous exactness will soon be established.

Hints to Young Wives.

The authoress is well aware of the difficulties which surround a young wife on her first setting out, particularly if situated at a distance from the kind mother who has hitherto directed her, with servants who watch every movement, and who will soon discover whether the new mistress is qualified for the task she has undertaken.

Accustom yourself to rise early; fix a certain hour, and let nothing but indisposition prevent your being up at the appointed time. By this means your affairs will all be arranged in good season, and you will have time for recreation, in walking, riding, or in reading such authors as will tend to strengthen and improve your mind.

Young persons removed from large families often suffer greatly from loneliness, whereas, if they were occupied with household affairs, they would not feel so severely the absence of their husbands while attending to business.

Be punctual to the hour that has been fixed on for your meals, and let good order prevail in every department of which you have the command. A mistress of a family is much happier, who knows how every thing is going on from the garret to the cellar. By inspecting every thing you soon become interested, and we all know when that is the case, the most difficult pursuits become easy and pleasant.

And with what pleasure will a young wife welcome her husband to his meals, when her conscience assures her that she has done her best, and that nothing is neglected; and how will it lighten his labors to reflect, when absent, that the partner he has chosen, is performing her duty at home.

I am fully persuaded that the formation of domestic happiness, is generally laid the first year of marriage: therefore, my young friends, act well your part; if you desire to be treated with confidence you must merit it. If you keep an exact account of all your expenses, there will be less danger of living beyond your income, of which there have been so many lamentable instances.

25

Never buy any thing because it is recommended as being cheap; many cheap things amount in time to a large sum. In selecting furniture, let utility, not fashion, govern your choice; some young persons furnish their parlors so extravagantly, that necessary and useful articles are neglected, for want of means to purchase them. Be persuaded that happiness does not consist so much in having splendid furniture, as in attending to the every day comforts of those around you. If you marry without the useful knowledge necessary for governing your family, lose no time in acquiring it.

There is a time when most young girls show a fondness for domestic affairs before they are old enough to go into company, when it would be an agreeable change to be absent from school and assisting their mothers; the knowledge thus acquired would never be lost.

Many a young man who commenced with fair prospects, has been ruined through his wife's ignorance of domestic duties, and she has suffered from the consequent diminution of his esteem and love.

I once knew a lovely and accomplished young lady, accustomed to every indulgence, who, on her marriage, removed several hundred miles from her parents, to reside in the country, where servants were difficult to procure. This delicate and sensitive young creature was much distressed by her ignorance of almost every thing connected with housekeeping; and after suffering repeated mortifications, concluded to learn to do the work herself; and when this dearly bought knowledge was acquired, she was able to teach her ignorant servants; and resolved, if ever she had daughters, to use every means in her power to teach them.

When a prudent wife is made acquainted with the

circumstances of her husband, she will endeavor strictly
to keep within their bounds; always remembering that
losses and events, over which he has no control, may
occur and greatly reduce his income. And how will
it assist her to bear a reverse of fortune, if she has
acted with discretion; it will strengthen the wife to
encourage and cheer her partner, and enable him to
struggle through difficulties which were thought insur-
mountable. Happiness will not forsake such a family;
though they lose almost every thing, the peace which
is the result of a good conscience will remain ; this will
strengthen them to begin anew, and the Divine blessing
will attend such efforts.

A few Remarks to Encourage Young House-keepers in their First Attempts.

As bread is the most important article of food, one
of your first attempts should be to make a few loaves
of good bread and rolls, of the most simple kind.
Bread rolls are very easily made. If you succeed
tolerably, it will encourage you to try again. When
you make cakes, begin with the simple kinds; plain
jumbles or cakes that you can roll out, or crisp gingerbread. Sponge cake is easier than those that have
butter in them; I have known young persons succeed
very well with it. Bread rusk is also easily made, or
a few plain pies. Do not trust the baking to an
ignorant person, but superintend it yourself. Sometimes baking in a stove, is protracted by the damp-
ness of the wood. Before you bake, have dry wood
prepared. Watch the time ; it is a good plan to have a
clock near the kitchen. Do not have too many things
on hand at once; but perfect yourself in the knowledge

of a few important dishes. If you make good yeast, you will be more certain of good bread, light cakes and rolls. To cook a steak nicely, is also important; and with a dish of potatoes well cooked, a dish of cold slaw and an apple pie, or a little stewed fruit, will make a good plain dinner.

When your family is small, you can have something nice every day, without cooking much. Veal cutlets, and mutton chops, are easy to cook, and may be prepared in a short time. If you have a fowl, and boil it, you can save the soup, and warm it over for the next day. A cold roast fowl may be hashed. On days that you have cold meat, a batter pudding, or plain rice pudding, is easily prepared.

If you wish to have an early breakfast, make every preparation that you can, over night; set the table, have the relish cut, ready to cook, or to warm over— and cold bread may be sliced, and wrapped in a cloth to keep it moist. Coffee should be ground, and dry fuel, and water at hand. With these preparations, breakfast may be ready in half an hour from the time the fire is made. If you have warm corn bread, or rolls, it will require more time; but if you have them made up over night, and put in a cool place, they will not sour, and can soon be baked. Maryland biscuit are very convenient, as they are always ready, and will keep good a week. I have found it a great advantage to set the table over night, particularly if you have a separate room to eat in; although it takes but a short time, every minute is important in the morning.

Where the mistress washes the breakfast things, and puts them in their proper places, and counts the spoons, and other articles, she can see when any thing is missing. A mop is useful for glass and china;

keep a pan, or a small tub, for the purpose of holding the water, which should not be too hot. If tea things are put in very hot water, it will be apt to crack them, or they will look smeared. Put a little soap in the water, wash the glass first, then the silver, then the cups and saucers, and lastly, the plates and knives and forks. If spoons have been used with eggs, put them to soak immediately, to prevent their turning dark. Have a common waiter for the pan to stand in, and on it drain your tea things. Spoons when used with care, require polishing but seldom, as it wears the silver away. Dinner dishes should be washed first in moderately warm water and soap, rinsed in hot water, and drained before wiping. Put every thing in its proper place, and inspect your pantry and cellar frequently. Sometimes things are forgotten, for want of attention, until they are spoiled. Air the cellar frequently; do not let refuse vegetables accumulate, or any thing that would be likely to cause sickness.

You should provide coarse towels of different kinds, for china and glass, and for the dinner dishes; also knife cloths; have them marked and kept in their proper places. Some persons have their towels washed out every day; but it is better to save them for the weekly wash. If towels are thrown aside damp, they are liable to mildew. You should keep dusters of several kinds. Old silk handkerchiefs, are best for highly polished furniture, or an old barege veil answers a good purpose. For common purposes, a square of coarse muslin, or check is suitable. You should keep one floor cloth for chambers, and one for the kitchen. Keep brooms for different purposes; always use a soft one for carpets; as soon as they wear stiff, they will do for the kitchen, or pavements. Pouring a little hot

25*

water on a broom, softens it for carpets. You may save tea leaves, to sprinkle over your carpet, when you give a thorough sweeping, this will brighten it; and occasionally to wipe it over, with a cloth, that has been wrung out of hot water cleanses it; of course, this is only required for carpets in constant use.

It is of great importance to health, that sleeping apartments should be well aired and swept. If you sleep in an apartment, where there has been fire during the day, it should be well aired before going to bed; or if the room is close, have a little air admitted, so as not to blow on persons that are asleep. A window that will lower from the top is an advantage. Beds should be well aired before they are made; take the clothes off, and leave them at least an hour. In pleasant weather, you may keep chamber windows hoisted, for several hours; and even in cold weather, the windows may be kept up a short time; and if on any occasion, you may be obliged to have the beds made without airing, turn the clothes half way down, and leave them for several hours. Some persons have cheap calico covers, to spread over beds, while the room is swept; this is a good plan, on account of the dust. Bolster and pillow ticks wear better, if you have a check case basted on; this should be changed, washed and starched occasionally. It is a good plan also to have check covers for matresses and feather beds; but the covers should not be kept on beds that are not in use, lest they should be liable to moth. In winter a blanket should be put next a bed that is not often slept in, or for a delicate person, and be particularly careful, that sheets are dry before they are put away.

In summer it is most healthy to have your chamber

floor bare, and have it washed occasionally. It is important to examine your clothes, after they come from the wash, and see that they are perfectly dry before they are put away.

CULTIVATION OF FLOWERS.

A FEW flowers and plants, when properly taken care of, are ornamental to the windows of a parlor, or sitting room; and will repay the care that is bestowed on them. Begin with a few that are easy to cultivate, and you will probably succeed. Persons that are fond of flowers, and have collected a number, are generally willing to give their young friends a few plants; and where we succeed in raising a fine plant from a slip, or cutting, we value it more than one that has been purchased at a green-house. Geraniums, cactus', wax plants, cape and catalonian jessamines, and some others, are easily cultivated in a parlor. Roses, camelias, and azaleas bloom best in a moderate temperature, as the heat of a parlor (unless very large) dries the buds, and prevents their coming to perfection. I have known these to bloom beautifully in a room that was very slightly heated—either over one in which there was fire, or in an apartment next a stove room. If the weather is very cold, they should be removed to a warmer room, until it moderates. The windows that are open to the south are best. When the blossoms have matured, you can bring them to the parlor; but if there is much heat, they will not remain perfect so long as in a moderate room.

Roses are sometimes troubled with insects, which should be brushed off with a feather, and the plants washed with a decoction of tobacco, (not too strong;) they will not bloom when thus infested. There is another insect that fastens itself to the bark of lemon trees, and other plants; frequent washing with soap-suds and brushing the stems, removes it; and sometimes wash the leaves with a sponge, when the weather is too cold to put them out of doors. Setting them out in a warm rain, or watering them well all over the foliage, is very reviving to plants. Be careful to have pieces of old broken earthen-ware at the bottom of each pot, to drain them, or the plants will not thrive. The earth should be sometimes removed, and an occasional re-potting, is an advantage; being careful not to disturb the roots. A mixture of charcoal and sand, and rich earth of more than one kind is thought best. Earth fresh from the woods is good for pot-plants, as well as borders, but should always be mixed with a stronger soil. Roses that are planted round a house, should have a deep and rich soil made for them, and they will then bloom beautifully all the season.

Pot-plants should in summer be placed in a situation where they will not be exposed to intense heat. Some persons place their pots in the earth on the north side of the house; others keep them in a porch where they can get some sun. They require much more water in summer. The wax plant blooms beautifully in summer, and should be kept in a sheltered situation, not exposed to the wind; it should have a strong frame of wood and wire to run on, well secured in a tub or box. Hyacinths and crocuses should be planted in pots, boxes, or small tubs, in rich earth, in October or November; a small painted tub is very suitable, and will hold a dozen hyacinths, and as many crocus roots. The most beautiful I ever saw in a window, were planted in this way, by keeping some in the sun, and others in the shade you can have a succession of blooms; they are also pretty in root-glasses, but this plan will exhaust the roots. After blooming in the house, they should be planted in the garden. The same roots will not answer the next year for parlor culture; they increase very fast in the garden by proper care.

There is something refining to the mind in the cultivation of flowers, either in a garden or in pots. Many hours that would be weary or lonely, are thus pleasantly occupied, and the mind refreshed.

I now take leave of the reader, with a sincere desire, that these remarks may be of use; and that the receipts which I have been at some pains in compiling and arranging, may be acceptable.

INDEX.

A.

B.

26

Corn Batter Cakes, 79.
Corn Beef, to Boil, 10.
Corn Dumplings, 98.
Corn Flour, Dry Yeast of, 63.
Corn Fritters, 44.
Corn, to Fricassee, 44.
Corn, Green, for Winter use, 44.
Corn, Green, to Boil, 44.
Corn Bread, 77.
Corn Gruel, 267.
Corn Meal Porridge, 78.
Corn Meal Pudding, 91.
Corn Muffins, 82.
Corn Pudding in Paste, 92.
Corn Starch, 193.
Corns, Salve for, 260.
Cottage Cheese, or Smearcase, 182.
Cough, for a, 228.
Cough, Remarks on a, 226.
Cough, Brown Mixture for a, 229.
Cougn, Lemon Mixture for a, 230.
Cough, Whooping, 233.
Crab Apples, to Preserve, 127.
Crackers, Soaked, 83.
Cracks in Stoves, to Mend, 214.
Cramp, 249.
Cramp in the Stomach, 248.
Cranberries, 132.
Cream, Almond, 107.
Cream, Cheese, 182.
Cream, Custard, 103.
Cream, Ice, Freezing, 108.
Cream Sauce, 101.
Cream, Snow, 111.
Cream, Toast, 269.
Cream, Poultice, 259.

Crisp Ginger Bread, 123.
Croup, for the, 233.
Crullers, 123.
Cucumber Catsup, 163.
Cucumbers, Cut, to Pickle, 162.
Cucumbers, to Fry or Slice, 51.
Cucumbers, to Pickle, 157.
Cucumbers, to Pickle, Small, 157
Cucumbers, to Preserve, 131.
Cultivation of Flowers, 291.
Cup Cake, 117.
Curds, Cheese, 105.
Curds, Skim, 105.
Curds, Whey Skim, 105
Currant Jelly, 136.
Currant Jelly, Black, 265.
Currant Pie, 88.
Currants, to Preserve, 127.
Currant Syrup, 137.
Currant Wine, 150.
Curtains, 207.
Custard, Apple, 102.
Custard Baked in Cups, 102.
Custard, Boiled. 102, 266.
Custard, to Boil in Water, 103.
Custard, Cream, 103.
Custard, Cold, 102.
Custard, Ice, 103.
Custard, with Raisins, 103.
Custard Bread Pudding, 93.
Custard Hasty Pudding, 94.
Custard for the Sick, 266.
Cutlets, Veal, 19.
Cutting Glass, 225.
Cuts and Wounds, Remedy for, 253.
Cymblings, or Squashes, 54.

D.

Damsons, to Preserve, 133.
Damsons for Pies, 143.
Damson Sauce, 141.
Deafness, 242.
Debility, Bitters for, 263.

Decanter, to Remove a Stopper from, 217.
Diseases, Summer, 236.
Domestics, on the Management of, 274.

G.

H.

26*

I.

J.

K.

L.

M.

N.

O.

P.

Paint, to Clean, 208.
Panada, 266.
Panada, Barley, 269.
Panada, Egg, 267.
Pan Cakes, 98.
Pan Cakes, Water, 99.
Papered Walls, 225.
Parsnips, 55.
Paste, Gum Arabic, 223.
Paste, for Puddings or Pies, 84.
Peaches in Brandy, 140.
Peaches, to Conserve, 141.
Peaches in Cider, 140.
Peach Dumplings, 97.
Peach Marmalade, 138.
Peaches, Pickled, 158.
Peaches, to Preserve, 132.
Peaches, Spiced, 165.
Peach Pie, 87.
Pears, to Conserve, 140
Pears, to Preserve, 136.
Peas, 53.
Pea Soup, 33.
Peppers, Green, to Preserve, 135.
Pepper Mangoes, 160.
Pickle for Butter, 180.
Pickle for Chines, 168.
Pickled Oysters, 42.
Pickled Pork, 167.
Pickles, Vinegar, &c., 147.
Pickles, Yellow, 159.
Picking Geese, 211.
Pie, Chicken, 28.
Pie, Beef Steak, 24.
Pie Crust, to Make, 84.
Pie, Currant, 88.
Pie, Mince, 85, 86.
Pie, Peach, 87.
Pie, Oyster, 40.
Pie, Pork Mince, 88.
Pie, Puddings, &c. 83.
Pie, Rhubarb, 87

Pie, Sweet Potato, 87.
Pies, to make Common, 83.
Pies, to Stew Fruit for, 83.
Pigeons, 16.
Pigs' Feet, 170.
Pigs' Head, 16.
Pig, to Roast a, 14.
Pine Apples, 128.
Pine Apple Syrup, 107.
Plaster, Adhesive, 259.
Plum Cake, 114.
Plum Cake, raised, 121.
Plums, Green Gage, 130.
Poached Eggs, 42, 268.
Poison, Remedy for, 254.
Pokeberry Juice, to Stain Ices, 109.
Poke and Greens, 52.
Pone, Cold Water, 80.
Pone, Lightened, 80.
Pone, Virginia, 80.
Pork, to Fry and Stew, 19.
Pork, or Mutton, to Corn, 174.
Pork, to Pickle, 167.
Pork, to Roast, 15.
Pork Stew Pie, 25.
Porter Beer, 153.
Porridge, Corn Meal, 78.
Porridge, Milk, 268.
Potatoes, to Boil, 45.
Potatoes, to Fry, 47.
Potatoes, Sweet, 46.
Potato Starch, 193.
Potatoes, to Stew, 46.
Potato Yeast, 64.
Potato Yeast, with Sugar, 64.
Potash Soap, 188.
Pot Pie, 28.
Pound Cake, 114.
Poultice, Bread and Milk, 258.
Poultice, Cream, 259.
Poultice, Flaxseed, 258.

Q.

R.

T.

27